PRIVATIZING
TOLL ROADS

PRIVATIZING TOLL ROADS
A Public–Private Partnership

Wendell C. Lawther

Privatizing Government: An Interdisciplinary Series
Simon Hakim and Gary Bowman, Series Advisers

Westport, Connecticut
London

Library of Congress Cataloging-in-Publication Data

Lawther, Wendell C., 1946–
    Privatizing toll roads : a public–private partnership / Wendell C. Lawther.
        p.   cm.—(Privatizing government : an interdisciplinary series, ISSN 1087–5603)
    Includes bibliographical references and index.
    ISBN 0–275–96900–2 (alk. paper)
    1. Toll roads—Florida.   2. Privatization—Florida.   I. Title.   II. Privatizing government.
HE336.T64 L38   2000
388.1′22′0975924—dc21   99–054744

British Library Cataloguing in Publication Data is available.

Library of Congress Catalog Card Number: 99–054744
ISBN: 0–275–96900–2
ISSN: 1087–5603

First published in 2000

Praeger Publishers, 88 Post Road West, Westport, CT 06881
An imprint of Greenwood Publishing Group, Inc.
www.greenwood.com

Printed in the United States of America

The paper used in this book complies with the
Permanent Paper Standard issued by the National
Information Standards Organization (Z39.48–1984).

10   9   8   7   6   5   4   3   2   1

To Cindi

For her love and support

CONTENTS

FIGURES AND TABLES

FIGURES

TABLES

INTRODUCTION

1

The decade of the 1980s witnessed an explosion of interest in the privatization of public services at all three levels of American government. Spurred by financial exigencies and tightening governmental budgets, privatization was hailed as a panacea for governmental financial woes. This interest has continued into the 1990s, as various surveys of state and local governments report an increasing percentage of formerly provided public services contracted out to private vendors (Dilger et al. 1997; Greene 1996; Miranda and Andersen 1994; Chi 1993; McManus 1992; David 1988).[1]

In addition, the literature analyzing privatization efforts in and issues as relevant to the experience of governments in the United States covers a wide variety of topics and perspectives. Much of the analysis of actual privatization efforts is very favorable, indicating that financial savings for governments, in some cases as high as 40 percent compared to public sector provision costs, are very likely (e.g., Fitzgerald 1986; Berenyi and Stevens 1988; Perry and Babitsky 1986; Ammons and Hill 1995). These same sentiments are echoed by authors who reviewed these and other studies (e.g., Barnekov and Raffel 1990; Donahue 1989; Wisniewski 1992; Bennet and Johnson 1980), although many of these reviewers also identify potential problems. They caution against contracting out unless city or state officials have made a thorough analysis of present and predicted costs prior to the decision to privatize.

Several other authors do not favor privatization, citing the lessening of citizen access to redress service problems (e.g., Moe 1987; Sullivan 1987; Morgan and England 1988), the negative impact on racial minorities, both in terms of a lessening of service (Lyons and Fitzgerald 1986) and increasing unemployment (Stein 1994); and the potential of privatization to increase costs, decrease quality of service, and even lead to corruption (Hanrahan 1983, echoed by Hebdon 1995).

Another relevant body of literature focuses much more on contracting, including a more generic, "how to do it" emphasis (Marlin 1984; Short 1987; Harney 1992). Others deal with contracting as it relates to various privatization issues, such as award, design, and monitoring (Gormley 1994; Martin 1993b); and contract management (Sappington and Stiglitz 1987; DeHoog,1990; Rehfuss 1989). Some authors specifically review the desirability of public employees competing directly with private contractors in response to a government's decision to contract out (Martin 1993a; Flanagan and Perkins 1995).

Still another emphasis in the privatization literature is placed on the public employees who are most affected by contracting out (Bennet and DiLorenzo 1983; Chandler and Feuille 1991; O'Leary and Eggers 1993; Denhardt et al. 1995; Becker et al. 1995). The general theme found here is that the fate of the public employees must be considered and that every effort should be made to ensure employment at comparable salaries and benefits, either with the government or the private contractor. Otherwise, opposition to privatization is highly likely, especially if public unions exist, and the social costs may be higher than desired.[2]

This proposed study offers a theory or model of the ideal privatization process called the privatization transfer process (PTP). The PTP consists of several steps. First, the privatization decision stage, during which the government considers whether to privatize a service, requires considerable analysis of the costs of present public sector provision compared to private sector provision. Also, the public employees affected by the decision should be consulted, especially if there is a union or an active employee professional organization. Second, the service transfer stage contains several steps including the creation of the request for proposal (RFP) which must be made in light of several factors, such as the complexity of the service, the degree of change from present service provision desired, and the nature of the contract management process envisioned. Also, a review and evaluation of the bids received must be established so that there is no evidence of unfair bias toward any bidder and that there is evidence that the most highly qualified bidder is chosen to provide the service. Third, the transition stage includes consideration of which types of contracts can be offered to the vendor (winning bidder); any negotiation leading to the signing of a contract; and the mobilization and phasing efforts during which the service is actually given to the vendor. Fourth, the contract management and renewal stage must entail meaningful measures and standards of service provision with appropriate review and accountability systems. Overall, implications of the desired nature of the pub-lic–private partnership that is established by this PTP should be identified.

If the contracting out effort is to be successful and meet the goals of the public agency (e.g., to lower costs while maintaining or improving service quality), this privatization transfer process must be considered as tightly knit, coherent, and highly interdependent. Each stage or step of the process must be viewed in the context of those that follow it. The RFP creation must fully articulate the nature of the service to be delivered, for example, or the re-sponses to it will not be satisfactory, causing further difficulties when the public agency manages the contract after its award.

The value of a detailed case study analysis is several fold. First, it serves to help fill voids in the privatization literature and emphasizes the implementa-tion of an actual privatization decision as it relates to the contracting process. Second, even though the experience analyzed here is not entirely generaliz-able to all potential privatization transfer instances, many relevant insights and lessons are available to the reader considering privatizing a service. Third, additional similar studies in other policy areas could be performed, allowing for comparative analysis.

This study also intends to fill another gap in the privatization literature: an extensive documentation and assessment of an actual privatization transfer process. Much of the existing reviews of specific privatization efforts focus on cost comparisons of before and after privatization (e.g., Perry and Babitsky 1986; National Council for Employment Policy 1988), providing only super-ficial accounts of the dollars saved and the plight of public employees. There are no detailed accounts of an RFP creation process. No study has reviewed the contents of competing bids, nor has anyone analyzed the rating process used to evaluate the bids by a government agency prior to the bid award. Furthermore, there has been almost no case study analysis of the issues faced in managing contracts by public sector officials.

THE PLAN OF THIS STUDY

This study focuses on the efforts of the Orlando Orange County Express-way Authority (OOCEA) to privatize its toll operations. As explored in Chapter 2, the OOCEA sought to contract with a private vendor to replace the opera-tions services provided by the Florida Department of Transportation (FDOT). This process began in the late 1980s and took until October 1995 to com-pletely turn over operations of the ten toll plazas to a private vendor. Even though historically some areas of government service have had a great deal of experience in contracting services (e.g., municipal sanitation services), in the late 1980s privatization was an innovative concept in the toll roadways industry. The management staff of OOCEA faced several challenges in cre-ating an RFP that would lead to a privatized operation that would be more efficient and produce a higher quality of service. Furthermore, OOCEA knew that privatization should not occur until an electronic toll and traffic management (ETTM) system could be installed. Only through the use of this technology could appropriate accountability and responsibility for the collection of toll revenue be assured.

The issuance of a privatization RFP for toll operations, named Project 266, was made in 1992. It had to be rescinded before bids were received because the ETTM equipment was not ready to be installed. Giving SAIC/Syntonic additional time to complete needed software and hardware modifications, a second Project 266 was issued in May 1994. The team of OOCEA staff, FDOT, and consultants who wrote the second RFP learned from the experience of writing the first RFP and from additional knowledge about the ETTM system. After an extensive and thorough review of technical and price proposals from three bidders, Florida Toll Services (FTS) was awarded the bid in November 1994 and began its partnership with OOCEA by signing the Project 266 contract in February 1995. Transition of the ten plazas was completed by October 1995.

The privatization transfer process is developed in greater detail in Chapter 3, which reviews existing literature that supports each stage of the PTP. For many governments, the decision to privatize is primarily based on anticipated lower operation costs after a private vendor is awarded the contract. These lower costs are due to competition among bidders, providing an incentive for all respondents to bid at or below market rates in their responses to the RFP; the existence of a profit motive, absent among public managers; lower labor costs, because the compensation practices of the public agency leads to salaries and benefits that are above the rates found in the comparable private market; and economies of scale that are impossible for small governments to achieve in comparison with private vendors. This privatization decision must be made only after present and future costs are carefully identified by the government, taking into account indirect costs and impacts on current government employees.

Other reasons for privatization include increased managerial flexibility, improved service quality and responsiveness, labor–management relations, and the existing political climate. In many instances, civil service or personnel regulations prohibit the timely removal of poor performers, and they do not always support the quick hiring of additional permanent employees to meet effectively unexpected service demands.[3] Even though several authors have warned of service "creaming" and the lack of responsiveness to citizens (e.g., Morgan and England 1988; Sharkansky 1980), clearly specified contract incentives coupled with effective contract management can improve delivery of services. The existence of a union, if relationships are positive, may provide a strong reason not to privatize, but negative labor management relations may lead government officials to strongly consider privatization (Chandler and Feuille 1991).

The importance of the service transfer stage to the success of the privatization effort may often be overlooked. The ideally created RFP must clearly identify service delivery goals as well as the standards by which the performance of the private vendor in meeting these goals will be evaluated. Bids received must be accurately and carefully evaluated, guarding against complaints of due process violations.

The transition stage includes an examination of the issues that occur after the bid has been awarded and prior to the complete assumption of service delivery by the private vendor. The impact of the privatization effort on current public employees must be assessed, with specific solutions regarding salary and fringe benefits provided by the vendor, the implementation of bumping rights if appropriate, and the possible promotion, transfer, or lay off of specific employees. There are potentially several coordination challenges, depending upon the size of the service and the number of affected parties.

The contract management stage remains in many ways the most complex stage of the PTP, as it is continuous, developing, full of potential problems, and greatly dependent on the relationships among individual members of the contract management team and the vendor management staff and employees. If goals, objectives, standards, and measures have been already identified in the RFP, then contract management can be greatly facilitated. In many cases, however, it is difficult to identify specific measures and standards. The RFP may suggest that these must be developed by both members of the public–private partnership after the contract has been awarded. Both must be willing and open to suggestions for solutions that will lead to better goal achievement.

In the subsequent chapters of the study, the PTP is applied to the OOCEA case study, with each chapter providing a detailed analysis of each stage. The decision to privatize by OOCEA, reviewed in Chapter 4, was based upon several factors. First, operating costs were expected to be much lower with a private vendor. The increased overhead charges made by FDOT to OOCEA, the higher than expected operation costs for the most recently built toll plazas, and the suspicion that fewer management levels were needed were the major reasons in support of expected lower costs. Second, improved service quality, especially as reflected by the timely resolution of customer complaints, was anticipated. Third, with the introduction of the ETTM and AVI technology, both increased usage of the toll roadways and better service quality was assumed. Overall, there was the feeling that independence from FDOT would allow OOCEA to be more creative and innovative in influencing transportation policy for Central Florida.

Chapter 5 focuses on RFP creation. The ideal RFP must be fashioned in a way that clearly communicates the service goals to prospective bidders. It must also shape the nature of the public–private partnership so that the private vendor will attempt to achieve these goals as much as possible. The language found in the RFP can be viewed on a continuum, from specific to general. Specific language provides little flexibility to the vendor in choosing how to meet the very specific goals, measures, and standards that are reflected in the RFP. General language allows the vendor maximum flexibility in choosing how to achieve stated goals, and provides the opportunity for public–private partnership to be a dynamic, evolving one.

Whether the successful RFP is written with specific or general language depends upon at least three factors: (1) the complexity of the service provided; (2) the amount or degree of service delivery change desired or anticipated by the government officials; and (3) the amount of knowledge about the service held by government officials. A routine service for which little change is desired would result in a RFP containing very specifically written goals, measures, standards, as well as the methods and procedures needed to achieve them. A highly complex service for which an extensive amount of organizational restructuring is anticipated, for example, would require an RFP that contains very general language, allowing the bidders a great deal of flexibility in helping to shape the service to be delivered.

The greater the amount of knowledge held by government officials, no matter how complex the service, nor how much change is desired, tends to result in a RFP written more specifically. To some extent, however, this specificity is counterbalanced by the degree to which a viable public–private partnership is desired. In other words, even though there may be a great deal of knowledge about how service delivery personnel should be trained, for example, allowing the vendor flexibility to choose specific training methods may facilitate changes that are needed after the contract is awarded.

The RFP written in 1994 by the OOCEA to privatize toll operations contains a mixture of specific and general language. Goals of greater efficiency and quality service were clearly stated. The hours during which specific toll lanes must be staffed were identified. The winning bidder was required to submit approximately forty sets of policies and procedures within ninety days after the contract was awarded. This emphasis on general language, due to a combination of a desire for change and in some cases limited knowledge, allowed the bidders a great deal of flexibility in identifying how the specified goals were to be attained.

The responses of three bidders to the technical proposal is analyzed in great detail in Chapter 6. A thorough evaluation process was created, employing five general categories of criteria and thirteen more specific subheadings, broken down into over sixty specifically rated criteria. A five-member evaluation committee individually rated each response. Of the possible 280 total points, one bidder, Florida Toll Services, scored 240.1, consistently receiving the highest average score across most of the criteria. FTS proposed a management team that had the most experience and provided a staffing plan that employed fewer toll operations management staff than the other two bidders.

Chapter 7 reviews bidder responses to the pricing proposals. FTS provided the lowest bid, approximately $6 million lower than its nearest competitor (over a five-year period). FTS proposed a smaller management team, bid much less for direct expenses and mobilization, and did not require as much for toll operation labor costs because no assistant plaza manager positions were included in its pricing proposal. Because it costed out each item of direct expense, its bid also appeared to be based on a much more complete analysis of actual and projected costs.

The transition stage is discussed in Chapter 8. Issues relevant in the OOCEA case were made more complex because the number of parties involved was much larger than OOCEA and FTS. The transition of individual employees was a huge success, as Florida FDOT was able to pool state employees from the OOCEA toll plazas and nearby Florida Turnpike plazas, allowing all a greater variety of choice. As a result, those most senior employees (more than five years experience) chose to remain with the state, while many of the more junior employees signed on with FTS. More than 50 percent of the forty-nine supervisory positions with FTS represented promotions for former FDOT employees.

Since ETTM systems were also being installed at the same time that transition was occurring among FDOT, OOCEA, and FTS, coordination also involved representatives from SAIC/Syntonic. A group of key staff from all parties met weekly for eight months to complete the transition tasks.

The chapter dealing with contract management and renewal (Chapter 9) introduces the principal–agent theory to provide a structure to support this crucial stage that often is overlooked by governments (DeHoog 1990). To overcome tendencies for the vendor to engage in self-regarding behavior (Perrow 1986) or shirking (Kettl 1993), the public agency must provide incentives for the vendor to pursue public goals even in the absence of any monitoring or inspection. These incentives can be monetary for both management and nonmanagement staff; and they can appear in the form of processes or procedures that help to provide a sense of organizational identity.

To evaluate the OOCEA contract management efforts, programs and policies that affect goal achievement must be reviewed. These include those that were well established and those that were under review at the time of the study. Many of these affect the attainment of more than one goal. The incentive performance program, designed to provide additional pay increases to toll collectors in the form of performance bonuses, seems to be stimulating better quality performance as well as increasing efficiency.[4] The number of patrons using toll roadways continues to increase as written compliments increase and complaints decrease. Ongoing issues that could improve efficiency include the reduction of manned lanes as the use of E-PASS, the automated vehicle identification (AVI) system, increases; the reduction of the number of hours needed for manned lanes; and the reduction of the number of plaza managers.

A key program that has also contributed to higher service quality is the citizen complaint/compliment system established by FTS. The various aspects of the FTS installed Quality Management/Assurance Program, especially the quality management review meetings are also discussed. Ongoing issues are the ratio of full-time to part-time toll collectors, as well as the extent of employee turnover. The various reports generated by the ETTM system to achieve sound financial management practices are discussed, as well as the ongoing issues surrounding the vehicle enforcement system.

The concluding chapter provides an overall assessment and evaluation of what can be termed a privatization success. Greater efficiencies are obvious. The OOCEA has saved over $1 million annually in operating costs. Patron usage continues to climb while toll collection labor costs are shrinking as E-PASS usage increases. The success of the citizen complaint/compliment system is one indication of improved service quality. Increased managerial flexibility is evident by the ease that personnel changes were made, both in adding full-time employees and decreasing the number of part-time employees. The RFP creation and evaluation of bids can also be judged successful, as all three bidders were deemed qualified. For employees, transition has been successful, since many FTS employees are now bringing home more dollars because of lower benefit costs and the incentive performance program.

To the extent that both OOCEA and FTS continue to work toward the stated goals in the contract, OOCEA's management of that contract is also effective. The most valid test of these efforts may be the willingness of both to listen to each other's ideas and assessment and continue a dynamic, evolving relationship.

NOTES

1. As reported by Chi (1993), for example, a 1993 survey of targeted state agencies by the Council of State Governments found that the contracting out of a number of state services was likely to increase. These services included support services such as custodial, printing and information, public works and infrastructure services, and social services. For local governments, Greene (1996) compares the results of a 1982 ICMA survey with those from a similar 1992 survey. The average percentage of services privatized in 1982 was 12.6 percent, compared with an average percentage in 1992 of 28 percent, an increase of over 121 percent.

2. Social costs may be defined as those incurred by the larger society as the result of the privatization of an already existing service. For example, if health insurance benefits for private employees are much less compared with those of the public employees who had previously delivered the service, then these private employees are more likely to use emergency rooms for routine medical needs. Higher health care costs are the result. Also, the privatization of some services delivered to those in greatest need, may result in fewer services, especially if user fees are increased and/or creaming of service delivery occurs. See Wisniewski (1992) and Morgan and England (1988) for more discussion.

3. Many authors have noted the inflexibility of personnel or civil service rules

and regulations. One more recent discussion, for example, can be found in Ban (1998). Also, the growing literature dealing with reengineering and the "reinvention" of government touts the vastly increased managerial flexibility, which is part of the practices that are usually involved in these efforts. See for example Osborne and Plastrik (1997); Cohen and Eimicke (1998); and Linden (1994).

4. The incentive performance program is explained more thoroughly in Chapter 9.

TOLL COLLECTION PRIVATIZATION: THE OOCEA EXPERIENCE

2

In October 1995, the operations for the last Central Florida toll plaza were completely turned over to Florida Toll Services, the private vendor that had been awarded the contract to manage all ten toll plazas. This event marked the end of a process that has its origins in the minds of Orlando–Orange County Expressway Authority staff as far back as 1989. In another sense, it marked the beginning of a new era for the OOCEA, one marked by a shift to a role emphasizing management and monitoring and oversight for a number of different contracts with private vendors, including maintenance, armored car services, and landscaping.

Throughout this time period, the Florida Department of Transportation (FDOT) has been a necessary partner in this trend toward privatization. This partnership has existed in a number of different ways. In a very pragmatic, practical sense, the FDOT Office of Toll Operations (OTO) had contracted with OOCEA to operate all toll plazas, since they had been completed in the 1986–1988 time period. For OOCEA to privatize toll operations, FDOT has had to agree (by contract) to relinquish the authority to manage toll operations and approve the OOCEA privatization effort.

In a larger sense, FDOT is the state agency that is ultimately responsible for the continued operation of all toll roads in Florida. As such, it must continue to play a role of oversight, but in ways that are not yet fully defined and are continuing to evolve.

As OOCEA has worked toward privatization, FDOT has been a supportive, helpful partner. Former Secretary of FDOT Ben Watts had been supportive of OOCEA efforts since the beginning. OTO staff have spent many hours reviewing drafts of request for proposals (RFPs) for both the toll operations contract (Project 266) and the electronic toll collection and traffic management system (ETTM) and automated vehicle identification equipment contract (Project 256). Although it is difficult to suggest that all FDOT staff have been enthusiastically supportive throughout the last seven to eight years of the OOCEA privatization effort, the FDOT–OOCEA relationships remain positive.

Another important theme that permeates this privatization experience is the impact of technology on the public–private partnership that has been established. From the very beginning, it was apparent that new ETTM and AVI equipment must be installed on the Central Florida toll plazas before privatization could occur. With this equipment in place, the management, auditing, and oversight of the private operations vendor would be much easier and much more effective. The new equipment would allow for quick access to operations records by OOCEA staff.

BACKGROUND

The OOCEA, established in 1963 as a state agency, has been given a wide range of powers that pertain to the establishment of an expressway system. These include: purchase of land; construction of roads, extensions or additions to the expressway system; authorization to issue bonds for the purpose of financing expressway construction; and authorization to charge and collect fees for the use of its facilities.

By 1986, three projects had been completed (see Figure 2.1). The first was the Martin Andersen Bee Line Expressway, which connected the south Orlando area with the Orlando International Airport and the Cocoa–Cape Canaveral area. In 1965, $7 million in revenue bonds were issued to construct the OOCEA's portion of the Bee Line Expressway, running from Sand Lake Road in the west to SR 520 in the east. This section was first opened to traffic in July 1967.

The second project was the Spessard L. Holland East–West Expressway, constructed primarily to facilitate east–west commuter traffic across Orlando, as well as to provide easy access to the downtown area. Financed with $70.5 million in revenue bonds issued in 1970, the East–West Expressway opened in 1973.

The Orlando International Airport interchange and Bee Line corridor improvements were the third project, funded with bonds issued in 1980. This project provided for a highly functional interchange for the Orlando International Airport. In addition, the project included a three-mile limited access facility running from the airport interchange westward to a connection with the Bee Line West (that portion of the Bee Line Expressway from Sand Lake Road to Interstate I-4). The airport interchange opened in July 1983.

Figure 2.1
Expressway System Map

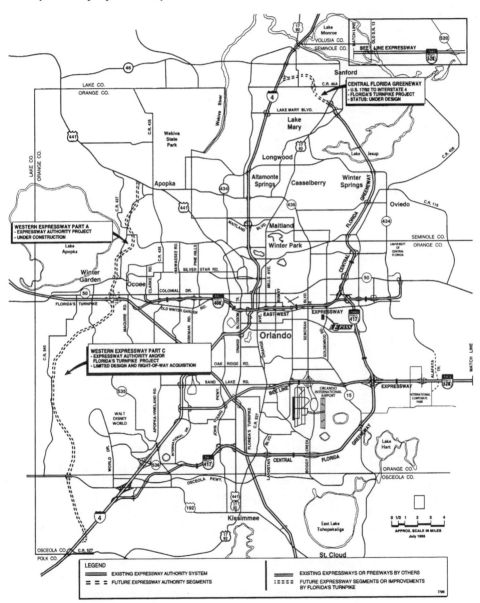

Source: Orlando–Orange County Expressway Authority.

THE 1986 PROJECT

In 1983, the OOCEA adopted a long-range plan that included the building of six additional expressways (see Figure 2.1). Because of successful refunding of outstanding bonds, the total annual debt service needed was reduced, thereby allowing the first four expressways to be combined into what has become known as the 1986 Project. These are (1) the eastern extension of the East–West Expressway; (2) the western extension of the East–West Expressway; (3) the north extension of the eastern beltway; and (4) the south extension of the eastern beltway.

On November 6, 1986, $433 million in revenue bonds were issued to complete these four expressways. The roads were completed, including toll plazas as noted below, and opened to traffic at the following dates:

North Section—Eastern Beltway	December 1988
South Section—Eastern Beltway	June 1990
Eastern Extension—East–West Expressway	June 1989
Western Extension—East–West Expressway	October 1990

The toll plazas for each expressway are:

North Section	University
South Section	Curry Ford
Eastern Extension	Dean
Western Extension	Hiawassee

East–West Expressway

The original East–West Expressway was 13.8 miles long, extending from the west side of Orlando at an intersection with State Road 50 at Kirkman Road to an interchange at State Road 551 on the east side of Orlando. East and west extensions were built as part of the 1986 Project. The East Extension is a six-mile expressway that extends eastward from Chickasaw Trail to an interchange with State Road 50 at Alafaya Trail. Construction began in late fall 1987, and toll collection began in May 1989. The West Extension is a five-mile expressway beginning from Kirkman Road to an interchange with the Florida Turnpike. Construction began in early 1989 and was completed in October 1990.

In addition, as part of the 1986 Project, improvements were made to the East–West Expressway. In January 1987, the number of toll lanes increased on the east-side toll plaza from twelve to fourteen, while the east-side toll lanes were expanded from eight to twelve. By October 1989, four ramps were also converted to manned facilities at Mills Avenue, Bumby Avenue, US 441, and State Road 436.

Eastern Beltway—North and South Extensions

The North Extension of the Eastern Beltway included construction of approximately three and one-half miles of four-lane highway, beginning at the Goldenrod Road (SR 551) interchange on the East–West Expressway and ending at the Seminole County line, just north of SR 426. (Seminole County subsequently completed a connecting toll road from SR 426 north to US 17-92.) A toll plaza was built just south of University Boulevard.

The South Extension of the Eastern Beltway included highway that connects the Eastern Extension of the East–West Expressway with the Bee Line Expressway. A toll plaza was built just south of Curry Ford Road.

PRIVATIZATION: THE BEGINNING

The June 14, 1990, issue of the *Engineering News Record* contains a small reference to the desire of OOCEA to privatize toll operations:

Public toll roads in central Florida, which now contract with the state Dept. of Transportation to operate and maintain their facilities, are reported to be seeking private quotes for contract operations. The high costs and onerous contractual conditions imposed by Fla-DOT are driving the discussions, sources say.

This apparent criticism of FDOT stimulated a response from OOCEA Executive Director D. W. (Bill) Gwynn to FDOT Secretary Ben Watts, which reads in part as the following:

The attached article from *Engineering News Record* is upsetting to our Authority as it appears to cast a bad light on the good relations that our organizations enjoy. It is certainly factual in that we are, with your knowledge and assistance, investigating the possibility of private enterprise operating our toll facilities. This is being done to determine if there can be a cost savings and an increase in efficiency to both of our agencies. (Letter dated July 2, 1990)

Although the letter may have been an attempt to placate any ill feelings on the part of FDOT personnel, certainly the position of OCCEA is made quite clear. Although there is nothing here that provides insight into what could be causing "high costs" and "onerous contract conditions," other documents provide clarity.

In February 1990, Bill Gwynn had requested authority from the OOCEA Board to advertise for an RFP to install AVI toll equipment. Greg Dailer, OOCEA Finance Director and a key player throughout the privatization effort, requested and received on March 8, 1990 operations cost information from FDOT. Subsequent to the above letter, in August 1990, Gwynn similarly stated to the Board that the cost of operations, billed by FDOT to OOCEA, is higher than anticipated. At the same meeting, he also stated that FDOT

Secretary Ben Watts has made it clear that he wanted the independent expressway authorities to handle their own toll operations.

In January 1991, Gwynn's conversation with the OCCEA Board indicated further activity toward privatization. He emphasized once again that rising FDOT operations costs are an issue and further announced that there was no agreement regarding FDOT operating the most recently planned Central Florida toll plaza, known as the Southern Connector. He thus requested (and received) authority from the Board for OOCEA staff to develop specifications for toll operations and once again related Secretary of FDOT Ben Watts's support. Concurrently, he identified a need for an OOCEA Director of Operations position.

A supplemental agreement to the general engineering contract between the engineering consulting firm of Post, Buckley, Schuh and Jernigan (PBS&J) and the OOCEA designated PBS&J in February–March 1991 to help develop the toll operations (266) RFP. A completed draft was to be ready by June 1991. The contract award was scheduled to be made at the September 25, 1991 meeting of the Board. RCH and Associates were hired as subcontractors, with President Robert Hawkins and Phil Burkhart as the primary consultants working with PBS&J.

In the meantime, the ETTM and AVI equipment proposal had been proceeding, with a contract awarded on July 24, 1991. SAIC was the low bidder at $15 million and was awarded the contract over TH Green and Lockheed.

With the ETTM–AVI piece apparently in place, in August 1991, Greg Dailer requested (and received) the Board's approval to proceed with the toll operations privatization effort. It may have seemed at the time that technological improvements and operations privatization efforts were reaching fruition. The first of many delays, however, was soon encountered.

In a meeting held on October 8, 1991 that included Board Chairman Bob Harrell, FDOT Secretary Ben Watts, Assistant Secretary Hal Worrall, and Greg Dailer, OOCEA and FDOT reached several agreements. First, OOCEA was to proceed with installation of its ETTM system. Since, however, FDOT planned to proceed immediately with an RFP for AVI equipment for the entire turnpike system, beginning installation in March 1992, the OOCEA agreed to postpone purchase and installation of its AVI portion of the ETTM system so that it would purchase the same equipment that FDOT would install on the turnpike. In addition, FDOT promised to install its AVI system on the OOCEA toll plazas prior to installing it on the turnpike. If it were not able to do so by March 1992, OOCEA would begin its own installation.

By the end of November 1991, Greg Dailer was able to announce to the OOCEA Board that a statewide committee had been established to develop an RFP for a statewide AVI system. This committee, he told the Board, hoped to have its work completed by January 1992, with a firm hired to begin work by April 1992.

In addition, at the October 8 meeting, OOCEA was informed that FDOT intended to develop its own statewide operations privatization RFP. Even though OOCEA had made much progress in developing its own 266 RFP (by November 28, 1991, Greg Dailer had announced to the Board that the RFP was "95% complete"), FDOT apparently wanted to write an RFP that would be sent out to prospective vendors in place of the one authored by OOCEA. The interrelated issues of (1) the scope of the RFP (statewide versus only OOCEA toll collection); and (2) who should issue the RFP and award the contract (FDOT or OOCEA) had yet to be resolved.

A group of FDOT staff reviewed a draft RFP devised by the OOCEA. After several meetings, Thomas Boyd, FDOT Comptroller, returned a FDOT revised draft to Greg Dailer on March 12, 1992. In the letter that accompanied the FDOT revisions, Boyd indicated that FDOT wished to discuss which agency should issue the RFP. Also, he identified an issue that became a key one throughout the privatization process: the ease of transition for toll operations personnel from FDOT to a private vendor.

The OOCEA team provided swift and somewhat critical response, furthering the review process. In general, the FDOT version was cited for being too general, not providing specific information such as the project schedule and the current FDOT budget and manpower resources. The original OOCEA draft was more specific, assuming that the more the bidder knew about the toll operations, the greater the likelihood that the end result would be a better proposal and a lower price.

In a response letter from Greg Dailer to Thomas Boyd dated April 2, 1992, the issue of who should issue the RFP is further clarified. Dailer states in part that

If FDOT issues the RFP and contract, an Interlocal Agreement will be drawn up assigning the contract and operational responsibilities to OOCEA after the contract is let. If OOCEA issues the RFP contract, an Interlocal Agreement will have to be drawn up assigning operational responsibilities to OOCEA before the contract is let. *It is OOCEA's preference to issue the contract.* (emphasis added)

Less than a week later, at a meeting held in Tallahassee on April 7, 1992, FDOT and OOCEA personnel agreed on several items, including the following:

1. OOCEA will issue the operations RFP and will contract with the operations contractor.
2. OOCEA will draft an agreement between FDOT and OOCEA for the transfer of operations responsibility.
3. There are between 275 and 300 FDOT personnel involved in operation of the OOCEA system, and they will be given first right of refusal by the successful contractor.

Several other specific details were agreed upon, including continuing the joint review of the RFP document as it continued to be revised. By all accounts, the meeting was harmonious, with both groups willing to work together.

It also had been decided that a statewide ETTM–AVI RFP was not forthcoming from FDOT. At a meeting on March 12, 1992, OOCEA was released from its agreement to wait until this equipment could be implemented on the turnpike and other FDOT state roads and given permission by FDOT to proceed with its own contract with SAIC.

It had been apparent for some time that the new equipment would have to be in place before the privatization contract could be implemented. Both OOCEA and FDOT realized that only in this fashion could adequate audit systems for a private vendor be established. With the in-place toll collection equipment, there was too great a danger that errors could occur without adequate detection.

The OOCEA team moved ahead, eliciting FDOT support and input. There were concerns about key aspects of the privatization RFP. In July 1992, Charlie Gilliard, Regional Manager for FDOT, indicated in a letter to Greg Dailer, that the toll accounting section is a "show stopper" and needed to be revised according to the comments on the accompanying RFP draft. Also, FDOT felt that the requirement of two years of corporate experience for bidders to be extremely restrictive and would discourage otherwise qualified bidders.

From July 10 to 16, 1992, the 266 privatization RFP was advertised and subsequently mailed to about fifteen prospective bidders, including the largest transportation consulting firms, as well as those who were known for bidding on operations contracts in the areas of maintenance. These included such firms as Morrison Knudson, Kiewit, Parsons Brinkerhoff, Lockheed, and Martin–Marietta. Two international firms, Confiroute, based in Paris, and Interpark, from South Africa, had also expressed an interest and were sent RFPs.

It was soon apparent that the original schedule for the receipt of bids and the contract awarding quickly needed to be extended. Bidders were notified that a preproposal conference was scheduled for August 5, 1992, with the final proposals due on September 19, 1992. Tours of the toll operations facilities were also held on August 4 and 5.

Almost immediately, prospective bidders had questions concerning the RFP, and OOCEA staff found itself responding to these questions and creating addendum to the RFP. A deadline to send questions was set as August 14. Charlie Gilliard had been hired by the OOCEA to be the Director of Operations on August 21, and he immediately began working on answers to questions and addendum. Answers to the questions were completed by September 28 and were first forwarded to FDOT for their review before being sent to prospective bidders.

Throughout the process of creating the RFP, the OOCEA team had discussed to what extent (1) the RFP should provide only general guidelines concerning toll operations; or (2) should be as specific as possible in identifying key aspects of operations, as well as identifying performance standards. Both options had positive aspects as well as potential dangers. A more general RFP would allow the winning vendor more discretion in creating an organizational structure, establishing policies and procedures, and in identifying ways to improve efficiency and quality that were not apparent to the OOCEA team. The difficulty and complexity of contract monitoring and management, on the other hand, would likely be greatly increased.

An RFP with more specified guidelines would take longer to create. Plus, since there were no privatized toll operations in existence, there was no already existing RFP or contract that could be used as a model. The OOCEA team felt that the value of being as specific as possible within the RFP would ensure that potential problems of contract management would be lessened as much as possible.

The resulting RFP was more specific rather than general. There was the expectation though, that the prospective bidders would "help write" the RFP through their questions. The necessity to respond to questions was certainly anticipated by OOCEA staff and to some extent even welcomed.

Throughout the next few months, seven addenda were finalized. For several, input from FDOT was sought. By October 3, 1992, the seventh had been sent to the bidders, and the deadline for final response extended to November 17. Further discussion between OOCEA and FDOT ensued, with one small controversy concerning whether SAIC and its sister organization, Syntonic, should be allowed to bid on the privatization contract. FDOT opposed their eligibility, indicating that since they designed the new ETTM–AVI equipment, they would have an unfair advantage over competitors. Although the OOCEA initially opposed this point of view, the problems that almost immediately surfaced with the ETTM–AVI contract, lead to a decision on the part of SAIC/Syntonic that it would not be appropriate to bid on the 266 contract.

During this period, apparent progress had been made on the ETTM–AVI equipment contract (256). At the July 1992 Board Meeting, it was announced that the AVI system had been named E-PASS. Subsequently, three months later, Hal Worrall, who had been hired as the new OOCEA Executive Director on May 1, announced that the OOCEA hoped to have the new equipment in place by June 1, 1993. A month later, on October 28, John Glazer of SAIC attended a Board meeting and stated there would be no problem in meeting the November 18 deadline for Critical Design Review.

As activities on both efforts began to coalesce, it became much more apparent that the privatization efforts would have to wait until the ETTM–AVI equipment was in place before the winning bidder for the privatization contract could begin to run the toll operations for OOCEA. Since this would not occur until June 1993, at least seven months away, there seemed to be some "breathing room" in the effort to award the 266 contract. Plus, as indicated by Charlie Gilliard at a staff meeting on November 2, additional work was needed to further refine the evaluation criteria for this contract. Once again, the deadline for bidders to submit responses to the privatization RFP was extended, this time to February 16, 1993.

A critical point was reached late in November–December 1992, when it became apparent that the SAIC software and equipment was not functional in its present state. Several meetings were held between OOCEA staff, Board members, and SAIC staff during this time. Ultimately an agreement was hammered out. At a special Board meeting held on January 15, 1993, a settlement, formally titled "Supplemental Agreement Number 4," was announced and approved. The key parts included the following:

1. $8.6 million would be returned to the OOCEA.
2. The schedule for development, production, and testing was extended.
3. OCCEA would obtain immediate title to all hardware on the Southern Connector toll operations plaza.

In short, SAIC and Syntonic would be permitted to complete the contract. Although some OOCEA staff expressed reservations, other staff and Board members were convinced that SAIC/Syntonic had the capability to fulfill their contractual agreements, even though the original contract deadlines for the development and implementation of equipment had not been met.

The new schedule identified that it would not be until at least Spring 1994 that the equipment would be ready. With this in mind, in a letter dated January 23, 1993, Charlie Gilliard stated that the RFP for the privatization of toll operations would be cancelled because of the delay in the completion of the 256 contract. OOCEA renewed its commitment to work with FDOT. Both wanted a fully integrated and operational system in place before the RFP could be reissued.

A YEAR OF PROGRESS

During the next year, much of the focus was placed on working with SAIC to develop software and hardware that would be acceptable. OOCEA staff made numerous visits to San Diego throughout this time. In addition, OOCEA and FDOT continued to work on an Interlocal Agreement regarding toll operations. The addition of the Southern Connector to the toll plazas under the jurisdiction of OOCEA also provided an opportunity to "experiment" with a partial privatization RFP and contract.

In late February 1993, it was reported to the Board that SAIC's efforts were now on schedule. The next month, Hal Worrall met with FDOT regarding the AVI schedule, including meetings with turnpike officials. In April, the OOCEA working team met with SAIC and their consultants, seeing a demonstration of the equipment on April 23. A month later, Hal Worrall reported to the Board that the initial software (Build 1.5) was installed in the lanes and will be tested. He subsequently went to San Diego June 15 to 17 for a final test of the more advanced software. Another trip was made on July 27 to 30 to finalize the critical design document and to accelerate the schedule for the ETTM–AVI implementation. In September, FDOT staff also visited SAIC operations in San Diego for an update on the AVI equipment.

Gradually, confidence grew in the probable success of the equipment, even though the actual implementation of the equipment on OOCEA toll plazas would be the ultimate test. At a staff meeting on December 20, it was reported that the installation of SAIC/Syntonic equipment was going well. At the same time, discussions concerning a reissuing of the privatization RFP began again with David Pope, the new Operations Manager, announcing that he hoped to have a completed draft ready by the end of January 1994.

Throughout the remainder of 1994, additional testing and finally installation of the ETTM equipment and software occurred. At the end of March, testing of the final phase took place in San Diego. At a staff meeting on June 6, David Pope reported that the thirty-day acceptance test for the final phase would be completed. Hal Worrall reported 99.96 percent accuracy. Installation occurred at various toll plazas, with David Pope reporting to the Board in December that installation was complete.

Concurrently, installation of the AVI system, or E-PASS, gradually took place. The OOCEA E-PASS Service Center opened on May 16, 1994. Installation of E-PASS first occurred on the Southern Connector and was followed by other plazas throughout the rest of 1994 and into 1995. By September 1995, all toll plazas had E-PASS capabilities.

OOCEA–FDOT INTERLOCAL AGREEMENT

It had been realized for some time that an agreement between FDOT and OOCEA would need to be created so that OOCEA could not only assume the responsibility for toll operations but also be allowed to privatize these operations. As early as April 1992, it was agreed that this interlocal agreement would be necessary, since OOCEA, not FDOT, would be issuing the privatization RFP. Such an agreement was not only essential legally, it also represented a significant change in that it would redefine the relationship between the two organizations. Furthermore, given that control and responsibility clearly was being shifted to OOCEA, FDOT had to clarify the degree of responsibility that it would have in this new relationship.

The process began with FDOT submitting a draft agreement to OOCEA in October 1992. A month later on November 30, Charlie Gilliard and Greg Dailer met with FDOT officials regarding OOCEA response to this agreement. Over five months later, Greg Dailer reported that FDOT had not yet responded. He subsequently contacted Bob Plant of the FDOT staff regarding the contract. Joe Berenis, OCCEA Deputy Executive Director, also contacted Bob Plant on May 3, 1993.

Throughout the rest of 1993, no correspondence was received from FDOT regarding the interlocal agreement. It was not until the Board meeting of February 23, 1994 that Hal Worrall was able to announce that agreement had been reached with FDOT regarding the schedule of taking over the toll plazas. Still, this did not mean a formal agreement was forthcoming.

It is difficult to state why nine months had transpired at this point without much activity regarding this agreement. Perhaps, since the privatization RFP had been delayed by the ETTM–AVI equipment delay, both organizations felt there was no urgency to complete this agreement. Also, FDOT may have wanted to wait until actual bids were received for the privatization RFP before committing to an interlocal agreement.

Southern Connector

The addition of the Southern Connector (SC) toll plazas, John Young and Boggy Creek, offered a test of operations privatization. Since FDOT personnel still operated all toll plazas, toll collectors were hired by FDOT. It had been long standing policy that no more than 40 percent of toll collectors should be hired on a temporary, part-time (Other Personnel Services [OPS]) status, with permanent state employees receiving full benefits constituting the remaining 60 percent. Although clearly the FDOT saved labor costs by hiring OPS personnel, this group of temporary employees experienced a much higher turnover rate and created many more personnel problems than did their permanent counterparts.[1] By contracting with a temporary personnel services agency for both full-time and part-time employees, additional funds would be saved by OOCEA because of lower salaries and a lower FDOT overhead charge. In addition, supervisors and managerial personnel would spend much less time on hiring, training, and other personnel issues for this group of employees. In addition, FDOT supported the contract with Norrell because it did not have sufficient career service (full-time) positions to allocate to the Southern Connector plazas.

As early as January 1991, Bill Gwynn had stated to the Board that the Bond Covenants in effect with the existing toll plazas had specified that FDOT was to provide toll operations but that no such provision was in place for the Southern Connector. Bids for the construction of the Southern Connector had been let in March 1992, with its opening scheduled for July 1, 1993. Under agreement with FDOT, the toll collectors were to be obtained under contract with a temporary personnel services agency, while FDOT would provide managers and supervisors. On April 9, 1993, an advertisement for temporary toll collectors was run, with an April 23 date set for response. However, OOCEA soon felt the RFP was not clear enough to encourage prospective bidders. The ad was rerun, with new bids received. Bids were received for the rebid RFP on July 7, 1993. Norrell Temporary Services was awarded the contract in late July. The experience with Norrell illustrates the difficulties with this arrangement. To some extent, Norrell was not comfortable with the role of providing employees who would be trained by FDOT–OOCEA, because it wanted to provide trained employees.

Even though there may have been salary savings because FDOT supervisors and management remained in place at the toll plaza, the extent to which this structural arrangement increased efficiency is questionable. The amount of managerial–supervisory time spent on personnel matters may have lessened in some respects. The contract with Norrell, though, meant that FDOT operations personnel had to deal with contract management in ways that posed unexpected challenges.

TOLL OPERATIONS PRIVATIZATION: A REALITY

On December 16, 1993, nearly eleven months after the first privatization RFP had been rescinded, OOCEA staff, the FDOT regional toll manager, and the consultant team met to plan and develop the second RFP. It was first assumed that only minor revisions would be necessary, and that the RFP would be issued within a few months. The RFP development team included OOCEA staff, FDOT tolls staff, consultants from PBS&J, and the Telos Corporation.

Accompanying this second opportunity to write another RFP, however, was the team objective to write a document that would reflect as specifically as possible what the winning vendor would have to accomplish. Early in February 1994, OOCEA staff and Phil Burkhard of Telos expressed several concerns about the original RFP and suggested changes (e.g., the scope of services needed more structure and organization).

Also, the team knew a great deal more about the new toll ETTM–AVI equipment, and could use this knowledge in fashioning the second RFP. The experience of writing the first RFP also had positive effects. Still, it apparently was felt that the envisioned changes would not delay the issuance of the RFP for any length of time. At the Board meeting in late February, Hal Worrall announced that the RFP would be ready by April 1. In addition, he stated that an agreement concerning the schedule for takeover of the toll plazas had been reached with FDOT. Also, he announced that the computerized toll equipment was coming on line soon and that weekly meetings would be held to coordinate the several projects that were ongoing.

At the March Board meeting, David Pope discussed the privatization project. He announced that the project had been reactivated in October 1993 after being suspended almost nine months previously. He sought and received Board approval for the privatization effort to proceed.

Meetings of the 266 working group continued throughout March and into April. Christine Speer, FDOT Toll Operations Director, expressed her concerns in a letter dated April 26, 1994. She identified areas in which apparent changes were made from the first RFP. In the area of employee benefits, the requirement that the vendor would now be required to provide "comparable" benefits rather than "equivalent" benefits was an error because it would lessen the amount of benefits required from the vendor. She also expressed concerns in the areas of vendor access to ETTM software, auditing systems, and the Violation Enforcement System (VES) and performance criteria. In general, she felt the RFP language needed to be clarified in these areas to allow the OOCEA to enforce better contract provisions as well as to prevent the possibility of vendor error. These concerns were seriously considered by the 266 team, with the appropriate changes made to the final document. On May 31, 1994, the second 266 RFP was issued.

The subsequent months followed a pattern similar to that of the first RFP. Site visits for vendors were held in June and July. Five addenda were written and issued during July and August. The first three primarily answered vendor questions. Addendum four, however, reflected a decision to remove plaza maintenance services from the contract, as the OOCEA had decided to issue a separate maintenance contract. Addendum five clarified this decision and changed the due date for proposals to September 23.

It was decided in late August to remove the maintenance services part of the privatization RFP. The reasons for this decision were several and reflect important issues in cost savings and contract management.

OOCEA had obtained agreement from FDOT to take over the responsibility for maintenance of the roadway and all toll plazas as of July 1, 1993, as well as to contract with private vendors to provide these services. Since agreements with many of these vendors were already in place, cost savings in plaza maintenance could be achieved by continuing this arrangement rather than allowing the vendor who operated tolls to subcontract for maintenance.

The breadth of administrative oversight and contract management increases, however, as a greater number of contracts must be managed than would obviously be the case if the operations vendor was held accountable for providing maintenance services. In addition, the OOCEA's policy of awarding maintenance contracts businesses owned and operated by women or ethnic minorities could be much more readily controlled and maintained. The decision to remove maintenance services prompted at least one prospective vendor to back out of the bidding, as Lockheed declined to send in a bid, expressing disappointment that these services were not included.

By the due date, three proposals were received. These were from Florida Toll Services, a Morrison Knudsen/Parsons Brinckerhoff Joint Venture; United Infrastructure Corporation; and URS Consultants. The process for evaluating, scoring and selecting the winning bidder for the 266 contract was specified with great care. Not only did the OOCEA wish to ensure a fair and equitable process, it also wished to ensure any potential protest would have no legitimate basis. To ensure these goals the RFP clearly described the criteria for evaluation and scoring, and great care was taken to establish a process that conformed to these criteria outlined in the RFP.

The evaluation criteria were placed into three groups: (1) the qualification statement, worth a maximum of 60 points; (2) the technical proposal, worth as much as 220 points; and (3) the price proposal, worth a maximum of 120 points. The total number of points was 400.

The selection committee consisted of Hal Worrall, chairman (nonvoting); David Pope, Operations Manager; Greg Dailer, Director of Finance, Bill McKelvey, Director of Construction and Maintenance; and two FDOT managers: Milissa Burger, Regional Toll Operations Manager and Joe Kerce, from the Office of Toll Operations. The OOCEA General Counsel (Tom Ross or Lynn White) and General Engineering Consultant Contract Administrator (Donald Erwin from PBS&J) were present at all selection committee meetings and provided legal and procedural guidance as needed.

Three selection committee meetings were held on September 30, October 5, and October 25. In all cases, discussions concerning procedure and clarification of criteria were held. At no time were the relative merits of one proposal compared to another.

In addition, discussions at the October 25 meeting centered on issues such as making certain that the privatization contract was written so that it was not considered a private business use, thereby jeopardizing the tax exempt status for the bonds used to construct the plazas. More specifically, there needed to be an analysis of REV Proc 93-191, which established the safe harbor criteria that would allow OOCEA to enter into a service contract while ensuring the bonds maintained their tax exempt status. Tom Ross, general counsel for the OOCEA, discussed preliminary issues with the committee.[2]

Of more immediate importance at that meeting was preparation for the oral presentations from the three proposers, scheduled for the next day. To ensure fairness, Hal Worrall first identified ground rules for the discussion of each proposal. Members of the selection committee were to raise issues, questions, or problems with each proposal, but in no way were they to indicate how they had scored a proposal on any criteria. Also, they were to develop questions for the oral presentations, as well as discuss general procedure.

On October 26, 1994, the three proposers presented oral arguments and responded to specific questions from the selection committee. Each proposer had approximately one hour for presentation and response to questions. The presentations were well attended by personnel from each of the three bidders. The presentations and the total experience went smoothly.

Two days later each member of the selection committee submitted his or her proposal evaluation booklet to Don Erwin, the GEC contract administrator. His responsibility was to tally the scores. That afternoon, the price proposals were opened at a public meeting at the OOCEA headquarters. They were immediately given to the OOCEA audit firm for tabulation and review.

On November 3, 1994, the first stage of the privatization effort came to a conclusion, as the grand total scores were posted at the OOCEA. Although one proposer posted an intent to protest notice, no protest was received within the ten-day legal time period. Florida Toll Services was awarded the highest number of points.

FDOT–OOCEA AND PRIVATIZATION COINCIDE

With the privatization process nearing conclusion, throughout the previous months OOCEA staff consulted with FDOT staff to finalize the necessary interlocal agreement that allowed OOCEA to privatize the toll operations.

Even though agreement had been reached concerning the schedule of OOCEA takeover of the toll plazas, no formal interlocal agreement had been forthcoming. From August through November, OOCEA staff meetings discussed the status of FDOT response to the OOCEA draft sent to FDOT in November 1992. Finally, on November 28, 1994, Greg Dailer announced at a staff meeting that FDOT had finally returned a draft that was not that much different from the one originally sent to OOCEA more than two years previously. The issue of whether FDOT could take over the toll operations at their option was a key point in this agreement. It was suggested that perhaps FDOT would agree to language that would allow them to cancel the agreement for cause.

Throughout the next two months, OOCEA staff pushed to finalize both the privatization contract with FTS and the FDOT interlocal agreement. Hal Worrall learned in early December that FDOT had unilaterally decided to increase the pool of state employee toll collectors that had to be given first right of refusal for positions with FTS. Central Florida turnpike toll collectors would also be given the right to transfer to the OOCEA toll plazas and work for FTS. It was felt that this would increase the financial obligation for OOCEA.

At a December 28 Board meeting, Hal Worrall requested (and received) the authority to grant approval of a contract agreement with FTS subject to the addition of a contingency clause making a signed interlocal agreement with FDOT a prerequisite. Negotiations with FDOT were continuing, as Worrall and Christine Speer met on December 19.

An agreement was finally signed on January 20, 1995. OOCEA could finally proceed legally with the privatization effort.

A TRANSITION YEAR

The year 1995 proved to be a year of positive results for OOCEA. A successful transition to privatized toll operations was achieved. The ETTM–AVI equipment was installed and was operating with few errors. The interlocal agreement with FDOT was completed, and relationships between OOCEA and FDOT remained positive and supportive.

The privatization contract with FTS was completed on January 9, with the final signatures dated February 28. Transition from FDOT toll operations to FTS was the next step, and it entailed the coordination of several elements. David Pope, who took charge of the effort, first met with FTS on January 20. A week later he met with FTS and Milissa Burger from FDOT to explain the process. Beginning on February 6, a transition team from OOCEA, FDOT, FTS, and PBS&J met every Friday through April.

A key issue was the transition of FDOT employees to FTS. To ensure that this would occur as smoothly as possible, a letter from FDOT was sent to all employees in February thoroughly explaining the transition process.

A job fair was held from February 27 through March 8 for all employees to help toll operations employees decide whether (1) to transfer to other FDOT positions, either outside of the OOCEA system or with the Florida Turnpike; (2) to become employees of FTS with the same or similar positions; (3) to seek employment elsewhere; or (4) to retire.

The job fair was deemed a success, as positions either with FDOT or FTS were found for all full-time operations employees that desired them. The approximately 182 FDOT positions were filled quickly. Employees at some plazas transitioned into FTS because they enjoyed working at those plazas and did not wish to commute a longer distance to other FDOT plazas. Many of the long-tenured supervisors and managers decided to remain with FDOT. In addition, employment was provided for almost half of the temporary employees.

During April and May almost all toll plazas were converted to FTS without major incident or problem. The April audit reports from FTS needed to be resubmitted and toll collectors were still not saying "thank you" as late as May. In response, FTS had established "mystery" drivers that would report toll collector courtesy. An employee incentive system, known as the incentive performance program was established, as well as a customer "3-C" system (complaint, compliment, or comment).

CONCLUSION

The OOCEA has achieved many of its goals in privatizing toll operations. Savings are significant, as OOCEA has saved approximately $1 million per year. Quality of service has increased, as the efforts by FTS to improve courtesy are working. The ETTM system has greatly facilitated a successful audit process. Transportation services to Central Florida have also been greatly improved with the increasing popularity of the E-PASS system.

It remains unclear what role FDOT wishes to play in contract oversight or management. As the experience with privatization of 266 continues, the newly created relationships among FDOT, OOCEA and FTS continue to evolve.

NOTES

1. In addition to the higher turnover rate, since many OPS employees would accept permanent employment elsewhere when it was offered, other problems included lower levels of performance, greater numbers of rules infractions, and an overall lack of commitment to quality service.

2. Subsequent rulings by the IRS allowed the privatization process to proceed.

PRIVATIZATION TRANSFER: THEORY AND PRACTICE

3

Privatization of government services has been viewed as a significant strategy in response to governments' interest in "doing more with less." Of the great variety of privatization methods, contracting with private or nonprofit firms remains the most widely used method.

The process of transferring public sector service delivery to the private vendor can be viewed as containing various stages, including: (1) the privatization decision stage; (2) the service transfer stage (which includes many steps, ending with the signing of the privatization contract); (3) the contract management stage; and (4) the contract renewal or reassignment stage. Existing literature has not fully examined the privatization transfer process from a theoretical perspective in which an ideal process would be identified. Throughout such a process the values of efficiency, responsiveness, and effectiveness must be examined for each of the above mentioned stages.

A decision to privatize can be based upon many factors, including (1) lower costs, (2) greater potential responsiveness, and (3) greater quality of service delivery. The service transfer stage includes various "nuts and bolts" steps, many of which need careful planning and analysis if the three values are to be reflected adequately. These steps include (1) the creation of the privatization RFP, in which specific delivery processes, procedures, and policies must be identified as much as possible, along with the standards of quality and responsiveness; (2) the rating of vendor responses, in which the criteria for rating must be identified and assessed in terms of fairness and adherence to legal and ethical standards; (3) the awarding of the contract; and (4) the formal transition to the vendor, in which the experience of the public sector agency employees is examined. The third stage deals with contract management and entails issues such as the effectiveness of the monitoring or management effort made by the government agency to ensure that the vendor adheres to the contract. Finally, the contract renewal or reassignment stage focuses on the extent to which an analysis or evaluation of vendor performance is performed along with the resulting decision.

Although each stage will be reviewed separately, it must be recognized that the stages of the service transfer process are closely related. The decision to privatize should not be made, for example, without a full understanding of the tasks and challenges associated with the contract management stage.

THE PRIVATIZATION DECISION STAGE

The decade of the 1980s reflected a growing trend among all governments to privatize services. Although privatization includes a wide variety of public–private arrangements (e.g., Farr 1989), contracting out public sector provided services to private vendors remains the most widely used.

It is expected that privatization will remain a primary tool to provide services and facilities during the 1990s (MacManus 1992). The primary reason for its attractiveness is cost savings. In a 1987 International City Management Association (ICMA) survey of local governments, 60 percent responded that citizen demand for more services without tax increases led to greater privatization (David 1988). A similar survey in 1988 indicated that "internal fiscal pressures" was the leading reason for over 80 percent of cities and 74 percent of counties to consider privatizing services (Farr 1989).

Although a great many local, state, and federal services are contracted out, the privatization decision should be made only after careful review of a variety of factors. The following discussion of each factor or criteria presents factors that favor privatization as well as potential dangers or problems that may influence a decision not to privatize.

Cost Savings

The most widely cited reason for the privatization decision is that it will cost the government less to deliver a service if it is contracted out to a private or nonprofit organization. These savings can come from a variety of sources.

Increased Competition and the Profit Motive

Much has been written concerning the positive impact that competition among private vendors has in minimizing costs. The cost savings come from two sources. First, the existence of alternative suppliers of a service will provide an incentive for the current private vendor to maintain lower costs and be less wasteful, or else risk losing the contract when it is time for rebid (Barnekov and Raffel 1990; Worsnop 1992). Quality of performance will also be maintained at higher levels if the private vendor realizes that if contract performance standards are not met the government can invoke the performance bonds that had to be posted and rebid the contract.

Concurrently, by keeping costs as low as possible, the vendor is likely to achieve higher levels of profit. Efficiencies and cost saving measures will be discovered and implemented because the profit motive provides a sufficient incentive (Bennett and Johnson 1980).

The lack of competition, because the government provides monopolistic services, plus the lack of a profit motive and other incentives, also suggests that the public sector manager has little reason to lower costs. In fact, incentives are likely to exist that stimulate public managers to spend more than is needed. If less than the allocated budget is spent in a given fiscal year, there is no "reward" other than a "pat on the back" and a lower budget for the coming year. Public managers will likely discover innovative ways to spend the entire allocated budget rather than identify ways of reducing the budget and returning funds to the city treasury (Harney 1992).

In fact, there may be incentives for public managers to increase their budget beyond what is needed to provide a service. The compensation for a public manager may be directly related to the number of employees in the department, the size of the budget, and the span of control. Without a share in the profits as an incentive to reduce costs, the public manager may feel that a higher salary and potential career advancement may be based upon increasing services and therefore spending more, not less (Jensen 1989; Downs 1967).

Labor Costs

Much of the reduced costs are derived from reduced labor costs. There are two sources of potentially lower labor costs: compensation, including fringe benefits, and labor practices.

The assumption here is that private vendors will pay employees lower salary and benefits than will the public sector counterparts for performing the same tasks. This is accurate because public sector compensation practices may lead to higher salaries that exist in the private labor market of a given community (Lawther et al. 1993). If, for example, the salary structure of a city contains steps that reward longevity with consistent annual raises, the maintenance worker who has been employed by the city for twenty years will command a salary that is above the going market rate.

Civil service provisions have been adopted to eliminate patronage and to compensate employees according to their performance. In attempting to do so, however, public sector wages are often inflated above levels that adequately reflect productivity (Hirsch 1989).

The studies that have compared public sector wages with those of private sector counterparts after privatization show widely varying results. If the data reflected differences in labor market wage rates, then these results should be expected. In a study undertaken by Stevens (1984), the employee wages for eight different municipal services in ten California cities that contract out were compared to wages in ten California cities that provide services in house. For street cleaning and tree trimming, the differences were negligible, with 2 percent and 6 percent lower salaries. Wages for janitorial services, however, were 29 percent lower when contracted out, while wages for asphalt overlayers were 58 percent higher in the private sector.

In a General Accounting Office study (1985), 53 percent of federal workers remaining in the same positions affected by service contracts received lower wages than they did prior to contracting. A review of these and other studies by the National Commission for Employment Policy (1988), concludes that wages are lower, but not significantly.

In the area of fringe benefits, however, numerous studies have indicated that these costs are higher in the public sector. Brotman (1992), in a study of mental health services in Massachusetts, found that employee fringe benefit packages were reduced by 40 percent after privatization. In an earlier review, Ferris and Graddy (1986) similarly noted that private sector packages were much less generous that those found in the public sector.

The more specific issues are clearly discussed in Becker et al. (1995). The authors indicate that efforts to privatize mental health services in a large metropolitan county in Florida floundered primarily because the county provided a much larger contribution to a fringe benefit package than community (private and nonprofit) vendors providing similar services. The county provided an almost 17 percent retirement contribution, while the highest similar private sector contribution was only 6 percent. For family health care coverage, the county required only a 9.7 percent contribution from the employee, while contributions required by private sector providers ranged from 27.1 percent to 77.3 percent.

Additional labor savings will also accrue from the much greater flexibility of labor practices that exists in the private sector. It is more likely that there will be more levels of supervision in the public sector than in the private sector. The phenomenon of "grade creep," which characterizes many governments, results in more positions than are necessary. In attempt to provide promotional opportunities as well as salary improvements, the creation of additional classes as well as the invalid reclassification of positions to higher salary grades has been frequently noted in government.[1]

Removing one or more unneeded, supervisory levels will be much easier in the private sector. There are fewer civil service or personnel rules and regulations that would hinder the removal of positions. In addition, the existence of "bumping rights" in the federal government and many others will further lessen the savings if the government attempts to eliminate positions (Hebdon 1995).

It is likely that the private vendor that bids on a contract to delivery services will specify fewer levels of supervision and personnel (Savas 1987).

One study (Berenyi and Stevens 1988) suggested that private organizations are more likely to allow first line supervisors the authority to hire and fire employees. Without the often extensive rules and regulations governing discipline and dismissal as found in the public sector, private organizations can demand more productivity from their employees. Lower turnover is likely to occur as well.

Flexibility of work schedules is often greater with private vendors, leading to better capacity utilization. Often governments maintain a workforce large enough to meet peak load demand and handle crises. Small cities especially have much less flexibility in managing labor costs to avoid underutilization (Ferris and Graddy 1986). This may mean, for example, that city employees who cut grass in the summer are maintained in employment during the winter months, clearing snow from streets. Private organizations are much more likely to utilize temporary labor pools to provide additional capacity when needed, maintaining a workforce that is less than peak load demand would require.

Economies of Scale: Equipment and Materials

If a large portion of the service provision costs are in equipment and materials, then large-scale producers may be able to purchase these at a lower price than small-scale producers (Ferris and Graddy 1986; Stein 1990). If a larger number of recipients can be served, economies of scale are possible (Ammons and Hill 1995). A private vendor serving a wider geographical area including several municipalities will normally have lower costs than any one specific government (Rehfuss 1989).

Technical Feasibility

If a government does not presently have the capability of providing a service, it is more likely that contracting out that service will be less expensive than developing the in-house capability (DeHoog 1985). This would be true for newly incorporated cities or special districts (Rehfuss 1989). This is even more the case if the service is technically complex (Carver 1989). Also, similar to the discussion of utilization of capacity mentioned above, if the services are needed only on an occasional basis, contracting with a consultant may be less costly than hiring a full-time employee.

Potential Dangers and Challenges

In reviewing actual costs of current government service delivery and in estimating costs of privatization, those in charge of making the privatization decision must first be aware of all potential costs. They must also anticipate various situations or conditions that may arise in the future and plan how to deal with them accordingly. There is always the issue of the level of service quality that is currently provided compared to that of a contractor. Much of the analysis at this point can result in contract provisions that will guard against unexpected costs.

Present Costs

Although it may seem reasonably simple to identify salaries and fringe benefit costs, as well as the cost of services and supplies, other direct provision costs and indirect costs may be more difficult to measure accurately. The costs of capital equipment must be assessed. Both replacement and repair costs must be identified. If there is an equipment replacement program, the present day cost of replacing equipment in the near future must be estimated. If there is a preventative maintenance program, its costs must be estimated as well, since it will have a direct impact on estimated repairs. If lower cost, less durable equipment is currently used, and is overused and under-maintained, repair costs are likely to increase if the current service remains in the public sector (Harney 1992).

In addition to the equipment and materials used on the job, two other indirect costs may be noted accurately to estimate present costs. These are departmental charges that cannot be charged directly to the direct provision of services, including travel, data processing and printing; and overhead services provided by staff agencies such as personnel, accounting, the legal department, and auditing. Plus, it may be that one or more internal service funds (ISFs) exist that would include motor pool charges based on the number of miles driven; and data processing charges based upon the number of hours of central processing time used (Coe and O'Sullivan 1993).

For the purposes of a privatization decision, it can be argued that indirect costs must be identified only to the extent that contracting out would actually reduce or eliminate positions (Farr 1989). If the effect of contracting out a service is only to reduce the workload of municipal support personnel without any lessening of actual costs, then this viewpoint is supported. To the extent that ISFs are in existence, however, and the funds used to support various support services are a recognized part of the budgetary process, then these indirect costs cannot be ignored. A decrease in departmental or overhead charges because one service is privatized may mean that charges to remaining services may be increased to offset these charges.

Future Costs

There are two categories of future costs that must be estimated prior to making the final privatization decision: (1) costs incurred by the government, and (2) costs incurred by the contractor that would be charged to the government. The former category includes compensation costs that will not be eliminated, plus additional costs associated with contract management. The latter category includes costs identified by the winning contractor who is awarded the contract, plus costs associated with requested contract changes and potential bankruptcy or service interruption.

When a service is transferred to a private or nonprofit contractor, government employees may be given the option of working for the contractor or being reassigned to other positions within the government. In accurately calculating future government costs, the salaries and fringe benefit packages for any reassigned employees must be considered. If the reassigned employees would be filling vacancies the government expected to fill within the current fiscal year, then there are no future costs that need to be part of privatization. If they would be filling vacancies the government had no intention of filling in the near future, then their salaries must be included as part of future government costs.

A key future cost that may be underestimated is that associated with contract management. There is the danger that the government expects that monitoring and managing contractors will be assumed by current employees as another task added to their already assigned duties. Although this may be a reasonable assumption if the contracted service is small and intermittent, there are many reasons that should compel the government to hire an additional full-time contract manager. If the tasks are assigned to a current employee, management efforts may be inconsistent, thereby increasing the risk that poor performance may not be noticed in a timely fashion. If serious problems arise, requiring a great deal of contract management time, then other assigned duties will suffer. If the service is complex and/or quality standards are imprecise, the need to renegotiate many of the contract provisions even after the contract has been awarded may require a full-time position.

In estimating what the cost of bids would be from contractors responding to an RFP for the privatized service, both expected costs bid and anticipated costs throughout the life of the contract must be considered. The ease or difficulty of estimating these costs depends upon several issues.

First, the source of the expected cost savings must be identified. If salaries of current government employees are higher than the market rate because of longevity and the service is one for which there is an abundance of temporary employees with sufficient skills, such as garbage collection, then savings will occur because the same number of personnel will be needed to perform the same tasks; the contractor employees will simply be paid less. A similar logic may hold true for fringe benefit costs.

If there is the assumption that the contractor can perform the service with fewer personnel, or with fewer levels of management, then the anticipated bid amount is more difficult to estimate. Likewise, if it is expected that economies of scale and equipment and materials costs will be less, these costs will also be difficult to estimate since the actual cost to the contractor will not be known.

Uncertainty concerning estimated future costs can be lessened somewhat by RFP specifications. Comparable levels of fringe benefit packages may be required. Minimum staffing levels can also be identified. If comparable private sector services (e.g., lawn service) exist; or if neighboring cities, for example, have privatized the service, then a more accurate picture of future contracted costs can be obtained.

Ultimately, the degree of certainty concerning the expected level of service quality, as well as the understanding of how to perform the service, will affect the accuracy of the future cost estimate. Ideally, the costs need to be identified prior to the decision to begin the service transfer process by creating and issuing an RFP. If it is difficult to obtain accurate cost data, however, and other factors support proceeding with the contracting effort, such as a lack of political opposition, then it may be feasible to issue the RFP with the expectation that it would be withdrawn if the cost savings are not as high as expected.

Sufficient Competition

Several studies, including MacManus (1992), have suggested that unless there are a sufficient number of "willing and able" private sector suppliers, privatization should not be attempted. The lack of competition will increase the cost of the privatization contract, since a "monopolistic" situation may exist. There is likely to be a lessening of the incentive to be as efficient and service quality conscious as possible. Furthermore, if the vendor approaches the government for more funds after the contract has been awarded, citing increased and unexpected costs, these requests are likely to be granted if sufficient alternative suppliers do not exist.

If the vendor goes bankrupt or cannot deliver the service in a timely enough fashion, the responsibility for providing the service falls back on government.[2] Without sufficient alternative suppliers who can quickly provide a similar service, the government should reconsider any privatization decision. Or, alternatively, the government may wish to retain some in-house expertise or equipment to counteract the threat of service interruption.

Increased Managerial Flexibility

Private managers will have greater flexibility in labor practices, which will mean that labor costs will be lower for private firms than governments, as discussed earlier. The same incentives that exist for private employees to be productive also allow greater managerial flexibility that is likely to occur in the public sector.

There is often little incentive for managers and employees to be innovative in the public sector. In fact, there is considerable evidence that these employees have a great deal of discretion in resisting change if they desire. Rules and regulations found in procedural manuals are difficult to change quickly. New technology may introduce the need for additional training and skill updating that may be met with resistance. Conversely, because private employees realize there is a much greater likelihood they may be fired for poor performance and rewarded financially for improved performance, they will be more willing to accept change and innovative practices.

Changes dictated by varying user demands and needs as well as technological improvements can be introduced and accepted much more rapidly in the private sector. To help facilitate these changes, incentive systems that reward employees more quickly are also much more likely in the private sector.

There is the potential danger that the contractor will use the managerial flexibility to "cut corners," finding ways to maximize profit by lessening service quality. An incentive contract plus effective contract management can limit the use of managerial flexibility in this fashion.[3]

Improved Service Quality, Effectiveness, and Responsiveness

To the extent that there are few if any incentives for government employees to strive for a higher quality of service and effectiveness and to be responsive to citizen complaints, there is the potential for improved service quality with a private vendor. If there is sufficient competition, the private vendor should be sensitive to citizen complaints, for example, fearing that the contract may not be renewed (Rehfuss 1989).

In the area of health and human services, if the contractor is a nonprofit organization, there is also the perception that clients needs will be better met. If the nonprofit organization has close ties to the community which it serves, citizens as well as clients may feel that better quality service is more likely than if government or private vendors provided the service (Ferris and Graddy 1986).[4]

There is a great deal of concern, however, that a lower quality of service and less responsiveness will occur with contracting out. Morgan and England (1988) suggest that citizens will have less opportunity to participate in the service delivery process if a private vendor provides the service. The assumption is that citizens will still complain to the government if service is inadequate, for example, and means of direct communication to the private vendor will be closed or limited.

Many authors, including Sharkansky (1980), have mentioned the danger of "creaming," in which services will be provided only to those citizens or clients who have the fewest needs and whose problems are the least costly to solve. The issue of service access and equity then arises as services to disadvantaged citizens may be of lesser quality than to others. As Murin (1985) argues, however, contracting out may prevent providing services to only the least needy. If there is sufficient competition, and if specifications are written into the RFP and contract, governments may be able to ensure greater equity of service with contractors than if public sector employees provided the service.[5]

Public Employee Opposition and the Political Climate

In the 1987 ICMA survey of local governments, 47 percent of the respondents identified government union and elected official opposition as a major barrier to privatization (David 1988). A major reason for this opposition may be the loss of power, prestige, and membership by the union, coupled with the threat for elected officials of being voted out of office.

Two related factors that impact on the degree of potential employee opposition are (1) the degree to which the service is highly visible, and (2) the existence and strength of a union (Farr 1989). The more visible the service to a community (e.g., garbage collection), the more likely that media attention will be given to the privatization effort. Without considerable communication with employees as well as the press, the government risks a lessening of public support. The existence of a union further requires careful handling, in that without continual communication with employees and union leaders, public employee morale is likely to suffer.

Yager (1994) indicates that the nature of labor management relations can have a significant impact on the type of analysis performed for a city council considering the privatization of solid waste collection. As it becomes known that the council is considering privatization, if the labor management relations become adversarial, then the information presented to the council can vary substantially. In two cities studied, Riverside, California, and Brownsville, Texas, management presented analyses indicating substantial cost savings, while labor, through union representatives, stressed the potential for lower quality service and lowered employee morale. Only in Ann Arbor, Michigan, where the union was given the option of considering a "city bid," were labor management relations not adversarial, and the city council was given a more objective analysis of cost and service quality issues.

If it is unclear how much cost savings will accrue because a lack of an accurate analysis of public and private costs, then government will find it difficult to overcome this opposition. Furthermore, if there is the actual or perceived threat that jobs will be lost and/or salaries or fringe benefits reduced, then a political climate that supports privatization may not exist.

THE SERVICE TRANSFER STAGE

Once the decision to privatize has been made, a variety of implementation issues face public sector decision makers. The service transfer stage includes the RFP creation, rating of contractor responses, awarding of the contract, and transfer of production control to the contractor. All of these steps must be analyzed in terms of how they affect the management of the contract, the subsequent stage.

First, the RFP must be written. The degree of specificity in the RFP has significant implications for the ease and nature of the ability of the government to effectively manage the contract. Second, the way in which contractor responses are rated impacts on the choice of the winning bidder. This has a significant impact on the bid award, especially concerning the issue of whether the lowest bidder will be awarded the contract. Third, the nature of the contract itself, especially the degree to which incentives are included, will impact the degree of motivation among employees and managers to provide services in the most efficient and effective manner possible.

Finally, the nature of the transition or mobilization effort where current government employees are transferred to the private vendor also impacts on the morale and motivation of these employees once they leave government employ. During this stage the locus of everyday managerial control is also handed to the contractor. Carefully monitoring is needed to ensure operations continue with few service quality concerns.

The Request for Proposal

Before reviewing RFPs, it is valuable to review the spectrum of methods by which the government may solicit bids from private or nonprofit bidders. The invitation to bid (ITB) is more appropriate for the procurement of goods rather than services, as it specifies the exact scope of work to be performed. In its applications for service contracting, it would not be used often, since it infers that there is only one way to accomplish very specifically identified goals and objectives. The contractor provides only a price bid.

At the other end of the spectrum, if there are few if any clearly specified and measurable goals, many acceptable methods available to achieve those goals exist, and it is expected that the standards of quality are unknown or cannot be specified, then a multistep bid process can be used (Harney 1992). In this case, the government can enter into negotiations with the bidders concerning the technical proposals. Price bids can be kept separate. When the government is satisfied that all bidders can perform the services, then price bids are opened, and the lowest bidder is awarded the contract.

The RFP represents a middle ground between these two extremes. Any RFP for services contracting must include at least three aspects: (1) the goals or objectives of the government in providing the service, (2) the standards by which the private vendor will be judged regarding how well these goals are met, and (3) the activities which the vendor must perform in order to reach the goals. The extent to which these three aspects are specified precisely indicates the range of RFPs that are possible.

A more general, shorter RFP has the advantage of letting the vendor provide the detail, especially with regard to the activities needed in service provision. The government can identify the service goals in broad terms, and the bidder responds with more specific statements of how to accomplish the service (Fitch 1988). This approach may also be preferred if the government wants to change the ways in which the service is delivered, but may not be certain of the best way that innovation or change could take place. In this manner, the private vendor will help to "write the RFP."

The disadvantage of a general RFP is that the vendor may not clearly understand the priorities of what the government wishes to accomplish. Responses in terms of cost and service activities may be unrealistic. If standards are unclear or omitted from the response to the RFP, contract management difficulties are likely to occur.

An RFP that provides great detail may preempt wishes to change or innovate, as the vendor must provide cost estimates and identify service activities that are as close as possible to those outlined in the RFP. The advantage of such detail is that contract management becomes much easier since there is likely to be fewer unanticipated conditions or situations that will cause conflict between the vendor and the government.

An ideally written RFP contains both general and specific aspects. Although goals may be general (e.g., providing the service in the most cost efficient manner), standards can be specific, especially those that refer to vendor performance or service activity. Service provision can be authored in both specific terms, if the activity is routine, for example, and in general terms with regard to the number of personnel needed to perform the service, if it is suspected that innovative managerial techniques may be feasible.

Rating of Bidder Responses

There are at least three main criteria by which bidder responses can be rated. These include (1) bidder qualifications, (2) technical proposals, and (3) price. There is a variety of ways to review and rate responses for these three criteria. A choice of methods depends in part on the issues of goal clarity, standard specificity, and the degree of detail needed to identify the activities used to provide the service. In all cases, the need to avoid bid protest is of paramount importance.

Bidder Qualifications

Determining bidder qualifications can be done before technical and price proposals are opened; as part of a process in which all three are rated simultaneously; or after technical and price proposals are opened. The postqualification determination is the most common for local governments (Harney 1992). This does not restrict anyone from bidding. After price proposals are opened, qualifications are reviewed. If the lowest bidder is deemed qualified, the contract is awarded. In this case, the number of bidder qualifications to be reviewed is limited. The disadvantage of this process occurs when the lowest bidder is not qualified. Often a protest will be lodged when the bid is awarded to the next lowest bidder. The more routine the service, the greater the advantage of a postqualification process.

A prequalification process, often characterized by a separate request for qualifications (RFQ), allows only those qualified to bid (Seader 1986). Although protests are possible here, disagreements may be more easily resolved since price bids are unknown.

If it is important to encourage as many bidders as possible, and the degree of competition is uncertain, and if it is possible to rate the degree of qualifications, then the preferred way to judge qualifications may be to employ a clearly specified rating system. The degree to which experience and backgrounds of specific management personnel are rated, compared to the past experience of a private firm, may suggest this process is preferable.

The choice of qualifications must be sensitive to the nature of the service and the availability of bidders. For a service such as grass cutting, qualifications can be relatively minimal. In the area of social or mental health services, in which goal achievement and quality of service is difficult to measure and for which a variety of methods are acceptable, bidder qualifications need to be set at a higher level.

Rating of the Technical Proposal

The rating of the extent to which the bidder meets the requirement set out by the RFP involves several factors. First, the bidder may be disqualified or given few rating points if clearly identified requirements are not met, such as providing a fringe benefit package that is comparable to that provided by the government; if the minimum levels of service identified by the RFP are not met; or if the activities identified (scope of work) do not seem to be able to accomplish the service goals.

For those types of services for which the RFP can be very specific, it may be relatively easy to provide a valid rating. The bidder's response meets the requirements, or it does not. For services toward the more general end, the rating becomes more complex. The activities needed to perform the service may not be spelled out in detail, if the RFP requires a procedures manual to be created within ninety days after the contract award, or a performance evaluation system is to be created, or a quality management system set up. To the extent that the government wishes to require these activities, but recognizes there may be more than one way to implement them, the more general RFP may make it more difficult to accurately judge the response.

Rating of Price

In one sense, the rating of price is easy, as the lowest bid is rated higher than the next lowest bid. To the extent that the rating system used allows the award to be given to a private or nonprofit firm that is not the lowest bidder, which is possible if a point rating system is used, the rating of price for each must be proportional: If the lowest bid is 20 percent lower than the highest bid, then the lowest bid should receive 20 percent more points in a rating system.

There are several goals for the bid evaluation or rating process. All bidders must be given a fair, nonbiased opportunity to be awarded the contract. The point rating system, if one is used, must be carefully developed to give appropriate weights to qualifications, technical proposals, and price. The rating process should choose the bidder who will effectively perform once awarded the contract. Finally, the rating system should ensure that the winning bidder be capable of operating within the costs as presented. A bid that is "low balled," or one in which the bidder provides below actual costs in anticipation of later convincing the government to increase payments, should be identified by an accurate and valid rating process.

The Contract

There are a variety of contract types that can be offered. These fall into two categories, the most common one being fixed price and contractor cost (National Institute of Governmental Purchasing 1986).

Fixed Price

With fixed price contracts, vendors deliver a specific level of service for a set price. Any cost overruns are absorbed by the vendor, while any cost savings are also kept by the vendor. Variations of fixed price contracts include the following:

Firm Fixed Price. If there is little expected uncertainty in the future service provision, and the government is assured that a fair and competitive price has been provided by the vendor, this is the most appropriate type. Often these contracts are for duration of less than one year (Harney 1992). Price increases are not permitted.

Fixed Price with Escalation (or Deescalation). This type is most appropriate when there are uncertainties with regard to the future need for labor and materials. It reduces the need for vendors to include in their bid upward cost adjustments that become excessive profits if the needs do not occur. Similarly, if labor or materials needs are reduced, then the vendor will receive less than originally bid.

Fixed Price with Incentives. An agreed-upon fixed ceiling price plus profit serves as the base for this type of contract. Any savings from projected costs are shared between the vendor and the government according to an agreed-upon ratio. If the actual costs are higher than the base, then the vendor profit is reduced. In this type, both cost savings and cost overruns are typically shared by both vendor and government.

Cost Plus Contracts

If there is so much uncertainty with regard to service quantity, and therefore labor and material costs cannot be accurately predicted with a firm-price type of contract, then a cost-plus contract must be used. If there is a financial risk to the service, one in which revenue or user fees are anticipated to offset costs, this type of contract is less preferable because the contractor is guaranteed cost reimbursement up to a certain predetermined level. There is little incentive for the contractor to reduce costs (Farr 1989).

There may be an advantage to cost plus contracts if the government wishes to change future labor costs by lowering the level of service, replacing labor with new technology, or increasing the level of service and thereby requiring additional labor costs. The flexibility inherent in these contracts may make them preferable to fixed price contracts.

Cost Plus Fixed Fee. The contractor is reimbursed all costs plus a fixed fee or "profit." If costs are lower than anticipated, then the fixed fee amount is a higher percentage of the total contract price.

Cost Plus Incentive Fee. The contract price reflects an agreed-upon cost and fee. If costs are lower than anticipated, then the contractor and government share in the savings, with the contractor receiving a higher fee. If costs are higher, then the amount of fee for the contractor is reduced (or eliminated) but the costs would still be reimbursed.

In reality, a contract may reflect a combination of various features of more than one of the types discussed above. A contract may contain an estimated cost for labor, for example, because the amount of labor time needed to provide the service cannot be estimated accurately. To maintain high levels of service and prevent the contractor from "cutting corners" by not quickly replacing employees who have resigned, labor is reimbursed on a cost basis. Materials and equipment, however, could be handled on a fixed price basis.

In many respects a contract with incentives, whether it is cost plus or fixed, is ideal. A high level of performance is ensured, as the vendor searches for ways to reduce costs, knowing that profits will increase. Employee incentive systems can be established to further improve the likelihood of reduced costs.

There must be assurances, however, that quality of service is maintained. Clearly defined and understood measures, ideally included in the RFP, must be identified and placed in the contract. It is also more crucial that contract management efforts focus on collecting the data relevant to the measures chosen, and analyzing it on a more periodic basis.

THE TRANSITION OR MOBILIZATION STAGE

There are a variety of issues relevant to this stage. These include the future of the current government employees and the transition from public to private control.

Impact on Current Employees

If an underlying goal is to provide continuous, uninterrupted service provision, and maintain or increase performance levels, attention must be paid to how current employees are treated throughout the process. As noted, lines of communication with current employees should remain open while the government is considering whether to privatize. Overcoming employee and/or union opposition may require agreements regarding salary and fringe benefits that must be part of the RFP. Finally, during the transition stage, easing employees into employment with the contractor or alternative employment will help allay fears that may negatively affect performance.

Options concerning what will happen to current employees after the contractor delivers the service should be considered from the very beginning of the privatization process. First, alternative employment options are often guaranteed. In many cases, the contractor is required to give the current government employees the "right of first refusal" for any position with the contractor for which they are qualified. Depending upon the number of employees and the nature of the service, current employees could be promised employment with the government in another department or agency. Outplacement services could be provided.

Contractors often accept this type of requirement. Experience and knowledge of the service and the work environment are obvious advantages held by current employees. If there are few trained, experienced potential employees in the appropriate labor market, the contractor may desire to hire current employees, and would likely do so even if not required.

The issues of salary and fringe benefits are more critical issues for which there are few guidelines. If one of the reasons privatization occurs is because government employees are being paid above the market rate, then to require that the contractor provide no less than current salaries for each government employee hired is undesirable. Similarly, especially if there is reason to believe that fewer levels of supervision or management are needed than are currently in place, requiring that the same number of employees at the same positions is also undesirable. Still, the Reason Foundation (1992) reports that many RFPs stipulate that salaries of any current government employee hired by the contractor cannot be at a lower amount. Contractors may agree, replacing higher paid employees with lower paid ones as attrition occurs. If those in supervisory or management positions decide to remain in government employ in other positions, then promotional opportunities would open for those who choose to work for the contractor.

There is the strong possibility that some employees would have to accept a lower salary if with the contractor. The job security that was present with the government will not be transferable as well. Although unions may argue in favor of guaranteed security as a condition of support for privatization (Becker et al. 1995), it seems unlikely contractors would agree.

When reviewing the labor cost pricing that is part of the bidders' response to the RFP, the government must be sensitive to the salaries that are paid. If they appear to be lower than the appropriate market rate, suspicion of "low balling" may occur. If they are lower because the bidder will hire temporary employees, given that such employees may not be as productive as permanent employees, the bid may be rated lower or deemed unacceptable. If possible, it is best to identify the desired policy regarding salaries and the use of temporary employees in the RFP.

The issue of fringe benefit packages may be complex. If the RFP states that "comparable" health and pension packages have to be offered, then the bidders response must be judged on the degree of comparability. If the government fringe benefit package is much greater than that of the private sector, then there is the risk that no firm will respond to the RFP.

Transition from Public to Private Control

There are a variety of transitional issues that face governments after the private vendor has been chosen. The contract manager or management team that will monitor the contract must devote close attention to the transition period to ensure that the activities promised by the contractor can be delivered. These include scheduling of when the contractor will take over service provision at what sites; the need for personnel training, especially if new employees are hired; establishing service provision policies and procedures; and other issues as identified by the RFP.

There is a variety of factors that influence the transition process. If the service is routine and there is confidence that the contractor employees possess the skills to provide the service, then the transition requires the least amount of time and effort. Much of the already existing information such as written procedures and employee schedules can be simply adopted by the contractor as a basis for establishing his or her own procedures.

To the extent that the service is not routine and/or there is a lack of confidence that the contractor employees can provide the service without appropriate training, then the transition period will be time consuming and potentially difficult. This may be the case when new equipment must be adopted, the contractor does not have extensive experience, or there is a change of technology needed to provide the service. If there has been great dependence on historical or institutional memory with few written policies or procedures, the transition will be much more difficult. Transitioning in steps, or in a few sites at a time, is imperative under these circumstances.

Although contract management has been separated from the rest of the privatization processes, in a real sense it begins with the transition from public to private or nonprofit contractors. Although the frequency of performance monitoring may lessen as the contract manager becomes confident that the service can be delivered, there are many other more complex policies and procedures that will take time to create and implement. The process of establishing these policies will only begin during the transition period.

Problems and Dangers

Critics of privatization often cite problems with the service transfer stage. Worsnop (1992) among others discusses the "low balling" problem so prevalent in DOD contracts, with cost overruns the norm. At the local level, the same phenomenon can occur if the equipment needed to perform the service (e.g., garbage collection), is sold by the city to the contractor. Thinking that the city has few alternatives, since it is without equipment, the contractor can raise the rates that he or she charges.

Sometimes the government may decide to contract out a service even though bidders are not experienced. As Hames (1984) points out, there may not always be the skills necessary to provide the service in the private sector. The government must be prepared to cancel the RFP if sufficient bidders do not exist. Similarly, a contract should not be awarded if there is doubt concerning the potential contractor's capabilities.

CONTRACT MANAGEMENT

The underlying values of efficiency, effectiveness, and responsiveness must be maintained throughout the contract management stage. Much of the criticism of privatization transfer focuses on the difficulties of maintaining contractor accountability after the contract has been awarded (DeHoog 1985). Yet it is possible to achieve greater control over service delivery in dealing with contractors than with government employees (Murin 1985).[6]

After the contract has been signed, the role of the government changes to one of contract administration or monitoring or to one of contract management. If contract monitoring characterizes the chosen role, the government risks losing effective control over the contractor, with problems in reaching stated goals a likely danger (Kettl 1993). Contract management, a more complex, dynamic, and often more difficult role, offers a greater opportunity for an effective partnership between the government and the contractor. The degree of success or failure during this phase of privatization also depends upon factors such as the degree of uncertainty inherent in the service and the degree of change that can be expected once the contractor assumes service provision responsibilities. The differences between contract monitoring and contract management are developed in more detail below.

Contract Monitoring Versus Contract Management

Harney (1992) identifies three types of output monitoring: (1) direct monitoring, which occurs during actual work performance; (2) follow-up monitoring, which occurs after work is finished; and (3) monitoring by exception, which can be direct or follow up but occurs only after complaints have been received. Direct monitoring, or observation of work performance, seems much more appropriate for contracts involving the production of visible outputs or products, or for contracts that provide a routine service. It is of limited use after an initial contract period unless there is the expectation of errors or in response to a complaint. Follow-up monitoring would seem more useful, especially if there is a review of a product according to written specifications, or records of services provided during a specified time period are easily obtainable. Monitoring by exception would provide the most infrequent, least visible role, especially if few complaints are received or few reasons to expect poor performance are identified. Many critics of contract monitoring point out the lack of consistent review, suggesting that many governmental monitors respond only when there are complaints (Rehfuss 1989).

In terms of more specific duties, the contract monitor or administrator ensures that (1) required reports are filed in a timely manner; (2) expenditures are within budget; (3) insurance certificates, bonds, and licenses are current; (4) contracts and related documentation are on file; and (5) payments are made to the contractor according to agreed upon deadlines. Contractor performance may be judged, but only according to contract provisions (Harney 1992).

Contract management entails a much more dynamic, evolving role, one that attempts to resolve issues that involve a variety of personnel from both government and the contractor. The contract manager establishes criteria and systems of evaluation and analysis. He or she also reviews reports and data for the purpose of suggesting service delivery improvements as well as the resolution of problems or complaints. Negotiations with the contractor ensue, leading to contract amendments or mutually accepted agreements concerning acceptable changes.

Contract monitoring suffices as an effective governmental role only if there are well-established specifications for the product or service; clearly specified, easily measured goals and standards; sufficient competition to ensure a high level of contractor motivation to maintain acceptable levels of efficiency and service quality; and few if any complaints from customers or citizens. Even under the unlikely event that all these conditions are present, contract monitoring abrogates much government control of service production to the extent that needed changes and possible improvements are likely to be overlooked. If problems occur, the monitor is likely to blame the contractor and insist that contract provisions be once again followed according to the existing contract.

It is essential that contract management occurs when changes in service delivery policies and procedures are needed or expected, and when the service or product is highly complex and/or can be greatly influenced by technological changes. Under these conditions, it is likely that goals and standards are unclear, not easily measurable, or need adjusting over the life of the contract. The RFP may allow for a significant amount of contractor discretion over service delivery policy, deliberately recognizing that a partnership between contract management and the contractor must be created that will allow for evolvement of policies and procedures in a dynamic relationship.

Contract Renewal or Reassignment

Successful privatization assumes that the relationship between the government and the contractor remain positive, with both parties working toward the goals of efficiency and improved service quality. For a variety of reasons, however, the performance of the contractor may prove to be unacceptable. Bankruptcy can occur, as the contractor may have underestimated the real service costs. There may be delays in service provision because of staffing inadequacies. Efforts to achieve efficiency may lead to decreased service quality.

The government must have a contingency plan in case the current contractor proves unacceptable. This is especially true if the service is provided on a continual basis and interruption is not legally possible. Prior to making such a drastic decision, however, the government must at a minimum consider establishing a process to deal with poor performance. In doing so, criteria that would lead to possible sanctions must be identified.

Part of this process includes consideration of the standards that are part of assessing the extent to which the stated contract goals are met. If a customer survey shows a decrease in satisfaction with the level of service quality, for example, the contract manager would note this drop, investigate the causes, and negotiate with the contractor to correct performance problems.

Such interactions would be similar to those that characterize the "dynamic partnership" discussed earlier. A distinction must be made, however, between actions that lead to greater cost savings, for example, because of improvements in procedures that are already operating at an acceptable level, and actions that occur because performance has dropped to levels that are less than acceptable. In this latter situation, it is necessary to establish a clearly identified process, because the likelihood of contract default is greater.

Characteristics of the process may include written correspondence sent to the contractor that may constitute formal notification of poor performance and/or lack of corrective action, formal meetings at which minutes are recorded, and a notice of contract default. The process is also important because documentation must be established that may ultimately be used to convince a bonding company that the contractor is not in compliance with the contract (Harney 1992).

The sanctions that are available to the government may be limited. The ultimate sanction, cancellation of the contract, is always risky for the government because there is no expectation that the bonding company will "bail out" the government by agreeing that the contractor is in default. Months of negotiation and/or litigation may ensue. More important, it invokes imple-menting the default contingency plan. The logistics in bringing in other per-sonnel and contractors to provide the service may lead to unacceptable levels of service interruption. A second sanction may simply be not to renew the contract of the current contractor. This may be a viable option if the contract is within a few months of completion. Other sanctions may include withhold-ing payment of management fees or profit; delaying payment until accept-able work is provided; providing part of the service by hiring personnel that are not employed by the contractor.

There are several options available within the default contingency plan. These include contracting with the next lowest bidder from the original so-licitation, using another contractor, using in-house personnel to deliver all or part of the service, and contracting with another government to deliver the service.

The choice of any option depends upon several factors, including the avail-ability of alternative contractors, legal ramifications of service interruption, and the size and complexity of the service.

CONCLUSION

Much of the literature reviewing privatization has focused on the privatiza-tion decision, often providing case studies of success or failure of privatiza-tion efforts. For the remaining three stages of the privatization transfer process, there is a paucity of accounts of how government should transfer services, manage contracts, and consider contract renewal.

Much work remains in reviewing these three stages. The conceptual un-derpinnings of an ideal RFP, for example, need to be explored in more depth, especially considering the type and nature of the service that is privatized. The various contract types can be described, but there is little analysis con-cerning which are best under what conditions and situations. Finally, con-tract management remains virtually unexplored in terms of how the various procedures and practices that could occur relate to the values of efficiency, quality of service, and accountability.

Ultimately, privatization should lead to services that are provided at the least cost while maintaining the specified quality of service. As public policy goals change, there should be the flexibility inherent in these services to re-flect different policy priorities, while maintaining appropriate accountability. More research and study remains to assist governments in achieving these goals.

NOTES

1. Tompkins (1995) has defined grade creep as the process by which more and more positions are over classified, primarily to provide the incumbents of these posi-

tions a higher salary. An increase in the number of separate positions that constitutes a government's classification system also may be a sign of a lack of managerial flexibility. Chi (1998), for example, reports that half of state governments have shown an increase from 1986 to 1996.

2. There are few, if any, instances in the literature that discuss examples of vendor bankruptcy leading to government "taking back" the service. Dilger et al. (1997), in an analysis of responses to a nationwide survey of local government officials, notes that some governments report resuming service delivery after privatizing a service, but bankruptcy is not cited as a reason. In instances where public sector employees are allowed to compete with private vendors, such as in Phoenix, Arizona, Flanagan and Perkins (1995) report that these employees have "won back" contracts that had been awarded to private vendors.

3. Incentive contracts typically indicate that any savings identified, either by the vendor or the government, will be shared by both parties according to a formula that is specified in the contract. See Harney (1992) for more details. There are a number of contract management techniques or requirements that can be implemented to help prevent the vendor from inappropriately cutting back on quality to achieve savings. For example, if the vendor has hired a management team to deliver the service, and a member of this team resigns, the government should insist that a person of similar qualifications (and at a similar salary) should be hired as a replacement. Contract or RFP language that allows the government to approve (or disapprove) all key personnel changes should be sufficient. Similarly, a more difficult contract management challenge occurs if the vendor wishes to reorganize the management team, saving salary dollars as a result. The government may wish to require revised job descriptions and appropriate changes in policies and procedures to ensure that the vendor has thoroughly considered all aspects of the altered workloads that reorganization would create.

4. See Smith and Lipsky (1993) for a much more extensive discussion of these points.

5. Morgan and England (1988) indicate that the term "creaming" originates with studies done by the sociologist Peter Blau. He observed that employment counselors spent more attention on finding employment for clients that were the easiest to place. Since productivity was measured by the number of clients placed, employees were reacting to incentives identified by the organization. Martin Lipsky, in his work *Street Level Bureaucracy*, argues that this behavior is valid for all organizations. Furthermore, there is a natural tendency to sacrifice service quality in the name of greater efficiency. Concerns about creaming by contractors can be alleviated by performance measures written into contracts by government officials. An emphasis on outcome measures rather than output measures would help. For example, a contract with a vendor providing health services could provide incentives that reward "number of patients cured" rather than "number of patients processed." In addition, any service that charges user fees (or increases already existing fees) once it is privatized risks reducing access to those who are less advantaged.

6. Many authors provide a wide variety of examples of actual privatization experience, including contract management. Two sources are Rehfuss (1989) and Lavery (1999).

OOCEA: THE PRIVATIZATION DECISION 4

Even though privatization of toll operations did not occur until 1995, the decision to privatize had its origins in the late 1980s. Three major factors influenced this decision. A large amount of cost savings was expected. This became very apparent when the operating cost billed to OOCEA by FDOT for the 1986 bond issue toll plazas was as much as 400 percent higher than estimated. Second, OOCEA was certain that it could ensure better quality service, especially in terms of greater responsiveness to citizen complaints. Third, with the introduction of the ETTM and AVI technology, both increased ridership and better service quality were anticipated. Overall, there was the feeling that independence from FDOT would allow OOCEA to be more creative and innovative in influencing transportation policy for Central Florida.

COST SAVINGS

Although cost savings may not have been the primary driving force behind the privatization decision, it soon became evident that OOCEA would pay lower operating costs with a private vendor than with FDOT. Once the 1986 Project plazas begun to collect tolls, OOCEA became much more aware of operating costs than they had been previously. A retrospective cost analysis indicates that savings could have been viewed as substantial.

Unanticipated Increase in Operating Costs

A lease purchase agreement between the OOCEA and FDOT provided for leasing the expressway system to FDOT. As authorized by Section 348.757, Florida Statutes, operations and maintenance of all parts of the expressway system are the responsibility of FDOT. As reflected in Table 4.1, prior to the 1986 Project, all operation and maintenance costs were to be paid by FDOT, with the exception of the operating costs of the Bee Line Expressway. With the supplemental lease purchase agreement for the 1986 Project, however, operating and maintenance costs were to be paid by the OOCEA.

In the "Traffic and Earnings Report for the Orlando–Orange County Expressway Authority," issued on September 25, 1986 by Vollmer Associates, it was estimated that the Bee Line operation expenses would continue at approximately $.4 million per year from 1985 through 1987. From 1988 through 1989, the cost of operations would rise to $.5 million per year; and from 1991 to 1994, the cost would rise from $.6 million to $.8 million per year. These operation expenses included salaries of toll collectors and supervisory personnel, toll equipment rental, utilities, insurance, and other supplies.

This same document also estimated that operations and maintenance expenses for each of the toll plazas that were part of the 1986 Project would total no more than $.5 million for the first full year of operation, with the expenses of each of the four no more than $.6 million by 1994.

The actual expenses charged to the OOCEA by FDOT were considerably higher than was estimated in 1986. The operating costs for first full year of operation of University Plaza, for example, 1990, were $1.68 million, more than 300 percent higher than original estimates. For 1991, the $2.03 million cost was more than 400 percent higher! Similar costs representing amounts three to four times higher than original estimates were also charged to operate the other three plazas (Curry Ford, Dean, and Hiawassee).

There are several reasons for the difference between original estimates and actual costs. First, it seems likely that the original estimates were inaccurate. It may have been that the operation cost estimates for the 1986 toll plazas were based upon the historical data reflected by the expenses for the original Bee Line Plaza. These had risen from a low of $.2 million in 1981 to $.4 million in 1985. The Vollmer report had projected increases of approximately 5 percent per year resulting in an estimated cost for the Bee Line of $.5 million for each year from 1988 through 1990, with $.8 million the predicted operating costs by 1994. Since the amount of the estimate for the four 1986 plazas was the same for 1990, for example, it seems likely that the Bee Line and the Holland East–West estimates were used as a basis.

The implied assumptions underlying these estimates was first that the number of open lanes and open toll ramps that were manned (requiring toll collectors to collect tolls) would be the same for the 1986 Project plazas as was for the Bee Line and the original Holland East–West plazas prior to the con-

Table 4.1
Division of Financial Responsibilities for Expressway Authority System

Project	Operation	Maintenance
1965, Bee Line Expressway	Authority	FDOT
1970, East-West Expressway	FDOT	FDOT
1980, Airport Interchange and Bee Line Expressway	FDOT	FDOT
1986, Eastern Beltway	Authority	Authority
1988, Central Connector	Authority	Authority*
1990, Southern Connector	Authority	Authority

*Financial responsibility for maintenance of the Bee Line/Central Connector interchange to rest with FDOT.

struction of these plazas. This assumption proved to be incorrect. As indicated in the data furnished in addendum one of the 1994 RFP, for example, the Bee Line Plaza operated eight open lanes, six of which were manned at least part of each day, for a total of 736 manned open hours per week. (The two ICP Boulevard off–on ramps, built in 1990, were not manned.) Eight lanes were also built for the University Plaza, with six of them manned. The number of needed manned hours per week, however, was listed as 784. The need for manned off–on ramps at University is also much greater than for the Bee Line. Of the ten off–on ramps (at Valencia, Colonial, and University), four of them are manned, requiring an additional 352 manned hours per week.

It seems likely that no analysis was performed that compared the number of estimated manned hours needed for the 1986 Project plazas with the Bee Line plaza. If this had been done, the conclusion that 54 percent more manned hours were needed at University than the Bee Line, for example, would have resulted in a higher original operating cost estimate.

A second reason that contributed to higher than expected operation costs was the increase in tolls. Effective July 1, 1990, tolls for two-axle vehicles were raised from $.50 on the East–West Expressway to $.75. The same increase occurred for University and Dean (those 1986 Project plazas completed before July 1, 1990). FDOT concluded that additional manned lanes were necessary because more patrons would likely require change because of the increase. In other words, the automobile driver was much more likely to have exactly $.50 in change than $.75. To prevent longer lines at manned lanes, since fewer cars would be using exact change (unmanned) lanes, FDOT opened more manned lanes than originally estimated.

A comparison of the 1989–1990 FDOT estimated operating budgets for the 1986 Project plazas with those for 1990–1991 supports this analysis. The data from University Plaza illustrates a dramatic increase in operating costs. The overall operating budget rose from $1.68 million in 1989–1990 to $2.03 million in 1990–1991, an increase of over 20 percent in one year. The major portion of these budgets was allocated to toll collection salaries, which rose from $1.16 million in 1989–1990 to $1.55 million in 1990–1991, an increase of over 33 percent. The number of employees needed to operate the manned lanes was four supervisors and thirty-eight collectors in 1989–1990, compared to six supervisors and forty-eight collectors in 1990–1991. The rental for automatic toll equipment fell during this time from $183,276 to $143,508, further supporting the supposition that fewer automatic lanes were used after the toll increase.

Perhaps the most significant contribution to this unexpected higher cost was the increased overhead charges made by FDOT to OOCEA to operate these toll plazas. From July 1986 through May 1987, the overhead rate charged against direct salary costs, for both administrative and toll collector personnel, was 30.65 percent. From June 1987 through April 1988, however, the overhead percentage jumped to 81.60 percent, and then again to 94.44 percent from May 1988 through January 1989. From February 1989 through June 1989, the overhead charge was 65.71 percent.[1]

A COST ANALYSIS OF TOLL OPERATIONS PRIVATIZATION

From a cost savings viewpoint, privatization would save money for OOCEA if the cost of operating all toll plazas under the jurisdiction of the OOCEA were less than the amount reimbursed to FDOT for the operation of the four 1986 Project plazas plus the Bee Line Plaza. In addition, other costs would have to be considered: the cost charged by consultants to help write the RFP; one-time transition costs incurred by the private vendor in assuming the operation from FDOT; and the contract management costs that OOCEA would assume after the privatization contract had been signed.

Although it is difficult to estimate what costs would have been considered by the OOCEA in 1990, the hindsight allowed by the actual figures bid by FTS (the winning bidder) provides some indication of what may have seemed appropriate at the time. First, the cost of writing the RFP must be considered. The consultant team that devised the RFP consisted of OOCEA staff and outside consultants from PBS&J, plus consultants hired by PBS&J. Assuming that the contribution of time from the OOCEA staff would be part of their normal workload, the only additional cost would be the outside consultants. A figure of $200,000 would not be unreasonable. As supported by Martin (1993a), it is best to amortize these figures over the life of the contract. For a five-year contract, the amount needed for this would be $40,000 per year.

Second, the one-time transition costs could be required by the RFP, and again amortized over the five years of the contract. The approximately $795,000 charged by FTS equals $159,000 per year.

Third, the contract management costs associated with a private vendor operating the toll plazas could be construed as the same or similar to the costs of managing the operations contract with FDOT. Various members of the OOCEA staff, including the director of toll operations and the chief financial officer, would simply shift from dealing with FDOT to dealing with the private vendor. It would have been difficult to estimate whether additional OOCEA staff would have been needed. It could have accurately been assumed, however, to be no more than the cost of salaries for one or two additional staff members.

The approximately $100,000 of additional annual cost needed to privatize would be offset by expected lower operating costs from a private vendor, primarily because the cost of profit charged plus the administrative costs would be less than the overhead charged by FDOT. A quick analysis of the operating costs for the four 1986 Project plazas plus the Bee Line Plaza shows the likelihood of significant savings. Of the $8.58 million total operating cost of these five plazas for 1990–1991, $6.94 million can be attributed to salary charges. Assuming an overhead cost of 65 percent, $2.73 million of the salary was attributed to overhead charges.

If the operating costs of a private vendor would be the same, assuming exactly the same personnel and salaries, these costs (without overhead charges) would be $5.85 million annually. Again using the management and support staff costs, plus expenses furnished by FTS, the average amount per year is $1.09 million per year. With an additional 10 percent profit (or management fee), the total operating charge to the OOCEA would be $7.63 million. Even adding the $100,000 of additional costs, the $7.73 million amount is still approximately $850,000 less than what FDOT would have charged.

Even though it could not be predicted what a private vendor would bid to operate these toll plazas, significant savings could be expected. As indicated below, however, there were more compelling reasons to privatize.

The Perceived Likelihood of Higher Quality Service

In addition to higher than expected operating costs, a second reason that contributed to the privatization decision was the perception that a private vendor may be able to provide better service to patrons of the toll roads than FDOT. This perception was based in part on the certainty that OOCEA could have more influence over the daily operating procedures of a private contractor than it could have over FDOT operations. Second, the ability of either FDOT provided sanctions or incentives to improve customer satisfaction seemed lower than what could be provided by agreed-upon OOCEA–private vendor customer satisfaction systems. Finally, as will be discussed in the next section, the implementation of ETTM systems of toll collection would likely quicken toll collection processing times and improve overall performance of toll operations.

OOCEA staff had little input into the FDOT operating procedures, policies, and how they were applied. A patron that had a complaint and wrote to the OOCEA for its resolution had to be referred to FDOT. Although there was the perception that this complaint resolution system improved over time, it proved to have little effect in changing toll collector behavior, as incentives were virtually nonexistent and sanctions were largely ineffective for full-time employees.

For the 40 percent of toll collectors that were hired as temporary employees (other personal service employees), dismissal was an ever-present threat. This possible sanction may have lead some temporary employees to improve their behavior after a complaint had been lodged.

For full-time FDOT employees, however, there were few incentives associated with working for the state of Florida. Raises were provided by the Florida State Legislature, and during this time of economic recession any raises were minimal or nonexistent. Promotional opportunities were few, especially since the majority of the employees working after 1990 had only a few years of experience, having joined FDOT only when the 1986 Project plazas opened.

Sanctions were ineffective as a means to improve customer service. Even though an employee could be "written up" for any number of violations, few full-time employees were fired. An existing grievance procedure, which allowed for many appeals that could prove time consuming, and the presence of a public employee union further dampened the willingness of supervisors to apply sanctions.

Overall, the motoring public experienced long delays at toll plazas such as the East–West Expressway, especially during rush hour. Toll collectors were often uncommunicative and unfriendly to patrons as they passed through the plazas. Although there was a complaint resolution system in existence, it did not seem to result in improved service.

ETTM TECHNOLOGY

A third reason for the belief that privatization was a more efficient and effective way of achieving OOCEA goals involved the implementation of the ETTM System and the AVI technology. It had long been recognized by both FDOT and OOCEA that an ETTM system needed to be in place before privatization should occur. The system would allow for a much more accurate counting of each vehicle that moved through the toll plazas. Reporting of the amount of tolls collected would be much more accurate, with less room for error. The private vendor could also be held to higher standards of accountability.

With the implementation of a violation enforcement system (VES), vehicles that did not pay tolls would be identifiable. An administrative system would be established to notify all those who were delinquent, requesting payment of due tolls and issuing a uniform traffic citation, which would include a fee to cover administrative costs.

With the implementation of the automatic vehicle identification technology, named E-PASS by the OOCEA, it was felt that better service and increased ridership would likely occur.[2] Those vehicles with transponders would travel through the toll plazas much faster, at a speed of 25 miles per hour, and would be unlikely to experience delays. Also, there were two other conveniences that patrons would find attractive. Exact change (or any cash) would not have to be a concern for the patron each time he or she would travel through the toll plazas. Also, receiving a monthly statement could facilitate record keeping if travel were done for business purposes.

CONCLUSION

Cost savings were only one of the major reasons underlying the decision to privatize. With an expanding number of people moving to Central Florida and with all traffic projections indicating increased use of tollways, the income received from collected tolls was expected to be more than enough to meet bond payments and support administrative and operational costs.

With privatization, OOCEA felt that it would have more control over toll operations. This control would allow greater opportunity for OOCEA to be more innovative and creative in a variety of ways. A more responsive patron satisfaction system could be implemented, one that would result in improved service. Incentive systems could be established that would reward employees for friendlier, better service, as well as for identifying ways to be more efficient. The new ETTM technology and the E-PASS system would not only collect tolls more accurately, it would allow patrons to travel more quickly through toll plazas. Ultimately, as more patrons used E-PASS, fewer manned lanes would need to be opened, thereby saving additional funds.

There was still a great deal of uncertainty in 1989–1990, however, concerning whether privatization would be successful. At that time, no toll operations in the United States had been privatized. Even though there were informal indications that private firms would be interested in responding to a privatization RFP, a sufficient number had to respond to make the effort a success. By 1994, when the second RFP was finally issued, the Southern Connector plazas had been opened, thereby adding to the operations cost. If all the private firms bid at levels that were higher than the cost charged by FDOT, and no cost savings were to occur, then the privatization decision may have had to be reconsidered.

Much depended on the creation of a successful request for proposal, one that would lead to a contract that would represent a successful partnership between the OOCEA and the private vendor. The RFP that was created and issued in 1994 is the subject of the next chapter.

NOTES

1. FDOT had recently undergone a revision of its indirect cost allocation plan, primarily to take full advantage of all indirect costs that were reimbursable by the federal government under the guidelines set out by OMB Circular A-87 and Code of Federal Regulations Title 23. As a result of these changes, the overhead charge in the area of toll operations rose significantly.

2. Although the implementation of E-PASS was not necessary prior to privatization, it is an essential part of the ETTM technology that was deemed necessary to achieve optimal revenue collection and accountability.

REQUEST FOR PROPOSAL: THEORY DEVELOPMENT AND PRACTICAL APPLICATION 5

The ideal request for proposal, pertaining to the contracting out of a service, must be fashioned in a way to communicate clearly the service goals to prospective bidders that the agency wishes to achieve. Once the contract is awarded, the partnership that results should be one in which both agency and the vendor strive to achieve the same goals. This partnership can be dynamic, with both parties changing policies and procedures to solve problems.

The primary goal of an RFP is to define the nature of the public–private partnership between the contracting agency and the private vendor. There is the desire to create a partnership that is positive, efficiently managed, and cooperative. Most important, both partners should maintain the goal of providing quality public service as efficiently and effectively as possible.

Another goal of an RFP is that it will effectively shape a contract that will require the vendor to meet the goals of the agency. As discussed by many (e.g., Kettl 1993), there are often many reasons that the vendor wants to strive for goals that are in his or her best self-interest. These goals may often conflict with those espoused by the agency. The goal of the RFP and the contract is to provide incentives to ensure that it is in the best self-interest of the vendor to engage in activities that meet the agency goals.

An RFP can be written in terms that range from specific to general. The specific methodology provides little flexibility; it clearly identifies measures, standards, and/or goals from which the vendor may not deviate. Toll Lane X at Plaza Y must be open twenty-four hours per day, and the grass must be cut once every week. Often, though, RFPs may not specify the procedures by which the standard is met or the activity occurs. This is true for those activities for which there are generally acceptable means of reaching the goal. No RFP, for example, is likely to specify what machinery will be used to cut the grass.

Generally written RFPs (or sections of RFPs) provide a great deal of flexibility not only in how a goal is achieved, but also in defining or measuring to what degree a goal is achieved. Directing the vendor to establish an employee performance evaluation system (PES) to help achieve a high quality level of performance is one example. This statement allows the vendor a great deal of latitude in creating the PES, but it also allows the vendor to determine what behaviors constitute different levels of performance.

The more general the terminology, the more the RFP invites the winning vendor to enter into a partnership to achieve the goals desired by the agency. There is the implication that this partnership will not be fully defined until after the contract is awarded and signed. The agency must have a certain degree of trust that the vendor will abide by the goals set forth by the partnership. If the RFP states that the agency wishes to provide a more efficient, higher quality service, then there is the trust that the vendor awarded the contract will try to achieve these goals, or, at a minimum, not engage in activities antithetical to them.

The efficiency and quality service goals of any RFP are reflected by the degree of specificity found in the terminology. To some extent, specific language reflects a belief that the goals of the vendor may not coincide with the goals of the agency unless the standard or measure is precisely identified. The frequency of grass cutting (e.g., once per week), is mentioned instead of a more general phrase (e.g., the grass should always be neatly trimmed), because it seems likely that the vendor would not always meet this more general standard.

The more general the terminology, however, the more the vendor and the agency will enter into a public–private partnership, in which both parties could work toward common goals. Not only would this kind of partnership be desirable, it may be that the agency may not have a choice, given various characteristics of the service or factors that would influence the ways in which the RFP must be written.

There are several factors that will influence the RFP creation which defines the partnership. These include first, the nature of the service, including the complexity of (1) the processes needed to provide the service, and (2) the valid measurement of goal achievement. Measurement of this factor could be made on a continuum of routine to complex. The second factor is the degree to which change from the present system of service provision is desired or anticipated by the contracting agency. This desired change could be relevant to many areas, such as service provision policies and processes, management practices, staffing levels and practices, or equipment required. Measurement of this factor could be made on a continuum of low to high.

As shown in Figure 5.1, both of these factors can be placed on continua that can intersect, producing four quadrants by which services can be classified and which provide guidance concerning how an effective RFP can be written. In quadrant I, the nature of the service is routine, and the government agency has determined that a great deal of change is required. The RFP should be written to provide little opportunity for the contractor to exercise independent judgment. If the government agency feels, for example, that the garbage could be collected with a driver and one collector instead of the driver and two collectors currently required, then the RFP should specify no more than one collector per truck. If each current city maintenance crew has two levels of supervision, for example, and the city feels that only one is needed, then the RFP should specify no more than one level of supervision.

Other considerations influence those services in quadrant I. The more the government agency is familiar with how similar services are provided in the private sector, the more specific the RFP can be written. No matter how much change is desired, if the RFP is written in such a way that no private vendor wishes to bid in response, then the RFP will have to be reissued. On the other hand, if the agency desires fewer levels of supervision and chooses not to

Figure 5.1
Factors Affecting the RFP Creation Regarding the Privatization of an Already Existing Public Service

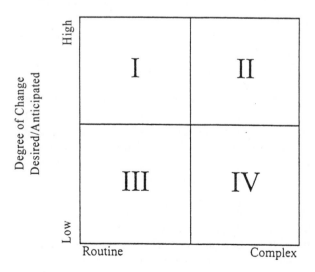

Nature of the Service

specify how many levels are required in the RFP, the agency risks a situation in which all vendors bid the cost of the same number of levels of supervision that presently exist.

Another consideration concerns the major anticipated source of cost savings if a service is privatized. If they will come from increasingly flexible work rules, resulting in fewer employees needed on a permanent basis, for example, then the RFP must be written generally to allow for the bidders to identify innovative, changed policies and procedures. If the cost savings will come from lower wages simply because the market wage rate in the private sector is lower than that paid to the current government employees, then the RFP can be written very specifically, no matter how much change is required. In the former case, the service would fall into quadrant I, while in the latter, quadrant III would likely be more appropriate.

Quadrant II services are those that are highly complex (e.g., computer support services), for which a high degree of change is anticipated because of changing technology; or for which a high degree of change is desired because new technology is being adopted. The RFP should be written very generally, in a way to elicit new, different ideas from the bidder. It should also be anticipated that the contract management relationship will be a period during which additional change can occur as part of a public–private partnership.

The reasons that influence whether a service is in quadrant II or IV depends in part on the considerations identified above. In many cases, however, there may be few services that would fall into quadrant IV. Only if the agency feels that the salaries of the present employees are above market rate, and little needs to be changed in terms of procedures and numbers of supervisors, for example, would the service be categorized in quadrant IV. It would seem likely that the complexity of the service may require that the RFP be written in more general terms, even if little change is anticipated.

Knowledge of the service provision process by both agency and projected bidder is the third factor. If both agency and vendors have a great deal of experience in providing the service (e.g., garbage collection), then the RFP can be written in very general terms, focusing on outcomes or goal achievement. If the agency has much less knowledge, and there are many potential bidders (e.g., a new service that the agency has not provided), then the RFP will have to be written generally, but the responses may vary, and the evaluation of those responses becomes more difficult. If both agency and potential bidders have less knowledge (e.g., a new service, a highly complex service, or a high degree of change is anticipated or desired), then the RFP will invite bidders to help write the RFP through questions that will result in additional addenda or changes to the RFP. In addition, the partnership that characterizes the contract management period will be characterized by negotiation and continual potential clarification and further contract adjustments. Measurement of this factor could be made on a continuum of low to high.

In reality, for many RFPs the degree of service complexity and the amount of knowledge are likely to vary throughout various aspects of the service provision. Providing management services, for example, is more complex than routine functions. Similarly, the degree of change desired may be small for the part of the service provision that is routine, while great for the part that is not. The amount of knowledge, conversely, may be great for routine functions, while a great deal of uncertainty may characterize those functions that are not routine.

Also, the agency must take into account the degree to which there may be a better way of providing the service than is presently occurring. If there are a variety of methods to achieve agency goals, and the agency is not certain which may be the most efficient and produce the highest level of performance, then the vendor may be given the discretion to choose from among a variety of alternatives. Under these conditions, the RFP must be written generally, encouraging the vendor to be innovative and to submit policies that may be different from those presently performed.

THE OOCEA EXPERIENCE

The following section discusses the application of these more conceptual ideas in light of the OOCEA experience in creating the RFP for the privatization of toll operations (Project 266). The unique feature of this process is that there were two RFPs, one was issued in July 1992 that had to be rescinded in January 1993 because the ETTM and AVI toll equipment could not be in place as early as initially anticipated. A second RFP was issued in May 1994, which was ultimately successful in attracting bids and awarding the privatization contract. Much of the contents of the 1994 RFP represented a greater understanding of the requirements needed for an RFP that would more clearly outline a more viable partnership relationship.

Work on the 1994 RFP process began in December 1993, with the issuance of the RFP in May 1994, culminating in the contract award in November 1994. Initially it was thought that the 1992 RFP could be quickly revised and reissued. It was soon realized that more structure and organization was needed, especially in the scope of services, especially since the RFP writing team had a great deal more knowledge about the ETTM–AVI system that OOCEA would be implementing.

SCOPE OF SERVICES

The 1994 RFP outlines a scope of services section that includes a general (introduction) subsection, and sections on mobilization, program management and administration, auditing–accounting, toll operations, and facilities maintenance. Each section would require different responses in terms of the criteria outlined above. Mobilization is unique, in that OOCEA staff would have to coordinate with FDOT as well as the contractor, plus ensure that the new ETTM and AVI equipment were in place and working satisfactory as well. Program management and administration was an area where change was anticipated, as levels of staffing and other policies and procedures were likely to be different from that provided by FDOT. Toll operations in terms of functions were likely to be routine, assuming that appropriate training regarding how to use the new equipment was provided to the collectors. The concern with collectors providing a high quality level of service, though, was seen as potentially different from that espoused by FDOT. Finally, facilities maintenance is a routine function.

General

The purposes of the privatization effort are clearly stated in a way that provides general guidelines for the public–private partnership envisioned by this effort. These purposes include

1. Efficient toll collection operation including a reduction in current operating costs.
2. Sound financial accounting of revenues and assets.
3. Responsive, courteous customer (patron) service.
4. Serving the best interest of the people of Central Florida and the OOCEA (2-5).

Furthermore, this section states that "It is not the intent of the Authority to recreate the current operation, but to provide a more creative, efficient Toll Operations Management Program, particularly during the second and third years of the Contract" (Orlando–Orange County Expressway Authority 1994, 2-5).

It is clear that positive change is desired from these statements. A more efficient service must be provided. Perhaps more important, though, is the implied desire for a partnership that is more flexible and more open to change and innovative ideas and practices than had existed. The OOCEA also reserved the right to change the scope of services, as long as changes were in the intent of the contract. The implication may have been that the contractor should agree to changes, as long as they did not lessen the "management fee" or "profit" incurred by the contractor. Also, if these objectives are not met, the contractor can be "declared in default of Contract." The OOCEA clearly wished to be in charge of the partnership, by providing ideas and requiring that the contractor be receptive to them and by requiring the contractor to submit plans and reports regarding various aspects of the toll operations.

The remainder of this section informs the prospective bidder of the arrangement with FDOT for operations for all toll plazas, including the Southern Connector, indicating that the contract with FDOT for operations would terminate as of the date that the contractor took over operations. Also, the potential bidder was informed of the need for coordination with the installation of the new operations equipment, Project 256. Finally, during the first year of operations, the takeover of the toll plazas would occur in phases, not all on a given date. This aspect of the scope of services was later realized to be a key to the smooth transition to privatization.

Mobilization

In any transition from a public agency to private contractor, there is the expectation that the contractor will be able to provide services from the first day of operations. Even if the contractor has extensive experience in providing the exact service elsewhere, there still must be a period of time in which the contractor must learn the specific characteristics of the operations and create a set of policies and procedures that will be implemented. This learning may take place either prior to responding to the RFP, during a mobilization phase prior to the actual takeover of operations, or after the actual transition of control of everyday operations.

In the second section under scope of services, the 1994 RFP lists forty documents (plans, standard operating procedures (SOPs), and reports) that will be required to be submitted after the date for the notice to proceed has been identified, and, in most cases, prior to the actual date of the beginning of operations.

As listed in Table 5.1, these documents fall into the general categories of administration, audit–accounting, operations, and facility maintenance. They are also referenced to information that follows in the RFP under each of these four areas. For each, after the document has been submitted, the OOCEA had the right to review and respond within ten days by requesting additional changes.

In some cases as indicated, the RFP requires an "preliminary outline" of the document to be included in the response. These are for the plans dealing with systems operations transition, toll operations contractor (TOC), and toll operations. Most of the other documents are due either thirty days or forty-five days from the notice to proceed (NTP) date.

Any analysis of these documents and the time period by which they are required must include consideration of why the information was not requested as part of the response to the RFP. To some extent, the policies and procedures requested were those that were not critical to being in place on the first day of operations. Second, to some extent the request represents both a lack of knowledge on the part of the agency in terms of what is desired and a willingness to allow the contractor time to introduce innovative changes that would meet the desired purposes of the partnership. Third, they represented knowledge that the contractor would not necessarily have known unless a great more detail was placed in the RFP than existed. Finally, to some extent requesting these documents after the contract has been awarded represented a gamble by OOCEA that a viable partnership between the agency and contractor could be established.

Table 5.1
Listing of Required Documentation[1]

SECTION	TYPE	DESCRIPTION	DATE DUE
Volume 1 - Administration			
B.2.2	Plan	System Operations Transition[1]	45 Days from Contract NTP
B.2.3	Plan	Toll Collection Hiring	Updates due 30 days prior to each phase take-over
B.2.4	Plan	Administrative Hiring	45 Days from Contract NTP
B.2.3	Plan	Staffing	45 Days from Contract NTP
C.3.1	Plan	TOC Operations Office Layout and Security System Plans	45 Days from Contract NTP
C.3.6	SOP	TOC Operations Office[1]	45 Days from Contract NTP
C.5.0	Plan	Human Resources Management	45 Days from Contract NTP
C.6.0	Plan	Training	45 Days from Contract NTP
C.7.0	SOP	Customer Relations	45 Days from Contract NTP
C.8.0	SOP	Security and Investigations	45 Days from Contract NTP
C.8.0	Report	Security Inspection Report	15 Days after Security Inspection
C.8.0	Report	Security Improvements/Repairs	Every 6 months starting 45 days after NTP
C.10.0	Plan	Emergency	45 Days from Contract NTP
C.11.0	Plan	Safety Progrm	45 Days from Contract NTP
C.12.0	Plan/SOP	QM/QA	45 Days from Contract NTP
Volume 2 - Audit/Accounting			
D	SOP	Audit/Accounting	45 Days from Contract NTP
D.1.2	Report	Transaction Accountability Exception Report	45 Days from Contract NTP
D.1.4	Report	Account Verification	45 Days from Contract NTP
D.2.1	Report	Job Cost Accounting	45 Days from Contract NTP
D.2.2	SOP	Invoice Processing	45 Days from Contract NTP
D.2.3	Report	Deposit Reconciliation Report	45 Days from Contract NTP

Note: Some required plans listed include standard operating procedures (SOPs) as part of the document. Section references that call out specific SOPs as part of the overall plan shall be prepared and submitted by the TOC according to the contract.

1. A preliminary outline of this document shall be submitted with the technical proposal (Orlando–Orange County Expressway Authority 1994, 2-15–2-17).

Transition

Transition from FDOT operations to the TOC is discussed in this section, as well as end of contract transition. Both aspects represent a mix of OOCEA control of the process and a certain degree of trust that the TOC will abide by the conditions in the RFP and the resulting contract.

A key element of the transition period from the OOCEA to the TOC is the creation of a staffing plan. Noting that the minimal requirements are listed in

Table 5.1 (*continued*)

Volume 3 - Operations

E	SOP	Toll Operations[1]	30 Days from Contract NTP
E.1.1	SOP	Toll Collection Operations	30 Days from Contract NTP
E.1.3.1	SOP	Manual Lane	30 Days from Contract NTP
E.1.3.2	SOP	ACM Lane	30 Days from Contract NTP
E.1.3.3	SOP	E-Pass Lane	30 Days from Contract NTP
E.1.3.4	SOP	Attended ACM Lane	30 Days from Contract NTP
E.1.3.5	SOP	Ramp Collection	30 Days from Contract NTP
E.1.3.6	Report	Collector Shift	30 Days from Contract NTP
E.1.3.7	SOP	Shift Operations	30 Days from Contract NTP
E.1.3.8	SOP	Money Handling & Counting	30 Days from Contract NTP
E.1.3.9	SOP	Deposit Prep and Verification	30 Days from Contract NTP
E.1.3.10	SOP	Discrepancy Reporting	30 Days from Contract NTP
E.3.0	Design	Uniforms	45 Days from Contract NTP

Volume 4 - Facility Maintenance

F	SOP	Facility Maintenance	60 Days from Contract NTP
F.6.3.3	Plan	Preventive Maintenance	60 Days from Contract NTP
F.7.0	Listing	Tools and Equipment	60 Days from Contract NTP
F.8.0	Listing	Spare Parts	60 Days from Contract NTP
F	Budget	Annual Budget	30 Days prior to each year begin

Appendix A of its *Request for Proposal* (Orlando–Orange County Express-way Authority 1994), the OOCEA stated its desire that the TOC give all FDOT toll collectors who were career service employees the "right of first refusal." Also, the TOC was encouraged to consider the FDOT part time employees and the contract labor from the Southern Connector when filling positions.

What is not included is any reference to a minimum salary or to a guaranteed minimum length of employment after toll collectors become employees of the TOC. The TOC is thus given the flexibility of hiring employees at a salary that may be closer to the comparable area labor rate than what may be paid to FDOT employees. There are also no restrictions on the number of supervisory or management positions that must be filled by the TOC.

There is a certain amount of risk reflected here, as there is nothing to prevent the TOC from hiring career service employees, firing them within a reasonable period of time, and then hiring replacement employees at a lower rate of pay. If a stronger employee union had existed, this may have been a part of the RFP that would have caused problems for the OOCEA.

However, as indicated previously, both OOCEA and FDOT expressed concern that the FDOT toll collectors, over 400 employees, should not lose their jobs nor receive lower health care benefits because of privatization. In addition, one likely assumption is that, at least in the early period of the contract, the TOC would want to hire the FDOT experienced employees, since (1) there were no alternative employees to choose from in the local area, as other area toll facilities were already under FDOT management; (2) the likelihood that recruiting toll collectors from out of state would be more costly than hiring FDOT employees; and (3) once the operations were running and the human resources plan had been submitted, arbitrarily firing employees for reasons other than poor performance was likely not to occur.

In addition, the majority of the more than 400 toll collectors had been hired since the implementation of the 1986 Project toll plazas. Most of these had five or fewer years experience, and thus their salary was at or below the average $6.73 per hour. When the transition did occur, most of those with more than five years experience stayed with FDOT, transferring to the Florida Turnpike or other FDOT plazas outside the control of OOCEA.

If the TOC is to be replaced by another after the contract expiration, or OOCEA wishes to terminate the contract, there is a need to provide an orderly a transition as possible to the new TOC. The RFP states, "The TOC agrees to exercise its best efforts and cooperation to effect an orderly and efficient transition to a successor" (Orlando–Orange County Expressway Authority 1994, 2-20).

The employees would be released from working with the TOC at a mutually agreeable time, presumably to ensure that services are not interrupted. The intent here is that the toll collectors would prefer to remain in their present positions during a transition time, most likely provided a "right of first refusal" with the new TOC.

This section represents the OOCEA's attempt to plan for the contingency that the TOC may have to be replaced. The benefit of this language in the RFP is that the TOC is aware that a plan does exist and that cooperation with OOCEA is necessary to avoid the termination of the contract.

Program Management and Administration

In this section the RFP requires only that the TOC "provide adequate key management-level staff and resources" needed to meet the purposes and goals of the privatization effort. It does not state specifically which positions are needed. The expectation here is that the type and number of positions needed may be fewer than existed under FDOT. More important, the TOC is given the flexibility to decide which positions are needed. This is a gamble from the viewpoint of the OOCEA; the hope is, however, that the number identified will be sufficient to provide high quality service.

In terms of establishing a level of quality control, the OOCEA reserves the right to approve any personnel changes and to request the dismissal of any employee. In this manner, replacement of a more qualified management employee with one less qualified but who can be paid a lower salary may be prevented if the OOCEA feels it would lead to a lowering of service quality.

The Staffing of Toll Lanes

The desire for flexibility and change in the area of toll lane staffing is stated clearly. With the expected increase in the number of lanes dedicated to E-PASS, the number of lane attendants is expected to decrease. Both the TOC and the OOCEA will conduct periodic reviews of staffing needs. The staffing plan, developed and implemented in accordance with OOCEA approval as one of the plans listed, will be modified.

In addition, the staff needed to perform all tasks listed under each section of the scope of services must be listed, along with an identification of what tasks each staff member is assigned. In this way, the OOCEA can review and check workloads, ensuring that service quality is not decreasing as a result of the inadequate performance of an "overloaded" employee.

The TOC Operations Office

Since this contract is not provided to private vendors that service other similar agencies in the geographical area, the TOC is required to maintain a central office, complete with training facilities, office space for two OOCEA staff, and appropriate personal computer equipment to produce necessary reports and interact with the ETTM–AVI equipment.

The Human Resources Management (HRM) Plan

Although the HRM plan was to be fully delivered within the first forty-five days of the contract, the RFP provided the aspects that were felt to be most important. Given that the employees would be in a position to handle money, the RFP specifically insists that the selection process must include a screening process. This process must include a drug testing program and a background check that would prevent the hiring of employees who could jeopardize the TOC's ability to properly handle revenues collected. Since such a screening process may add additional expense to what the bidder would otherwise provide, it needs to be mentioned as part of the RFP.

Second, the TOC is required to provide a detailed job description for all employees that includes training requirements. It is noteworthy that no other detail is mentioned. The TOC is not required, for example, to use existing job titles or descriptions. There are also no requirements to maintain the same job description: By implication, job duties as well as job titles can be changed. Finally, there is no mention of how training requirements are to be reflected in the job description.

The third aspect of the RFP is perhaps the most significant: "The TOC shall provide its full-time employees all normal privileges, benefits and guarantees of employment that are afforded to the firm's existing regular and part-time employees" (Orlando–Orange County Expressway Authority 1994, 2-26).

By implication, the HRM plan must include a performance evaluation system, a compensation plan, an employee assistance program, and whatever employment guarantees are present for the upper management personnel. The TOC is provided the flexibility to create its own plan with few requirements or restrictions, yet a plan must exist.

Training

This section clearly delineates the training responsibilities of the TOC. The OOCEA will train all TOC employees in the ETTM system prior to the assumption of each phase of the transition process. Once the TOC has been hired, all subsequent training is the responsibility of the TOC. Clearly the perspective TOC realizes that training costs are to be in the budget, as part of the response to the RFP, or they must be absorbed in some other fashion.

One key aspect of the training content is in the area of customer service. Training needs to include directional information within a fifty-mile radius of Orlando, as well as effective communications training. This requirement complements the goal of improving quality service.

All training materials, submitted for the approval of the OOCEA prior to use, become the property of the OOCEA. There seems to be the intention that if a new TOC must be hired in the future, the OOCEA would have these materials to provide training for newly hired employees prior to contractual arrangement with another TOC.

Customer and Public Relations

To emphasize the relevance of customer relations to the quality service goal, a separate section of the RFP identifies the need for a customer relations procedure. Although not stated as such, one of the objectives of this procedure is to handle and resolve customer complaints.

This is clearly an area in which the OOCEA wishes to enter into a partnership arrangement with the TOC. Both organizations are to contribute to providing customer relations services. The TOC is to provide relevant data and information as requested by the OOCEA. In the area of public relations, the OOCEA must obtain consent in writing prior to issuing press releases or other information to the public.

Quality Management–Assurance

This section clearly emphasizes the need to provide service to customers that achieves the highest level of quality possible. The OOCEA is insisting on the creation of a quality policy that "shall include an organizational mission statement and/or managerial philosophy, along with goals and objectives linked to the quality assurance and management system" (Orlando– Orange County Expressway Authority 1994, 2-30). More specifically measurable goals–objectives are identified, including:

1. A high level of customer satisfaction by
   a. Minimizing delays through toll plazas.
   b. Implementing a customer complaint resolution system.
   c. Periodically surveying customer satisfaction.
2. Accurate collection of all tolls.
3. Eliminate the loss of funds collected through adequate financial controls.
4. Provide managerial and financial data and reports.
5. Operate grounds of the facility in ways that provide a clean appearance.

Furthermore, the TOC is required to identify appropriate procedures and policies that will achieve these goals, including quality standards of behavior, where appropriate. These would be part of a quality assurance program, one that would include activities such as planned inspections and other ways to achieve quality.

Along with implementing customer satisfaction surveys, the TOC also must create an employee performance assessment and evaluation system. In theory, this system creates behavioral standards and complements the quality management system.

Performance Monitoring

The final significant section of this part of the RFP states that a performance evaluation committee (PEC) will be established. Including a representative from the TOC, the PEC will perform duties which include monitoring and evaluating the TOC against the performance standards as agreed to by both the TOC and the OOCEA. The PEC will meet monthly or periodically to discuss deficiencies and ways in which these issues can be resolved. At the end of the evaluation period, the TOC will within ten days submit a self-assessment report, outlining the steps needed to correct any problems. Also, "The TOC will receive favorable ratings for identifying 'a better way' and for developing and implementing cost savings ideas and quality performance standards" (Orlando–Orange County Expressway Authority 1994, 2-34).

There is much that is vague about this section. First, performance standards will be developed by both parties, with everyone agreeing to which will be used. There is the implication that the process of agreeing to standards will be negotiated and that the policies or procedures by which the standards are changed will be flexible as well. By not specifying that evaluations will take place in a given period of time (e.g., quarterly), one implication is that meetings of the PEC will take place as needed. By not specifying the composition of the PEC in terms of who from the OOCEA staff needs to be on it, there is the implied flexibility that the PEC's membership may change depending upon the issues or problems that need to be resolved. By specifying that a representative from the TOC will be a member, though, the OOCEA is sending the signal that any resolution of problems will be made in conjunction with the TOC, preventing an adversarial relationship and underlining the need for a partnership.

There is the expectation that the TOC will perform at levels beyond the minimum (or satisfactory), and that "the TOC shall strive to attain the highest standards of excellence in executing its responsibilities under the contract as measured against performance standards" (Orlando–Orange County Expressway Authority 1994, 2-34).

If it is found that the TOC does not meet these expectations, a self-assessment report shall be submitted within ten days after the evaluation period, addressing both the strengths and weaknesses of the TOC's performance. Identified within the report will be actions that the TOC will take to overcome any deficiencies.

This section presents a complete evaluation "cycle," with problems identified as measured by previously set standards and solutions required. This section also discusses a key aspect of contract management, as the TOC understands that evaluation of performance will occur on a periodic basis. All of this language, though, is presented in a nonthreatening manner that invites a partnership relationship.

Finally, the section concludes with identifying sanctions. There are three: (1) withholding payment until acceptable resolution; (2) imposing "performance liquidated damages" and/or retaining 10 percent of the TOC's monthly invoice; and (3) "termination, suspension, or cancellation of the Contract" (Orlando–Orange County Expressway Authority 1994, 2-43). Although it is implied that no party wishes to invoke these sanctions, their identification as part of the RFP clearly dispels any doubt that the OOCEA is willing to award the contract to another vendor if the performance of the initial TOC is not satisfactory.

Audit–Accounting

This section outlines the content of what should comprise the audit–accounting plan. In doing so the potential respondent to the RFP not only understands what duties are required but also can estimate the number of employees needed to perform these needed tasks. In large part, this section writes part of the job description for these individuals. Also, auditing–accounting is one area in which little change can be expected from the procedures that have occurred in the past, with the exception that the ETTM system will provide capabilities that previously did not exist.

Audits

Daily audits or counts are to be performed for all money collected at each lane, as well as for each aspect of the toll operations that involves exchanging of funds: the change funds, shift banks, coin vaults, tour funds, and deposits. A copy of the reports of each audit collected is sent to the OOCEA on a daily basis. The OOCEA reserves the right to audit these reports monthly. It expects complete cooperation from TOC staff for all audits performed, including those performed by outside auditors or by FDOT.

Transactions Accountability

Every transaction, that is, every time a vehicle passes through a toll operations lane, must be identified by the TOC. These transactions include cash, E-PASS, prepaid, and nonrevenue or violations. It was expected that with the ETTM equipment very close to 100 percent of all transactions could be identified. Second, cash or payments received must match the number of paid transactions. The final element of accountability is found in the transaction accountability exception report (TAER). Any discrepancies that cannot be explained by the transaction count and/or to reconciliation of payment to transactions are identified in this report.

The TOC is required to establish a cost accounting system that serves (1) as the basis for all labor costs that would be billed to the OOCEA, and (2) for management purposes. Costs associated with accounts payable–receivable, invoicing, personnel, materials, utilities, subcontractor costs, budgeting, estimates, and inventory will be tracked as part of the system. Accompanying each monthly invoice sent to OOCEA for reimbursement, must be an approved job cost accounting report.

All cash must be deposited within twenty-four hours of collection. The deposit slips must be reconciled with the transactions processed and a copy sent to the OOCEA. The daily reports must be compiled into a weekly and monthly summary report that is also submitted to the OOCEA.

Toll Operations

As with the audit–accounting section, the toll operations section provides an outline of the toll operations SOP. A preliminary outline of the SOP must be submitted with the response to the RFP and must include the following aspects.

In general, the TOC is responsible for the hiring, training, and managing a toll collector staff that will perform the required duties associated with toll operations. To reinforce statements made earlier, there is a warning that poor performance may result in the imposition of contract damages or the withholding of a certain percentage of the monthly payment until all concerns are met.

If there is any revenue lost because of the TOC performance, there will be a deduction from the payment to the TOC. This statement carries a great impact, as it provides a significant incentive for the TOC to provide error-free transactions and reconciliations. If transactions for a given time period record an amount of expected revenue that is greater than the amount of corresponding bank deposits, then the TOC must contribute the difference. With total annual tolls approximating $60 million, an error rate of .5 percent, for example, means that there is $300,000 less income received by the TOC.

Again, the need for courteous as well as efficient and accurate service is emphasized. Reporting of financial transactions and related information must also be supplemented with reporting of all incidents and accidents that occur, along with a record of all actions undertaken to resolve these occurrences.

The remainder of this section outlines the procedures needed for each type of lane: manual, automatic coin machine (ACM), E-PASS, automated attended lane, and ramp collection. The TOC is directed to use the OOCEA's existing SOP, those created by Syntonic for the ETTM system, as the initial operating procedure.

Also, a minimum of 60 percent of all toll collectors must be full-time employees, scheduled over a seven-day week and for all shifts. A TOC supervisor shall be scheduled for twenty-four hours per day, seven days per week. These two requirements represent both quality and efficiency concerns. The 60 percent is a historically based standard. FDOT experience concluded that if fewer than 60 percent of the toll collectors were full-time employees with full medical benefits, the problems caused by the much higher turnover of the part-time employees without benefits would be unmanageable. In addition, there was the perception that quality of service among the part-time TSAs was significantly less than among the full-time employees. The TOC is thus prevented from hiring more than 40 percent temporary staff who will be paid minimum wage without benefits.

Second, given that FDOT operations typically contained more than one level of supervision, by implication the RFP is suggesting that fewer levels may be needed. By indicating the need for one supervisor at all times, but omitting any statement of the need for additional supervisory personnel, the OOCEA is clearly stating its preference. The respondent who identifies a need for more than one level runs a significant risk that the total dollar amount of toll collector and supervisory salaries bid will be higher than competitive bids.

The RFP shows minimum staffing requirements in Appendix F of the *Request for Proposal*, and the toll operations SOP is to include sample shift schedules for each facility. In line with the goal of providing efficient service, "It is the Authority's intent to reduce customer delay and congestion to the maximum extent possible consistent with efficient staffing" (Orlando–Orange County Expressway Authority 1994, 2-43). As indicated in Appendix F, during high volume traffic periods, more lanes must be opened than during low volume periods. The OOCEA reserves the right to review these schedules and approve any changes.

The final significant element of this section is the requirement that the TOC use the services provided by the OOCEA's existing banking services contract.[1] It is clear that the OOCEA wishes to retain control of banking services rather than allow the TOC to subcontract these services. Unless the TOC was committed to issuing its own RFP and choosing a bank in which to deposit funds, the OOCEA is assured of receiving a much less costly service by using already existing banking services.

ETTM SYSTEM

The TOC is required to use the OOCEA's electronic toll and traffic management (ETTM) system. It is to operate twenty-four hours per day, seven days per week. It will provide the TOC with accurate processing, auditing, and reporting of all transactions. All ETTM system reports will be run daily, maintained and filed at the TOC operations office, and made available to the OOCEA upon request. The TOC is to ensure that no ETTM system data is lost or corrupted; a backup tape system is to be maintained; and if there is any need for system maintenance and repair, the TOC is to work with the OOCEA's toll equipment contractor (Syntonic). The maintenance on-line management system (MOMS) automatically reports system failures or malfunctions.

The violation enforcement system is part of the ETTM. The VES records a video image of each vehicle as it passes through a toll booth, including a copy of its license plate. If a vehicle does not pay at a toll booth, the information on the license plate is recorded, and the TOC is required to maintain all captured video images. With the third violation, the vehicle is reported to the OOCEA, which issues all toll violation notices and/or uniform traffic citations.

For violators, the responsibility is divided. The TOC is required to identify these vehicles, while the OOCEA will issue fines and handle the administrative paperwork in issuing notices and collecting payment.

Facilities Maintenance

Even though the OOCEA decided to withdraw this section from the RFP, it is useful to review the general nature of the information in terms of its specificity and standards.[2] Since it was in the RFP as originally issued, the impact of this section on the vendors' response to the RFP needs to be reviewed.

The initial part of this section begins as follows:

The TOC shall be responsible for hiring, training, providing and managing a staff (including subcontractors) to perform all activities related to the maintenance of the Authority's toll facilities including, but not limited to, operations buildings, ramp buildings, tunnels, canopies, islands, lanes and booths. The TOC will not be responsible for maintenance of roadway lighting, parking lot lighting, pavement striping, attenuators, and signage (Orlando–Orange County Expressway Authority 1994, 2-47).

The TOC has the option of hiring maintenance staff or subcontracting all or part of the needed duties. This is one area in which, at least originally, the TOC was to be allowed to subcontract services. The TOC is to develop a facilities maintenance procedure which is to include the following aspects.

Repair Work

Unscheduled maintenance falls into three categories:

1. Incidental repairs: those repairs costing under $100. These are to be included as part of the TOC bid price.
2. Minor repairs: those repairs costing between $100 and $1,000. These are also to be included in the TOC bid price.
3. Major repairs: those repairs costing over $1,000. The work is not to be performed until the OOCEA and the TOC agree upon price. These repairs are not included in the TOC bid price.[3]

The parts, materials, and supplies needed to perform the repairs would be furnished by the OOCEA, or furnished by the TOC, the cost of which would be reimbursed to the TOC at the "established catalog or list prices, in effect when the material is furnished, less all applicable discounts" (Orlando–Orange County Expressway Authority 1994, 2-48).

There are several issues which are unclear. First, how is the TOC reimbursed for the use of equipment? Is it at current "lease" rates? Or is the equipment purchased by the TOC, and every time it is used, there is a usage cost charged to the OOCEA?

The current price for parts, materials, and supplies may be higher than if the part were purchased by the TOC in the past. Also, the TOC may be able to purchase the items in bulk at a much lower cost per item than what it would charge the OOCEA for the use of a smaller amount. It would seem that this may be an area in which the TOC could charge the OOCEA more than the actual cost of these items.

Custodial Services

These services are to be provided after normal working hours (7:00 AM to 6:00 PM). Cleaning schedules are to be provided to the OOCEA. This section describes the areas that are to be cleaned, with some specific instructions (e.g., "liner bags for waste receptacles are to be replaced daily" [Orlando–

Orange County Expressway Authority 1994, 2-49]). In general, though, specific instructions concerning how cleaning is to occur and what materials are to be used are not identified.

Similarly, there is little direction given to pest control directions. Frequency of service is every six months, with pesticides used to be those in compliance with federal law and regulations, and the pest control firm to be licensed as specified in Florida Statute 482.

Landscape maintenance must be performed on a routine basis, including mowing, edging, and trimming of grass and shrubs, as well as weed control. Mowing and edging are to be performed a minimum of twenty-six times per year but no more than once per week.

Trash cannot be kept on the premises for more than two weeks. The TOC must pay for disposal, but is allowed to keep proceeds from the sale of recycled materials.

Equipment operation and maintenance is to be provided by the TOC, including labor, supervision, scheduling, and coordination. All building equipment and systems must be maintained, with the temperature controls specified:

Temperature controls shall be set to maintain 68–70 degrees Fahrenheit during working hours in the heating season. Temperature controls shall be set to maintain 76–78 degrees during working hours in the cooling season. Computer rooms shall be maintained at a temperature range between 72 and 74 degrees Fahrenheit. (Orlando–Orange County Expressway Authority 1994, 2-54)

A maintenance program is to be developed, including a preventative maintenance program. Repairs are to be performed as necessary. All electrical systems must be inspected, tested, and maintained.

All plaza lanes must be pressure cleaned during the hours between 10:00 PM and 6:00 AM. No equipment, vehicles, or equipment is to be stored at the plaza, suggesting that the TOC will subcontract this service.

A section that may prove significant in terms of the implications for liability, states the following: "The TOC . . . shall be responsible for any and all damage to the property of the Authority and to the public moving through the toll facility caused by TOC's operations" (Orlando–Orange County Expressway Authority 1994, 2-58).

Depending upon the specific language of the contract, the implication here is that the TOC, not the OOCEA, will be liable for any damages caused to people and vehicles as they pass through the toll lanes, if equipment and buildings have not been properly maintained.[4] Finally, the TOC should maintain a stock of spare parts, as well as the necessary equipment, with the provision that renting little used expensive equipment is allowable.

There are many aspects of the services provided that would allow the TOC to charge the OOCEA an amount more than the actual cost. Charges for equipment usage may include a depreciation cost that over time may be more than the actual replacement value. It may be possible to charge for preventative services (e.g., inspections), that do not occur. The ability and concern of OOCEA's contract manager to actually monitor how many times the grass is mowed may be limited, and it may be likely that these aspects of a contract may not be fulfilled.

METHOD OF COMPENSATION AND PAYMENT PROCEDURE

This section spells out the methods by which the TOC will be paid. The contract represents a combination of cost and fixed price. In doing so, it provides for the maximum flexibility in terms of staffing while removing incentives for the TOC to lessen costs by potentially lessening quality. These two types are reflected in two categories of costs: (1) unit price items, defined as expended quantities during each month that the costs are incurred (cost); and (2) lump sum items, or those items that remain fixed throughout the contract, with a portion of these items reimbursed on a monthly basis.

At the beginning of the section, the OOCEA states clearly that it reserves the right to adjust quantities of the unit price items, primarily toll collector labor costs. The goal reflected in this statement is that as E-PASS customers increase, the number of automatic lanes will increase, and the number of toll collectors needed will decrease.

The prospective bidders still have complete discretion to estimate the number of toll collector employees needed and the salary amount. The contract amount will reflect the unit costs for the toll collectors as estimated by the winning bidder.

Other parts of the section include a description of the invoice processing system, and a statement concerning the right of the OOCEA to withhold or delay payment for reasons of unsatisfactory payment. Upon project completion, the OOCEA will perform a final audit, with any adjustment in the amount paid to the TOC occurring after the results of the audit.

Even if the need for some items decrease, and the amount of reimbursement to the TOC for these items decreases, the lump sum payment arrangements still allow for the profit (termed fixed management fee) and salaries of management personnel to remain constant. Under management, program management labor—including the program manager, the audit–accounting manager, the toll operations manager, and the maintenance manager—is to be identified in terms of man-months. The lump sum amounts include costs associated with support staff for the four managers noted above, plus those costs associated with the support staff for the ETTM system administration and management and the violation enforcement system. Costs for the TOC operations office lease and utilities, telephone, supplies, furnishings and equipment, vehicles, mileage, and other miscellaneous expenses are also paid in a lump sum format.

ADDENDA

Addenda are meant to furnish additional information in response to questions posed by the prospective bidders. In addition, the addenda may provide additional documentation that was not fully ready to distribute as part of the original RFP. If the OOCEA had deliberately changed its wishes regarding parts of the RFP, they could be reflected in the form of addenda. Addenda can also clarify points or correct minor errors.

Most important, addenda can provide a "dialogue" between vendors and the agency. The vendor can help "write" the RFP by asking questions about items that the agency has either omitted or has not fully considered. To the extent that such items cannot be fully resolved within the context of the RFP, they may become part of the contract, or even part of the public–private partnership that occurs after the contract is signed.

Addendum One

The first addendum was issued on July 24, 1994, approximately two months after the issuance of the RFP. Additional information was requested as preliminary outlines of the staffing plan, the TOC operations office, and the accounting–auditing plan were to be included in the response.

Florida Toll Services submitted 131 questions in a correspondence dated June 29, 1994. Issues that were clarified included:

- The TOC will provide the capital needed for the change fund (question 016).
- The TOC is not responsible for reimbursing the OOCEA for tolls missed because of violations (017).
- The TOC must provide a fireproof vault (027).
- The 60 percent–40 percent full time–part time split refers to regularly scheduled employees, not the number of hours worked (037).
- Benefits provided to part-time employees should be the same as those provided other part-time employees of the TOC (036).
- All ETTM equipment is the responsibility of the OCCEA's toll equipment contractor (SAIC/Syntonic).

Lockheed IMS submitted thirty-one questions in a letter dated July 5, 1994. Issues that were clarified included:

- Since the RFP requires that there be a reduction in operating costs, the question asked is this: What are the current operating costs? The answer will be provided in a later addendum.

To the extent that the addenda are to reflect a learning process that serves as the basis for a future, continuing partnership, some questions are asked that apparently have not been considered by the OOCEA, or they crystallize thoughts that need further development. One such question, for example, may be one such as number 144: "The RFP requires that the selected firm negotiate the transfer of any earned fringe benefits to the successor firm. Will any current FDOT or Norrell Services employees that have earned fringe benefits be eligible to transfer these benefits to the selected firm for Project 266?"

That the response is left blank seems to indicate that the OOCEA was still considering what options are available. The only significant fringe benefit that might be transferable are pension rights. No part-time Norrell service employee would have these. Only some FDOT employees would have vested rights in the state pension fund.

To some extent, some questions understandably ask for detail that OOCEA is not willing to furnish because the TOC should have some discretion to choose the manner in which the detail is created. For example, question 148 refers to the reports which must be processed through the ETTM system. More detail (e.g., all data elements), than that found in the sample report included in the user manuals is requested. The response from OOCEA is simply to "refer to user manuals." The implication here is that exactly how the required data is furnished in the reports is subject to further negotiations and discussions after the contract is awarded.

Two other parts of addendum one included the number of hours each lane on each plaza must be open on a weekly basis (Appendix F) and a contract entitled "Section 5 Toll Facility Operation, Management and Maintenance Agreement." Many of the questions left unanswered referred to the maintenance part of the RFP.

Addendum Two

One week later, July 28, 1994, addendum two was sent to prospective bidders. The primary purpose of this document was to (1) answer questions left unanswered in addendum one, (2) clarify changes to the RFP, and (3) clarify or provide more information concerning the responses to questions offered in addendum one.

The schedule for responses was extended, as proposals were to be received by September 14, 1994, with oral presentation scheduled for October 17 and 18, 1994.

Further clarification was offered concerning whether the TOC would be responsible for missed tolls collected, whether for violations, equipment failure, or armed robbery (017–019). The answer was no, providing that the TOC followed proper procedures in terms of providing appropriate personnel for manned lanes at the time indicated in the RFP as well as for security purposes and that appropriate and timely reports were made in the event of equipment failure or robbery.

A list of all subcontracts was provided, with the answer that all of these were available for review; telephone costs were estimated to be $700 to $800 per plaza per month; turnover rate of FDOT full-time employees is 5 to 7 percent; and again, the TOC is not responsible for the ETTM equipment.

The use of the 60 percent full-time employees was clarified as well:

TOC employees should be regularly scheduled for consistent, consecutive time frames, e.g., one week, two weeks, one month. When that schedule is developed a minimum of 60% of those toll collection employees must be full-time, scheduled during all shifts, for each day of the week. . . . It is not permissible to schedule all full-time employees four days per week and part-time employees the other three days. Nor can full-time employees be scheduled only during the day and part-time employees only at night. (037)

The intention here is that better performance of part-time employees will be obtained if they work shifts along with full-time employees. The TOC is not allowed to give preferable shifts (e.g., day shifts to full-time employees and least preferable to part-time). There must be a mix of both on each shift.

Addenda Three through Five

The issue of the portability of fringe benefits for FDOT will be discussed in a future addendum. In addendum three, further clarification is made, with the response that there is no anticipated transfer of benefits to the TOC. Addendum three, dated August 18, 1994, answers more questions and furnishes the salary data of all toll collectors.

In addendum four, dated August 24, 1994, the OOCEA announces that it has decided to eliminate the facilities maintenance part of the RFP, changing the name of the contract to "Toll Facility Operation and Management Services." The prospective bidder is instructed to eliminate all references to facilities management under scope of services and also as part of the price proposals.

On August 30, 1994, addendum five further explained that the OOCEA will manage the maintenance of toll plazas. It also reassured the prospective bidders that toll operations and accounting would not be eliminated from the proposal. Bidders were given additional time to submit responses, with September 23, 1994 designated as the final day for submission.

CONCLUSION

Three factors were proposed that determine the creating of an effective and successful RFP: (1) the nature of the service (routine to complex), (2) the degree of change desired or anticipated by the government agency (low to high), and (3) the knowledge of the service by both agency and vendor (low to high). All three influence the degree to which an RFP is written more generally or more specifically, and in doing so, eliciting various responses from vendors. To assess more fully the RFP, these factors will be applied to the various parts or aspects of the OOCEA RFP (see Table 5.2).

Mobilization and Transition

The mobilization and transition of operations from FDOT to a private vendor represents a situation of high complexity, a high degree of change desired, and a low to moderate knowledge of the activities needed to perform this service.

The complexity of services must be rated high because neither the OOCEA nor the TOC had any previous experience in privatizing toll operations. Also, a great deal of coordination would be necessary among a variety of parties, including the OOCEA, the TOC, and FDOT to effect a successful transition. The great variety of SOPs, policies, and reports that were requested as part of

Table 5.2
Analysis of OOCEA Privatization RFP

RFP Section	Nature of Service	Factors Degree of Change Desired/ Anticipated	Knowledge of Service Provision
Mobilization Transition	Complex	High	Low
Program Management and Administration			
Staffing of Toll Lanes	Routine	Moderate-High	Moderate-High
TOC Operations Office	Routine	High	High
HRM Plan	Moderate	Moderate-High	Moderate
Training	Routine	Moderate-High	Moderate-High
Customer and Public Relations	Moderate	High	Low-Moderate
Quality Management And Assurance	Complex	High	Low
Performance Monitoring	Complex	Moderate	Low
Audit/Accounting Audits			
Transactions Accountability	Routine	Moderate	High
Toll Operations	Routine	Moderate-High	Moderate-High
ETTM System	Routine	High	High
Facilities Maintenance	Routine	Low	High

the mobilization add to the complexity, even though for some (e.g., toll operations), it was expected that the TOC would adopt many of the already existing procedures found in FDOT's *Manual of Operations*.

The process of transitioning FDOT toll collectors and supervisors to positions with the TOC or to other FDOT positions was one that was potentially highly complex. Although the FDOT employees were to be given the "right of first refusal," and employee benefits were to be provided that were similar to those provided by the state of Florida, there were no restrictions placed on salaries that would be offered to these employees. Although there was an interest in a smooth transition expressed in the RFP, it was far from certain that everyone who wanted to remain with FDOT or transition to the TOC would retain employment.[5]

For a variety of reasons, a high level of change was also desired. It was anticipated that the number of supervisors would be fewer, leading to lower labor costs. Also, as stated in the goals of the RFP, toll collectors were to deliver a higher quality service to patrons.

Knowledge of how to transition services, plus the introduction of the ETTM technology, and the various reports, policies, and SOPs requested, also indicated that the knowledge of the service must be rated low as well.

Program Management and Administration

Staffing of Toll Lanes

Once the staffing plan has been submitted and approved during the transition phase, updating and changing the plan is routine. That the OOCEA wished the flexibility to change a lane from manned to automatic or E-PASS suggests that the anticipated change is moderate to high, especially since the criteria by which the change would occur is not identified in the RFP. The knowledge of how to staff toll lanes is rated moderate to high simply because neither the OOCEA nor the TOC had previously performed this task.

TOC Operations Office

The RFP states that there must be a TOC operations office that must be capable of operating the ETTM system. Setting up an office would be a routine service; the amount of change anticipated is high since one has not previously existed; and both the OOCEA and the TOC would know how to do it.

Human Resource Management Plan

Creating an HRM plan is not a routine function, but since it was anticipated that the TOC (or its parent firms) would have one in place for its present employees, adopting one for the toll operations would be relatively straight-forward. Change desired was high in at least two respects, since drug testing and a background check were not performed by FDOT. It was also antici-pated that since higher quality performance standards were desired, the per-formance evaluation system would be different from that currently in use. Knowledge of how to create an HRM plan is rated as moderate only because OOCEA may have less knowledge than the TOC because of its lack of op-erations experience.

Training

This is a function that can easily become routine, once the training content is fully linked to the behavioral goals required to be reached. The ETTM system introduces a degree of change from current practices, while it also means that both OOCEA and the TOC have only moderate knowledge of the service provided.

Customer and Public Relations

This service must be viewed as complex because it involves the lessening of customer complaints, and it clearly identifies the need for a partnership in the area of customer relations–public relations between the OOCEA and the TOC. The lack of a customer complaint system plus the lack of consistent interaction between OOCEA and FDOT concerning public relations issues indicates that a high degree of change was desired in this area. Given the high degree of uncertainty concerning how to improve this function, the knowl-edge of the service is rated low to moderate.

Quality Management and Assurance

This section requires the TOC to create a quality management system which encompasses the customer satisfaction function. Since it asks the TOC to identify quality standards of behavior and link them to quality performance goals, the nature of the service must be viewed as complex; the degree of change desired is high, since no quality management system had existed un-der FDOT; and a low knowledge of the service exists, as it would seem likely that this function would require negotiation between OOCEA and the TOC to create a system acceptable to both.

Performance Monitoring

Creation of a performance evaluation committee to monitor the perfor-mance of the TOC is an innovative way of resolving issues concerning deficiencies that have been identified. The vagueness of this section indicates a clear willingness by the OOCEA to enter into a partnership with the TOC to resolve difficulties. This section must be rated highly complex, with a high degree of change anticipated, and low knowledge of how it is to be accomplished.

Audits–Accounting

For both the audit and transaction accountability section, the service provided will be routine once the ETTM system is fully operational. In one sense the degree of change anticipated will be moderate, since the error rate with the electronic system will be much less than with the manual system. Knowledge of how to furnish the required reports will be high, since the ETTM system will produce them easily.

Toll Operations

Since the key aspect of this section outlines the procedures needed to staff each type of toll lane, plus it restricts the percentage of part-time collectors to no more than 40 percent, the rating for this section is the same as staffing of toll lanes: routine nature of service; moderate to high change anticipated; and moderate to high knowledge of the service.

ETTM System

This section simply identifies the ETTM and VES system, and states that the TOC will use it to issue financial reports: routine nature of service, high degree of change, and high knowledge, simply because the creators of the system (SAIC/Syntonic) will be responsible for its maintenance and repair.

Facilities Maintenance

The services to be provided are all routine, with the exception of the hiring, training, and firing of maintenance staff. There are few restrictions or standards, and it is assumed that the TOC will know how to accomplish the repairs, cleaning, and other maintenance activities: routine service, little change anticipated, and high knowledge of service.

Overall, the program management aspects of the RFP were judged to be not routine, with knowledge of the service to be low to moderate in part because neither the OOCEA nor the TOC had much experience in toll operations. Many other aspects of operations were routine, and the FRP was written reflecting this fact. The degree of change desired or anticipated was high for many of the services requested by the RFP because these represented aspects of operations that did not exist under FDOT.

NOTES

1. The complete title of this contract is "Armored Car and Depository Banking Services." The contract is between the OOCEA and a bank. It requires an armored car to pick up revenue collected on a daily basis and transport it to the bank. The amount of revenue is counted by bank employees and deposited to OOCEA accounts on the same day. Since the revenue is counted before leaving toll plazas, this process has the benefit of noting discrepancies between the toll plaza count and the bank count. All discrepancies are noted and investigated as part of the internal auditing process of toll revenue.

2. The OOCEA decided that the management of maintenance contracts would be more effective if maintenance duties were separated from the toll operations contract.

3. This language is standard for similar contracts. No matter what amounts are chosen to define the various types of routine maintenance, one overriding issue is the degree to which OOCEA would want to manage or monitor unscheduled maintenance repairs that are not expensive. The TOC should not expect to be reimbursed for low cost, incidental repairs and must include all such items in its overall bid. Repairs that cost more, however, must be approved by OOCEA on a case-by-case basis for additional payment.

4. The issue of liability if there is an accident or injury due to negligence on the part of the private vendor is complex, with state law governing how such issues are resolved. One analysis of this issue in the state of Florida, for example, concludes that recent court decisions have not provided clear direction.

5. At the time the RFP was issued, it was not certain that there would be sufficient positions with the private vendor for all FDOT employees. As discussed in Chapter 7, these concerns proved to be groundless, as the more senior state employees were given the option of taking positions with the Florida Turnpike.

BIDDER RESPONSES TO THE 266 RFP: THE TECHNICAL PROPOSAL

6

Three bidders responded to the 266 RFP. These were (1) Florida Toll Services, a Morrison Knudsen/Parsons Brinckerhoff Joint Venture; (2) United Infrastructure Company (UIC), a Bechtel Enterprises and Peter Kiewit and Sons' Joint Venture; and (3) URS Consultants, Inc. All three submitted separate technical and price proposals as requested. Proposals were received by the OOCEA on September 23, 1994. The OOCEA–FDOT Selection Committee, using criteria identified in the RFP, evaluated the technical proposal.

On November 3, 1994, the evaluation was completed and the notice of the intent to award was issued. FTS was awarded the most points, 360.1, followed by UIC with 265.8, and URS with 223.5. For the technical proposal, the rank order of the three bids was the same: 240.1 for FTS; 229.2 for UIC; and 223.47 for URS. The number of points allocated by section and subsection for the technical proposal is identified in Table 6.1.

Overall, FTS consistently scored higher than the other two bidders on most sections. Of the twelve subsections listed for which points were awarded, FTS scored the highest on ten. FTS provided more information, responding to each section with a greater amount of detail.

The most significant reason for the FTS highest score was the much higher rating given to its managerial, professional, and technical support staff. The members of the management team had many more years of related toll opera-

Table 6.1

Evaluation Criteria: Overall Major Sections—Technical Proposal; Average Points—Selection Committee

Item No.	Title	Available Points	FTS	UIC	URS
1-A	Qualification Narrative	45.0	41.1	38.3	39.4
1-B	Financial Statement	15.0	0.8	13.5	2.0
2-A	**Understanding and Approach**				
2-A.1	Clear Understanding of Project Objectives	30.0	26.7	25.6	26.17
2-A.2	Proposed Approach	50.0	45.6	43.0	41.5
2-B	**Ability and Professional Staff**				
2-B.1	Professional Management Staff	50.0	47.3	34.3	40.1
2-B.2	Technical and Support Staff	20.0	18.2	15.2	17.0
2-C	**Project Management and Organization Plan**				
2-C.1	Responsibility and Accountability	15.0	14.2	13.7	12.7
2-C.2	Work Program	15.0	13.1	12.8	11.3
2-C.3	Quality Control Program	5.0	4.4	4.5	4.3
2-C.4	Financial Control and Security	15.0	13.6	13.2	12.2
2-D	**Affirmative Action Program**				
2-D.1	Proposer provided specific levels of minorities and workmen in the composition of the Proposer's professional/technical workforce	10.0	6.5	5.9	7.6
2-D.2	Participation Goal of 15%	10.0	8.6	9.2	9.2
	TOTAL	**280.0**	**240.1**	**229.2**	**223.5**

tions experience. There was a clearer understanding of how management would transition from the mobilization period to normal operations. There were also fewer professional and technical staff identified, with a greater amount of information concerning the tasks and duties of all personnel.

Proposed toll operations staffing also contributed to the FTS score. It proposed a more efficient, "leaner" operation, indicating that no assistant plaza managers would be needed. It also identified the fewest supervisors and full- and part-time toll collector personnel. Its flexible benefits package more closely resembled that of the state of Florida than that indicated by UIC.

Finally, FTS started from a more advantageous position, as the breadth of experience of its parent firms, plus the amount of direct toll operations experience of these firms, was judged significantly higher than that provided by the other two bidders.

In another sense, however, the scoring was very close, with the 10.9 point margin of FTS only 4.5 percent higher compared to UIC. UIC did score significantly higher on the financial statement, providing information that gave it a 12.7 edge over FTS. UIC also provided a project management and organization plan and an affirmative action program that was rated virtually the same as FTS, receiving 59.3 points compared to the 60.4 received by FTS for these sections.

URS scored significantly higher than UIC on the managerial and professional staff section, and outscored both FTS and UIC on affirmative action programs. Since it lost by only 16.6 points, if it had provided more information concerning its financial statement, it would have scored a close second to FTS.

THE EVALUATION PROCESS

Care was taken to ensure as much as possible that the evaluation process was fair and without bias. To provide direction to the respondents, a description and discussion of the evaluation criteria were included in the RFP, specifying those items that were deemed most important during the selection process. Each of the five evaluation committee members was provided a packet entitled "Evaluation Guidelines and Scoring Forms" to be used in assessing and recording their scores for each aspect of the technical proposals. The scoring forms were separated into the various evaluation criteria, providing guidance in the form of specific questions that further detailed the evaluation criteria.

The instructions to the committee reflect a concern for maintaining a bias-free process. The nature of the interaction among committee members was discussed:

During the evaluation period the Selection Committee will meet as necessary to discuss the proposals and their content. Evaluators will be able to make qualitative comments or to raise questions about relevant aspects of the proposals. They may also bring to the attention of the Committee issues of concern or interest or which may not be clear to an evaluator. *However, no discussion shall take place regarding specific score values for various items.* (emphasis added) (Post et al. 1994, p. 3)

There could be discussion concerning what was meant by specific criteria. Also, clarification concerning what a bidder meant by certain sections could occur during committee meetings (as well as during the oral presentation). There was to be no discussion concerning what score any one member was considering giving a respondent on any given item.

In addition, there was to be no discussion concerning what a score of five measured, for example, on a ten-point item. Did it mean that the bidder met one-half the criteria for that item? Clearly many of the items were not easily quantifiable, so that the measurement standards used by each committee member were determined by that individual.

By employing a five-member committee and averaging the scores of each member for each evaluation item, this process should have resulted in a fair outcome. Even though the measurement standards were different for each member, if that person used the same standards consistently for all the criteria, no bias should be present. To further ensure a bias-free process, the committee was reminded that since all Florida government documents are a matter of public record, the individual rating scores could be scrutinized by any of the respondents. If a protest were to be filed, this was likely to occur.

Under a section entitled "Recommendations for Evaluators," committee members were directed to first read each proposal without scoring "to develop an overall understanding and familiarity with the proposal." A second review would result in preliminary scores. Each evaluator is encouraged to compare scores for the three proposals for each item.

The value of the oral presentations are reflected in two ways. A preliminary score for each evaluation criteria is given prior to the presentations. Afterward, the final score is recorded. In addition, separate forms are provided to list questions to be asked, with space provided to note the responses. If the presentation experience changed the number of points awarded, the evaluator was directed to make a note. Finally, each evaluator was encouraged to use the full range of points allowed, given partial credit, rather than assigning no points.

BIDDER RESPONSES

The following compares and contrasts the responses to the primary sections of the RFP, assessing the appropriateness of the response. For each of the major sections as listed in Table 6.1, those criteria weighted the most will be analyzed. Information provided in the responses is reviewed and summarized where appropriate.

In evaluating the responses to an RFP, a variety of approaches are possible. First, the extent to which the information provided directly responds to the information requested in the RFP can be assessed. The level of detail and resulting completeness of the information provided also constitute general criteria for assessment.

I-A: QUALIFICATION NARRATIVE

Section I-A of the evaluation criteria, titled "Qualification Narrative," contains seven items. These are (with maximum number of points) as follows:

1. Proposer's written narrative   2
2. Listing of reference   2
3. Listing of eighteen areas of experience   18
4. Tolls and revenue collector experience   10

5. Support services and security experience	5
6. Information management experience	5
7. Overall proposer experience	3
TOTAL	45

The RFP requests "full and complete" information from each responding firm, including all firms if a joint venture is proposed, as well as from any subcontracting or consultant firm. The more significant information requested is a qualifications statement describing all experience of the firm(s) during the past five years "in performing the variety of operations, management maintenance and support services inherent with a complex and state-of-the-art toll collection system, revenue collection operation, or comparable industrial operation" (Orlando–Orange County Expressway Authority 1994, 1-21).

A discussion of more specific experience is desired in areas such as toll collection operations, project management, customer services, accounting–revenue control, quality assurance–quality control staff recruitment and training, and contract management. The focus of the narrative, limited to no more than ten pages, should be on criteria such as: (1) size of operation managed, (2) technical complexity of operation managed, (3) financial control experience, and (4) number of personnel managed. Past performance should be addressed, including successes and improvements, innovations, or special areas of risk.

To obtain information concerning how experienced the bidders were with using advanced technology, the RFP also requests that bidders

Provide detailed information on the firms capability and experience in managing information resources including computing and telecommunications, planning and operations. Provide descriptions of automatic data processing equipment managed and the types of systems managed, e.g., toll collection, manhour tracking, payroll, property, project management. (Orlando–Orange County Expressway Authority 1994, 1-22)

In addition, there are eighteen areas of expertise listed that bidders were directed to describe specific experience. These are as follows:

Toll collection operations	Project support services
Revenue collection operations	Customer services
Project management	Public relations
Facility–equipment operations	Resource management
Facility maintenance	Utility management
Computer data center operations	Contract management
Accounting–revenue control	Staff recruitment
Quality assurance–quality control	Financial management
Staff recruiting and training	Business management
Safety management	

All three bidders represented firms that were either joint ventures (FTS and UIC) and/or involved relationships with subcontractors. All three also represented firms that had experience in providing services relating to transportation. Although all three noted they had some experience in toll operations, much of the experience noted was in construction and engineering design and management. Experience in revenue collection operations was mentioned as appropriate.

FTS

FTS, formed as a joint venture of Morrison Knudsen (MK) and Parsons Brinckerhoff (PB), offered the experience of the parent companies. In the transportation area, both were associated with the E-470 Toll Road project in Denver, Colorado, with PB having been involved "in the early phases of the planning, design and construction management services" for a project that was to be a forty-eight-mile, four-lane tollway. Responsibilities included "management of innovative design options for the automated toll collection system" (Florida Toll Services 1994, 2).

MK operates the present toll collection, facility and equipment maintenance, and roadway maintenance for the one toll plaza. Various innovations in staff scheduling and internal accounting procedures have been implemented. MK will be also responsible for similar operational functions on the full forty-eight-mile tollway once it is operational. Both parent companies are experienced in revenue collection, including collecting in excess of $6 million annually in billeting and dining halls at NAS Fallon, a Navy installation in Nevada. Other revenue collection and accountability systems were provided to the Naval Air Facility at El Centro, California.

Information is also provided about the two parent companies. MK is a general contracting firm, in existence since 1912, with approximately 3,000 key engineering and management staff supporting approximately 15,000 employees. Since 1920, MK has provided engineering, construction, and maintenance of highways. Examples mentioned include the $1.5-billion I-90 project in Seattle, and the $672-million Northumberland Strait Fixed Crossing, linking New Brunswick to Prince Edward Island via the eight-mile Prince Edward Island toll bridge. MK will operate the toll collection services upon completion.

PB is an engineering firm, with over 109 years of experience in the transportation industry. It has planned, designed, and built projects for a variety of turnpike authorities, as well as being involved in many of the newest toll road projects, including the E-470 project in Denver, the Dulles toll road expansion in Virginia, and the SR 125 project in San Diego County, California. In addition, the FTS technical proposal provided an experience matrix listing sixty-four projects and services, of which nineteen were related to toll facilities. Fifty-seven pages of narrative supported this matrix.

UIC

UIC, formed in 1993, is a joint venture partnership backed by Bechtel Enterprises and Peter Kiewit Sons'. For this project, UIC proposed to be the prime contractor, providing top level management resources. MFS Network Technologies (MFSNT) would provide program management and audit–accounting functions for the project. Wackenhut Services, a subsidiary of Wackenhut Corporation, would provide the toll operations services. In addition, Lyca and Associates would be responsible for training, PAB Consultants providing the temporary personnel, and Ms. Bertica Cabrera, an MWBE agency in Orange County, would assist with community relations and recruitment of personnel.

UIC indicated that it has been involved in two transportation privatization projects that involve financing, construction, and then operating toll facilities. These involve the Tacoma Narrows Bridge and a congestion pricing project in Washington's Puget Sound region.

Both parent firms participated in many relevant projects. Bechtel projects include providing a variety of construction and management services for Attiko Metro in Athens, Greece; the BART extension program in Oakland, California; and the Rapid Transit System, Taipai, Taiwan. Kiewit Construction Group Projects include new construction and modification of toll projects for the Florida Turnpike; airport construction in Honolulu, Hawaii; and construction of a passenger terminal, parking garage, and baggage handling areas for the Sky Harbor International Airport in Phoenix, Arizona.

MFS Network Technologies has been involved in a variety of intelligent vehicle highway systems, including those found in the Florida Turnpike System; the Cross Island Parkway in Hilton Head, South Carolina; the Walt Whitman Bridge in Camden, New Jersey; and various toll collection points in New York City.

Wackenhut Corporation provides toll collection and toll road operation services for four cities in Columbia, South America and for San Juan, Puerto Rico. In addition, it provides security forces and personnel for the Florida Turnpike, the Metropolitan Dade County Transit Authority, the New York Racing Association, and the U.S. Department of Energy.

Lyca Associates of Orlando is a minority, women-owned enterprise, providing training programs for organizations such as the Orlando Aviation Authority and the Orange County Sheriff's Office. PAB Consultants, Inc. is a disadvantaged business enterprise (DBE). It provides temporary personnel for the FDOT, Florida Turnpike, and the Tampa Hillsborough County Expressway Authority.

URS

URS proposed to be the prime contractor, providing overall management services as well as accounting and auditing services. U.S. Personnel, Inc., and Norrell Services, Inc., would provide toll collector staffing, while Communications Plus, Inc., would assist in the areas of customer service and staff development.

URS, an architectural–engineering firm formed over ninety years ago, currently manages several complex projects with fees in excess of $150 million. It currently employs over 1,200 professionals in a variety of professional areas, including toll road operations, revenue collection, mechanical engineering, program and construction managers, and architects.

More specifically, URS is providing multiprofessional services for the nineteen-mile Reversible and Concurrent Flow Bus–HOVB roadway system on I-64 and Route 44 for the Virginia Department of Transportation. Operations management services are provided, including the recruitment, training, and scheduling functions. In addition, URS provides support for the VDOT public relations program.

As traffic engineer for Florida's turnpike, URS provides a wide range of traffic engineering services, including traffic and revenue studies, transportation planning and traffic engineering analysis and administration, and improved project scheduling. It also serves as the general engineering manager for the San Joaquin Hills Transportation Corridor and the Foothill–Eastern Transportation Corridor which are part of the Orange County (California) Transportation Corridor Agency's Toll Road Construction Program.

U.S. Personnel services currently provides staffing for the SAIC on the OOCEA's ETTM project in Orlando. In addition, it has provided assistance to three state agencies of the state of South Carolina, averaging over 5500 billable hours of business per week. Norrell Services provides toll collector staffing to the OOCEA Southern Connector toll plazas, plus providing the Orlando centroplex all ticket takers and ushers since 1988.

Analysis

In evaluating the written proposal and the list of references, relevant criteria include the clarity and completeness of the information provided and the number of references. The degree to which past experience was judged to be relevant to the needs of the OOCEA was perhaps more closely reflected in the other items. As such, all three proposals rated high in clarity and completeness. The FTS proposal, when the experience of MK and PB are included, contains the most number of references and the most pages of narrative.

The greatly varied experience of the FTS parent firms enhanced the score given to "18 experience areas." Greater experience was apparent in toll collection (with the E-470 project), revenue collection (NAS Fallon), and project management. Experience in some areas seems to be present by implication. There are no discussions of programs dealing specifically with public relations, customer service, or safety management, with limited mention of quality assurance. Yet the number of awards won (e.g., U.S. Army's "Contractor of the Year") for outstanding base operation services would seem to suggest experience in these areas.

For UIC, a similar range of experience was reflected by the parent firms and those who would contract with UIC to provide toll operation services. There was a chart provided that indicated which of the eighteen experience areas was characteristic of each parent–subcontracting firm.

For toll collection operations, Wackenhut provided direct experience, with its 1,300 employees and forty toll plazas in Columbia as well as its experience in Puerto Rico. MFSNT was designing and installing toll collection systems in a variety of places, but apparently lacked operation experience. UIC stated that it will be operating toll collection facilities in the state of Washington, but had not done so at the time of the response to the RFP.

For the other experience areas, the amount of information furnished was much less than that provided by FTS. Although experience in project management, project support services, and contract management was apparent, for other areas, such as quality assurance, utility management, and customer services, much less information was provided.

For URS, the overall score of 16.4 matched that of FTS. Norrell provides toll operations experience through its employment contract with OOCEA on the Southern Connector plazas. Toll collection familiarity has also been gained by URS in its position as traffic engineer for the Florida Turnpike since 1954. In addition, URS has extensive project management experience, reflected by its management of the traffic management system for the I-64–Route 44 roadway system for the Virginia Department of Transportation.

Overall, of the three bidders, URS furnished the least amount of information. URS and its contractors do not have the depth and range of experience that can be offered by the parent firms of the other two bidders. Information regarding resource management, utility management, and quality assurance–quality control seems missing. Yet URS is in an unique position, given its relationship with the Florida Turnpike.

I-B: FINANCIAL STATEMENT

In order to "determine the financial adequacy of the firm," each bidder was directed to provide its most current audited financial statement (1-23). The evaluation criteria for this section included the following: a financial statement not over twelve months old; a CPA opinion that was satisfactory; a balance sheet; an income statement; a statement of cash flow; and financial adequacy–capacity. All criteria were worth two points each, with the exception of the last, which was worth five points. The total points for this section was fifteen.

FTS and URS provided little or no information concerning the financial capability of their firms, receiving 0.8 and 2.0 scores! UIC furnished the required information, scoring 13.5 points. For the former two bidders, apparently an oversight occurred.

2.0: TECHNICAL PROPOSAL

The evaluation criteria for the technical proposal clearly lists several components that the bidders are required to provide in their response. These include the preliminary documents as specified in the scope of services section of the RFP:

- Systems operations transition plan
- Staffing plan
- TOC operations office standard operating procedure
- Audit–accounting plan
- Toll operations SOP

In addition, two other deliverables are required:

- Flexible benefits package for employees
- Preliminary document submittal schedule

There are also several statements clearly admonishing the bidders to provide information "that is sufficiently detailed to enable the Committee to ascertain that the proposer understands the requirements and is able to furnish toll operations and maintenance services of a scope and complexity specified" (Orlando–Orange County Expressway Authority 1994, 1-23).

Statements that merely repeat the information contained in the RFP or that do not provide the necessary detail will receive no credit. Unlike the information requested in the qualifications statement, past experience not germane to toll collection operations should not be included.

Each of the specific evaluation criteria are outlined, with a narrative explaining each in more detail. Table 6.2 contains an outline of the criteria and the number of points allocated for each of the criteria.

Understanding and Approach:
1. Clear Understanding of Project Objectives

The bidder is directed to present the approach to meeting the objectives or goals as identified in the RFP, identifying difficulties and probable effectiveness in meeting these objectives. Efficient use of manpower, minimized use of OOCEA staff, and innovative approaches are to be discussed. The evaluation criteria include the following:

Effective toll collection operation	2
Reduction in current operating cost	2
Sound financial accounting	2

Table 6.2
Evaluation Criteria: Technical Proposal

A.	Understanding and Approach	(80 points out of 220)
	1. Clear Understanding of Project Objectives	(30 points)
	2. Proposed Approach	(50 points)
B.	Ability and Professional Staff	(70 points out of 220)
	1. Professional Management Staff	(50 points)
	2. Proposed Technical and Support Staff	(20 points)
C.	Project Organization and Management Plan	(50 points out of 220)
	1. Responsibility and Accountability	(20 points)
	2. Work Program	(10 points)
	3. Quality Control Program	(20 points)
D.	Affirmative Action Program and	
	Minority/Women/Disadvantaged Participation	(20 points)

Customer services	2
Operating environment that best serves the motoring public	2
Effective and clear understanding of work	10
Efficient–innovative manpower utilization	10
TOTAL	30

The evaluation criteria for this section are almost identical to the objectives stated in the RFP and the discussion that supports the explanation of the evaluation criteria. The criteria, as do the objectives, overlap in terms of the information they measure. For example, high quality customer services will significantly contribute to highly effective toll collection operation. Likewise, "efficient/innovative manpower utilization" will contribute to "reduction in the current operating cost" (Orlando–Orange County Expressway Authority 1994, 1-24).

The information provided in the responses to the first five more specific objectives, worth a total of ten points, overlapped considerably with the information relevant to the final two evaluation criteria, worth ten points each. The following analysis focuses on the responses to the specific objectives. All three bidders provided a general introduction to this section and then discussed each of the specific objectives.

FTS begins its presentation with an introduction to the subject of project understanding. Included in the introduction is an overview of the current toll collection operations, mentioning the use of FDOT and Norell Services personnel in providing collectors for the Southern Connector. It emphasizes the large amount of time spent by FTS personnel visiting OOCEA and gathering information about current policies and procedures. The transition phase is also stressed, suggesting that an initial draft of the SOPs required to begin the transition are included.

It lists the objectives and then states in one sentence "bullets" the ways by which these objectives will be achieved. Many of these methods are a rephrasing of the objectives (e.g., "improving the quality of operations," or "providing improved management abilities and financial controls"). Other ways mentioned, however, do provide some insight into the depth of the FTS proposal. "Providing strong commitment and loyalty to the Authority by developing a long term relationship through the 'partnering' concept," for example, is a statement that seems to suggest the interest of FTS in working with the OOCEA to reach common goals in a flexible and evolving manner (Florida Toll Services 1994, 4).

UIC's introduction highlights both the objectives reflected in the RFP and the UIC team approach. Ideas included in the approach are the following:

A TOC team composed of industry leaders in privatized infrastructure industry with particular emphasis in toll collection applications; a staffing plan that encourages employment of current toll collection personnel featuring a competitive employment and benefits package; our training approach stresses both operational procedures using the new Toll Management System and patron relations; a strong project management team that brings a high level of experience in toll systems and operations. (United Infrastructure Company 1994, 2-1).

URS provides a two-paragraph introduction, briefly describing the OOCEA toll operations services. URS states that it will develop and implement a training program, operate the toll collection systems, and maintain records and files.

Effective Toll Collection Operation

In terms of how to achieve greater toll collection operation effectiveness, FTS offers that "effective management and highly trained personnel" will be motivated to achieve the most efficient use of the ETTM system. The management team will develop a comprehensive training program, a system of key performance indicators and standards, a thorough system of internal controls, and safeguards that will limit employee errors.

UIC stresses the importance of customer relations, along with the need to employ the most experienced toll collection personnel. The establishment of a patron advisory committee to provide input on the quality and levels of service is another means of meeting this goal.

URS provides a similar approach, briefly listing responses to each of the four objectives and providing a more detailed discussion under a following section entitled "project requirements." In ways similar to the other two bidders, experienced and qualified senior management and toll collection staff are discussed. Staff recruitment, training, monitoring, and retention are also discussed.

Reduction in Operating Cost

To reduce operating costs, FTS suggests a few approaches. First, it suggests that "overstaffing, including toll collectors, supervision and administrative staff" was one of the common failures for not adhering to performance standards. To resolve this problem, "Expanded job duties and span of control for both supervisors and field managers will enable reduced staffing without any degradation of service" (Florida Toll Services 1994, 7). In addition, a computerized scheduling system will allow for optimal use of toll collection personnel.

Another identified problem is also relevant to efficiency (as well as to effectiveness). The "apparent confusion and an absence of organization for routine tasks" can be resolved through clearly identified and enforced SOPs, uniform training, and periodic rotation and cross training of employees.

UIC states thirteen ways by which efficient toll operations, including a reduction in operating cost can be achieved. These are presented in statement form, with most of them not explained or developed. The most relevant of these is "the use of state of the art computer modeling tolls to assist in a review of staffing levels." Referring to a discussion found later in the response, this approach will enable UIC to recommend annual or periodic adjustments to staffing levels. "Smart plazas" will be developed, using the ETTM technology, operational experience and statistics, and traffic information.

Second, using creative training methods, including "interactive workbooks," will help to provide greater knowledge and proficiency among the toll collectors. Third, employee quality work groups will be established to provide continuous quality improvement. Finally, an employee recognition program would stimulate high quality performance.

URS provides a one-sentence response to a statement of this objective. It stresses the elimination of waste from among the operating policies and procedures and the adoption of innovative ideas. This is followed by a discussion of efficient strategies in the "project requirements" section, such as possible changes in job descriptions to give more responsibility to lower staff positions and increased staff flexibility.

Sound Financial Accounting

FTS stresses a comprehensive auditing and accounting system that will include a strong system of internal controls. These include, first, the segregation of duties among those who are involved in the daily collection of revenue, storing of revenue, transferring of revenue to banks, and the reconciliation of revenue received from the vehicles that have passed through the toll plazas. Second, multiple systems of "determining and monitoring the correct amount of tolls to be collected" will be created. These include analysis of the ETTM reports, as well as unannounced field audits and employee observation.

Of the six statements that UIC lists under this objective, the separation of the audit–accounting function from the operations function seems the most significant. This statement is reflected by the identification of Wackenhut as the operations subcontractor and MFSNT as the accounting subcontractor.

URS mentions the need to enhance internal controls over cash collections. In addition, it promises to deliver comprehensive and timely audits, using the reporting systems that are part of the ETTM.

Customer Services

According to the response written by FTS, toll service attendants will receive training that "will emphasize accurate collection, accounting and security of tolls, together with friendly, helpful, courteous service" (Florida Toll Services 1994, 5). This training will include specific procedures for reporting and resolving patron complaints. The use of a performance-based education as the basis for all training programs begins with the desired behavior to be achieved and then developing the training methodology. FTS feels this approach will improve employee loyalty and morale.

UIC stresses the development of interactive workbooks as the basis of its training approach. A customer complaint system will be developed, as well as an employee recognition program that recognizes outstanding performance.

URS states that the OOCEA must be sensitive to public reaction to toll operations services. All staff will receive customer service training, and "standard measures of effectiveness regarding customer service" will be developed and monitored.[1] Additional ways to develop feedback from the public will also be developed.

Operating Environment That Best Serves the Motoring Public

This objective is the most general of the four and in many respects encompasses some of the aspects of the other three. Customer service must be a significant factor. Not only must there be a commitment to training, but there must be a regard for ways in which employees can be provided incentives to maintain a high quality level of service.

In addition, perhaps the best operating environment would be one that is flexible in ways that respond to the changing needs of the patrons who use the OOCEA toll roads. This would reflect a staffing plan that would be extremely sensitive to the changing road usage. As E-PASS usage increases, there may be less need for manned lanes. If there are increasingly long lines at the manned lanes at a given plaza, there may be a need for the opening of additional lanes. If traffic during certain periods of the day decreases, fewer manned open lanes may be required.

Ultimately, the degree to which an operating environment of a contractor approaches the ideal depends upon its relationship with the contracting agency.

To the extent that there is a willingness to engage in a partnership that strives to achieve goals and solve problems, the response of a bidder should be rated highly.

In the introduction to this section, FTS makes several statements that support the achievement of this objective. These include the following:

- Providing strong commitment and loyalty to the authority by developing a long-term relationship through the "partnering" concept.
- Improving image and morale of toll collection personnel and promoting esprit de corps.
- Assisting the authority in various programs to increase ridership and E-PASS usage (Florida Toll Services 1994, 4).

In its response to this objective, FTS adds the phrase "instituting policies and procedures that protect the investments of bondholders." It identifies another key element by mentioning the need for uninterrupted service. To achieve this, FTS states that procedures will be established to sustain operations during all types of emergencies. Plus, it emphasizes recognition of employee performance and the use of total quality management techniques.

UIC repeats information provided in responses to other sections, including the use of a patron advisory committee and the need for training to maintain high levels of employee satisfaction and performance. It also promises to use Orlando businesses and vendors to "promote local participation."

URS takes a different approach. It links serving the best interests of the people of Central Florida to efficient, less costly toll operations. It also reflects some of the themes identified by the other two bidders in a separate section entitled "URS Mission Statement," including the idea that "URS wants to serve the Authority for a long time" and "we will be extremely responsive and sensitive to the Authority's preferences" (URS Consultants, Inc. 1994, 6).

Overall, FTS provided a longer, more detailed discussion of the objectives and how they were to be achieved than did the other two bidders. FTS was the only one to mention expanded span of control for supervisors and field managers as a means of reducing operating costs. FTS provided examples of internal controls needed for sound financial accounting, while the other two simply mentioned the need for internal controls. To achieve high quality customer service, FTS would provide training based upon a performance-based educational approach.

Similarly, there was more information in the FTS narrative that indicated knowledge of toll operations. The discussion of the ways in which quality performance standards are not met, along with corrective actions, provided analysis that was not found in the other two responses. Two examples are "high violation rates during unattended periods," suggesting that the practice of "dixie cupping" needs to be met with vigilance; and "ground money littering lanes," indicating that, in the interest of patron safety, employees will not argue with drivers over dropped funds.

Understanding and Approach: Proposed Approach

This section asks each bidder to identify what procedures they would use to begin implementation of the toll operations if they were awarded the contract. Criteria include the schedule of activities, including the submission of required documentation, and the mobilization approach to starting the operations, the operations transition plans, and a preliminary listing of toll operations standard operating procedures (SOPs).

Of the fifty total points allocated to this section, the most significant subsection concerns the six points allocated to the flexible benefits package. It was very clearly stated that bidders were to provide health and medical benefits that were comparable to those presently received by FDOT employees. Furthermore, the RFP threatened to reject a proposal if it did not provide "an adequate benefits package" (Orlando–Orange County Expressway Authority 1994, 2-19).

In all cases, the amount of information furnished by FTS far exceeds that provided by UIC and URS. In response to the document submission schedule, FTS describes each document to be written, identifying overlapping time periods, promising that document submission would be complete by December 20, 1994. UIC provides a similar schedule, indicating that the necessary writing would be complete by December 12, thereby giving OOCEA more time for review and comment. URS simply lists the tasks that need to be accomplished, reproducing the timeline as indicated in the RFP.

The requirement of a preliminary toll operations SOP brought forth forty-eight pages from FTS, an amount of detail that seems close to what was needed for the final SOP. UIC provided a twenty-page outline, with a similar discussion (in much less detail) of the needed duties for toll collectors. URS responded with fewer than four pages, simply listing the title of each subsection of what would constitute an operations SOP.

There are common elements to each bidder's discussion of mobilization activities, which include the hiring of existing toll collectors and using approaches to operations that are already in existence. FTS does provide an additional promise that it will begin mobilization "between the dates of proposal submission and contractor selection notification" by developing contracts with subcontractors and readying purchase orders.

Flexible Benefits Package

Although it is difficult to directly compare all benefits, the major aspects of each bidder's package are noted.

FTS: Major Medical Including Dental. Cost per month for employee coverage is $10, with family coverage at $35 per month (two or more dependents). Dental insurance is also included for this cost. Eighty percent of all costs are paid until an annual out of pocket cost of $1,500 per individual or $3,000 per family is reached, after which the insurance pays 100 percent of costs. Annual medical deductible is $200 per individual or $400 per family, with annual dental deductible at $50 per individual and $100 per family. Although the option of an HMO is discussed, costs are not presented. Other benefits include life insurance at an amount equal to an employee's salary at no cost.

UIC: Major Medical Including Dental. The Wackenhut Corporation (TWC) offers a "traditional" indemnity plan with Blue Cross and Blue Shield and an HMO sponsored by Av-Med. The employee cost per month for the traditional plan is $45 (TWC's contribution is 75 percent or $135), with family plan cost of $510 (including the $180). Annual deductibles are $300 for an individual and $600 for a family. For the HMO, individual costs are $152, of which TWC pays 75 percent, and $450 per month for family costs. A PPO option is available. Dental insurance is available through Av-Med at a cost of $10.92 per month for an employee and $25.69 per month for family coverage.

Other benefits include $25,000 of life insurance at $.36 per $1,000 per month, of which TWC will pay two-thirds and the employee one-third. Short- and long-term disability insurance is available at additional cost, and a 401(k) plan is available to employees after one year of employment for those who work at least 1,000 hours per year.

URS: Major Medical and Dental. An analysis is provided comparing the URS medical plans with the state of Florida plans. URS costs are $30 per month for employees and $141 per month for families, with the URS contribution almost $200 per month for individuals and $472 per month for families. Although these amounts are slightly higher than the Florida State plans, URS argues that the benefits provided by its medical plan are greater. The URS plan has unlimited lifetime benefits (Florida's are capped at $1 million); no hospital admission deductibles (Florida's are $300 for non-PPC members) and lower out-of-pocket annual maximums (URS is $850 per individual and $1,700 per family; Florida is $2,500 per individual and $5,000 per family). Adoption, hearing, and vision benefits are also part of the URS plan. Dental premiums are also similar to Florida's, but with no cost for the individual (Florida is $24 per month, and $54 per month per family; and $58 per month for two family members or more). HMO options are almost exactly the same as Florida's, with an individual employee paying $30 per month and $97 per month for family coverage with URS.

Although the out-of-pocket expenses for FTS and URS are very similar for major medical coverage, the costs for UIC are considerably higher. The ratings of the evaluation committee reflected these differences, as the FTS and URS received the highest overall average of 5.2, and UIC followed with an overall average of 3.8.

2-B Ability and Professional Staff: Professional Management Staff

This section was the most pivotal in the entire set of bidder responses. To indicate the significant disparity in evaluator ratings, Table 6.3 shows the actual average ratings across all five evaluators for the three bidders. The

Table 6.3
2-B Ability and Professional Staff: Professional Management Staff;
Average Evaluation Ratings

Evaluation Criteria	Total Pts	FTS	UIC	URS
Provide Management Staff With Adequate Experience	10.0	9.4	5.4	8.2
Staff/Resumes with Projects Similar in Scope and Complexity	7.0	6.7	4.5	5.5
Staff/Resumes of Acceptable Performance History	8.0	7.2	6.0	7.0
Projects Demonstrate Proposer Experience	8.0	7.4	6.3	7.5
Resumes for All Key Staff Showing Adequate Experience	7.0	6.7	4.3	5.5
Staffing Plan to Encompass Key Elements of Proposed Organization Structure	5.0	4.9	4.0	3.9
Staffing Plan Adequate for Staff Loading Capability	5.0	5.0	3.8	3.5
TOTAL	**50.0**	**47.3**	**34.3**	**40.1**

subsequent discussion of each subsection clearly portrays FTS as the strongest of the three bidders.

Project Management Staff with Adequate Experience

The task of judging the ability of individuals who would comprise the top management team is a challenging one. It is difficult to judge the past performance of individuals from examining their resumes. It is even more difficult to ascertain the likelihood of future performance given past experience, as an individual with thirty years experience may not perform as well as someone with fifteen years of experience.[2]

Yet the knowledge, skills, and abilities (KSAs) needed to manage toll operations can best be learned from previous experience in that same field. To the extent that commitment, loyalty, and high quality performance accompany experience in a given field, it can be assumed that more years of experience are likely to be preferable to fewer.

This section asks the evaluation committee to rate the extent to which the proposed project management staff had adequate experience. Although each bidder proposed a slightly different management–organizational structure, a comparative analysis of the top three management positions can be made in terms of the relevant toll operations experience.

Program Manager

FTS: Edward DeLozier—six years as toll operations manager; twelve years turnpike authority experience

UIC: Marty Sas—one year as project manager, IVHS system

URS: John Ramming—approximately six years as executive director, state highway system; fifteen years as general manager and general counsel, state highway system

Toll Operations Manager

FTS: John Simonese—two years as maintenance director; five years as operations manager, state turnpike authority; twenty-six years as state toll collector

UIC: Debra May—five years as regional manager, state toll collection

URS: No one identified—

Stephen Moon, five years as project director (50% of the time) state toll collection;

William Wilfret, retired, to work only during mobilization

Accounting–Audit Manager

FTS: Monte Menard— two years as local toll operations

UIC: Donald Dillman—two years at MFS Technologies

URS: Donald Snoeblen—unclear experience

At the program management position, the FTS candidate had eighteen years of toll operation experience; the UIC candidate had no years; and the URS candidate had twenty-one years with transportation systems, although it was unclear how much of this was in toll operations. At the toll operations manager position, the FTS candidate had thirty-three years of toll operations experience; the UIC candidate had five years, and there was no permanent candidate proposed by URS, although the interim candidate had many (unclear) years of experience. At the accounting–audit manager position, the FTS candidate had two years of toll operations experience, while the candidates for the other two positions had none or unclear experience in this area.

Staff and Resumes with Projects Similar in Scope and Complexity

This criterion evaluates experience outside of toll operations (as well as toll operations experience), examining how previous experience compares with the scope and complexity of this toll operations contract. For FTS, neither the Dulles Toll Road (program manager) nor the E-470 projects (accounting manager) were as large in scope or as complex, while experience gained as a supervisor in the New Jersey Turnpike system may constitute a larger operation.

For UIC, Marty Sas's U.S. Army and private experience in communications could be larger in scope and complexity, but it would be difficult to judge given the information provided. An FDOT–OTO (office of toll operations) regional manager would have a position similar in scope and complexity, but experience in ETTM systems would be lacking. A position with MFS Technologies may be more complex, but smaller in scope.

For URS, executive director and general manager of state highway agencies would be larger in scope and complexity. Although Stephen Moon's role in the organization is unclear, his experience as director of the FDOT–OTO would indicate experience of larger scope and complexity.

Staff and Resumes of Acceptable Performance History

The evaluation form asks, "Has the Proposer provided a staff and resumes demonstrating *a history of acceptable performance*, specifically as it relates to completing program tasks *on time*, and with the resources allocated?" (Post et al. 1994, 15).

Without examining copies of annual performance evaluation ratings, for example, it may be impossible to adequately judge the quality of an individual's performance. An "acceptable performance history," though, may be reflected by a resume that indicates positions of progressively increasing responsibility over time, without unexplainable "gaps" of time without employment. Promotions within one organization could reflect this history, as well as movement toward holding similar positions with increasingly larger, more complex operations.

For FTS, the resumes of DeLozier, Simonese, and Menard all reflect growth in their performance history. For the former two, the fact that they both started as toll collectors and worked their way into top management positions seems more than acceptable. For Menard, moving into a management position with the E-470 project is clearly a more responsible position than his experience with Motorola.

For UIC, it is more difficult to trace Sas's performance history since his work with Magnavox to his present position with MFS. Perhaps the MFS experience is one of larger scope and more managerial responsibility. May more than acceptably progressed in her five years experience with FDOT, and since then has become part of the Wackenhut international tolls team. Dillman has progressed through increasingly more responsible accounting and managerial positions.

For URS, since no years are listed, it is difficult to trace an acceptable performance history. From the description of his experience, Ramming's history is more than acceptable, with positions as general manager and executive director in Indiana and Texas. For Willfret and Moon, progress has been shown in their performance history, although Willfret's interim status works against his performance assessment. There is not enough detail to review Snoeblen's performance.

Projects Demonstrate Proposer Experience

The evaluation criteria for this section seem to be asking the extent to which the past experience of the proposers, even if it is not in the toll operations area, is sufficient to operate a toll facility the size and scope of the OOCEA. To the extent that the projects operated by the parent companies of FTS and UIC can be taken into account, then these two proposers have an edge over that of URS. To the extent that this criteria asks the evaluators to judge the experience of the specific proposed management staff with operations of over 400 employees, much of the same analysis presented under the two previous sections is relevant here.

Resumes for All Key Staff Showing Adequate Experience

Not only were resumes to be submitted, the experience of key staff was to be judged for its adequacy and the degree to which it fit the needs of the OOCEA toll operations. In addition to the resumes for the project management team, all three bidders submitted resumes of other key staff. These other key staff fell into two categories: (1) managers from among the parent firms and subcontractors whose contribution to the project would be less than full time, and (2) members of the mobilization–transition team who would not remain as staff members after the contract was awarded.

During mobilization, the FTS Management Committee will be headed by Ed DeLozier. As project manager of the permanent management team, he will easily transition into the full-time position after mobilization is concluded. Along with the advisory role of the principals-in-charge from the parent companies, two members of the mobilization effort will work only during this period. Although resumes are not provided for both, a description of their background is provided.

The corporate mobilization transition team for UIC consists of one member of the management team, the permanent toll operations manager, and seven other members. No resumes nor description of the exact roles of these members are provided. For URS, the mobilization activities will be performed by a team of five members of the permanent management team, assisted by the principals-in-charge.

The members of the advisory committees for all three firms have more than sufficient management experience, although FTS and UIC members have slightly more experience that provided by URS. For mobilization team members that would not become part of the normal operation after the contract is awarded, each of the three provided different information. To a large extent, it seems as though for FTS most of the members of the program management team, headed by the program manager, would participate in mobilization, assisted by two other employees. For UIC, the toll operations manager would play a key role, with the program manager apparently absent from mobilization. Seven additional employees who would not participate in program management would assist in mobilization. For URS, the quality control manager would head mobilization, with the program manager assisting, along with a temporary toll operations manager and a few members of the program management team.

*Staffing Plan to Encompass Key Elements of
Proposed Organizational Structure*

Three elements were to be reviewed with this criteria: (1) the adequacy of the staffing plan; (2) the clear illustration of "key elements of the proposed organizational structure to accomplish management, technical, facility operations including ETTM and VES"; and (3) the adequacy of the required annual periodic staffing level review.

This section focuses on the positions identified by the proposers and the tasks and duties to be performed by the people holding these positions. In contrast, previous sections have emphasized the capabilities of the individuals holding key management positions. Information for this section is provided in the staffing plan furnished by each proposer.

FTS discusses five management team positions, in addition to the management committee. The program manager, who will supervise the remaining members of the team, will have complete responsibility and authority for toll facility operation and management. The toll operations manager will be responsible for all revenue collection and toll service attendant performance. The quality management–training manager will serve as primary staff advisor to the management staff in "interpreting, implementing and assuring compliance with the FTS Quality Control Plan" (Florida Toll Services 1994, 35), as well as developing training programs for all toll operations personnel. The administrative manager will be responsible for coordinating fiscal functions and administrative activities with other management staff members, OOCEA staff, and corporate offices. The toll audit–accounting manager will be responsible for all accounting processes and maintain quality control and audit capabilities for manual, ACM, and AVI transactions.

The staffing plan for UIC focuses primarily on the toll collection personnel, providing little information regarding the management team other than an organizational chart. The duties and responsibilities of the program manager, the toll operations manager, and the audit–accounting manager are outlined in the program organization and management section.

The program manager will "provide direction to all activities" as well as "maintain contact with OOCEA." The toll operations manager will head the management staff, with a public information officer as a staff position, a human resources manager, an accounting manager, a plaza operations deputy manager, and quality–safety inspectors, security investigations, and couriers.

For URS, once normal operations are underway, the program manager will be responsible for all operations. A quality assurance officer and a security investigator, who will hold staff positions, will assist him. In addition, the toll operations manager, the toll audit–accounting manager, the administration manager, and the customer service–staff development manager will report directly to the program manager.

In terms of the adequacy of the staffing plan, FTS and URS seem to have presented a better model. Both have the program manager as a full-time position, responsible for all activities associated with the toll operations. Both have three line managers reporting to the program manager, with quality control functions provided in a staff position also reporting directly to the program manager.

Since only the toll operations manager is reporting to the program manager under the UIC model (at least in one organizational chart), it is difficult to assess the importance of the program manager's role. In addition, the scope of responsibility for the toll operations manager may be too broad, as virtually all aspects of the operations would be under her control.

All three proposers, with organization charts and discussion, do provide a clear illustration of what positions will be required as part of the organizational structure. Also, all three, to varying degrees, discuss the need for review of staffing, in conjunction with OOCEA staff. UIC discusses its "smart plaza" computer simulation models that "analyze traffic growth, AVI (E-PASS) usage, and various manual/automatic lane configurations to determine optimal staffing and physical plaza configurations" (United Infrastructure Company 1994, 5-3).

Staffing Plan Adequate for Staff Loading Capability

There are two key issues for these evaluation criteria: (1) the number of personnel reflected in the staffing plan, and (2) the staff loading capabilities and resources available for this project.

This is one of the key criteria of the entire proposal, since the response reflects the proposers' understanding of manpower needs among the staff required to operate the ten toll plazas at an optimal level of efficiency. Previous studies (Lawther et al. 1993) had suggested that there may be too many levels of supervision in the FDOT toll operation configuration. On the other hand, there was the danger that a proposer may have indicated staffing levels that would be insufficient in an attempt to lower personnel costs.

Both FTS and UIC provide a breakdown of the number of hours to man each plaza, along with the number of personnel needed in various classifications. Using slightly different criteria, both arrived at approximately the same number of full-time and part-time toll collectors needed at each plaza during a given twelve-month time period. FTS indicates it needs 194 full-time and 127.7 part-time collectors, a total of 321.7 annually needed for 575,653 annual hours of coverage. FTS assumes that part-time employees work an average of 32 hours per week, while UIC assumes an average of 30 hours per week. UIC, rounding up the number of part-time collectors needed at each plaza, calculates its needs at 195 full-time and 130 part-time, for a total of 325 collectors, calculating the annual number of hours needed at 565,953.

URS does not provide a complete breakdown of how its needs were calculated for each plaza, thus a total number of hours is not reflected in the proposal as well. It does indicate that it will require approximately 10 percent more full-time collectors (219) than do the other two respondents, plus almost 50 percent more part-time collectors. Without knowing the total number of hours assigned to full-time and part-time personnel or the average number of hours worked per week by each part-time collector, however, it is impossible to determine whether the 60 percent full-time collectors–40 percent part-time collectors ratio was followed.

URS did not provide analysis for each plaza and arrived at a higher number of collectors using a methodology not fully explained. The greater number of employees could be based upon URS's identification of the need for mainline "breakers," ramp "breakers," and "lane walkers." The former two proposers did not identify the need for additional staff to provide breaks for other collectors. It is possible that this was an oversight by FTS and UIC or they assumed that supervisory personnel would provide breaks.

The number of management and supervisory personnel required differs drastically among the respondents, posing several issues that had to be considered by the five evaluators. UIC proposes the highest number of nontoll collector personnel, indicating that two assistant managers are needed for each of the ten plazas, along with a plaza manager for each. In addition, sixty-two supervisory personnel are needed, with a high of nine at both Holland East and West plazas and with a minimum of five being the lowest at any one plaza.

URS requires only nine plaza managers, apparently assuming that no manager is needed for Bee Line Main. Only one assistant plaza manager is needed for each plaza, with the exception of Holland East, for a total of eleven. The fifty-three supervisors range from a need of three for Bee Line Main to seven at Holland East.

The manning assumptions made by FTS are quite distinct from the other two. FTS proposes that one plaza manager is needed for each of the ten plazas, but that no assistant managers are needed! Also, it assumes that five supervisors will be needed for each plaza, for a total of fifty.

Without discussing the reasons underlying these different numbers with personnel from each of the three firms, it is difficult to accurately conclude why there are different numbers of supervisory personnel required. To some extent, URS and UIC may be following the manning model used by FDOT, not fully calculating the differing manpower needs once the ETTM and AVI equipment is in place. The electronic toll equipment would seem to lessen the need for close supervision of toll collector personnel, indicating that a minimum number of supervisors are needed. This fact may have been realized only by FTS. Also, the duties of the plaza managers may not have been fully considered. It could be, for example, that the FTS plaza managers will perform more direct supervisory duties than their counterparts would under UIC and URS.

Alternatively, it may be that FTS is making assumptions that are too "lean." At the larger plazas, for example, more supervisory personnel may be needed even with the introduction of the new ETTM technology. The danger is that

FTS may "underbid" the number of supervisory personnel needed and may have to seek a "correction" after the contract has been awarded.

The evaluation committee apparently felt that the assumptions held by FTS were realistic, as it received a perfect 5.0 score from each evaluator. UIC achieved a 3.8, and URS was third with 3.5.

2-B Ability and Professional Staff: Technical and Support Staff

The previous section dealt with management personnel. This section deals with the adequacy of the technical and support staff to carry out the tasks assigned. Included in this section is an evaluation of the proposed subcontractors.

Skills, Experience, and Time to Carry out Tasks

In many cases, unlike those who would become managerial personnel, the technical and support personnel have not yet been identified. Evaluators were faced with evaluating the title, the job description, and the value of a particular proposed position. In addition, some assessment could be made of the extent to which the scope of duties encompassed by all technical and support personnel was appropriate to fulfill the requirements of the contract.

FTS does not provide names for the following positions, but instead indicates that it would give the right of first refusal from among already employed FDOT personnel. Job descriptions are provided for each of twelve technical–support positions.

Four positions would report to the administration manager. These are a project accountant, a buyer, and two human resources–payroll clerks. The accountant will maintain "subsidiary ledgers" of accounting systems and balance accounts; review invoices and statements to verify information; and also maintain the job cost accounting system. The buyer will perform purchasing duties by receiving descriptions of items to be purchased, obtain price quotes, recommend vendors, prepare purchase orders, verify deliveries, and complete appropriate reports. The two human resource–payroll clerk positions will be cross-trained to ensure that the personnel programs will be administered and that the payroll function will be managed.

Eight employees would report to the toll audit–accounting manager. These are two toll auditors, one toll accountant, two VES clerks, and three vault couriers. The toll auditors' primary responsibility is to "verify annual and ACM cash deposit information, prepaid revenue, and AVI charge billings against actual lane transaction data, utilizing the ETTM System." The toll accountant will supervise the two toll auditors, coordinate necessary toll revenue reporting, and coordinate the reporting of any internal toll audit discrepancies. The VES clerks will operate the ETTM VES workstation, identifying and recording violations. Initially, the third violation will initiate a letter to be sent to the violator requesting payment. Vault couriers will work third shift, transporting ACM coin vaults from ramp locations to the mainline plazas.

UIC does not provide job descriptions for its professional management staff. A total of twenty-eight staff positions are identified. Five staff are required in the program management support area: an administrative assistant, a QA manager, a security manager, and one staff member in each of the areas of document control and customer relations. Twelve employees provide toll operations support: four human resource (HR) managers, one training manager, an operations account manager, a payroll clerk, a procurement staff person, a quality–safety manager, a security investigator, and two couriers. Another eleven personnel support the audit–accounting function: six auditing staff, two accounting staff, two VES staff, and one remote operations managers workstation (ROMW) operator.

URS provides a "normal operation organization chart," identifying a total of twenty technical and support staff. Nine staff would report to the toll audit–accounting manager: a supervisor of toll audit, who would supervise four toll auditors and two VES auditors; and a supervisor of reports and statistics, who would supervise one computer technician. Under the administration manager, an additional nine staff will be placed: two typist–receptionists; staff in the areas of purchasing and property, human resources, billing and disbursements, and job cost accounting, who will be supported by two assistants; and one health and safety officer. The customer service–staff development manager will supervise two staff: a public information specialist and a training specialist.

Analysis

FTS provides the most detailed job descriptions of the technical and support staff positions, while UIC provides the least amount of information. It is unclear, for example, what tasks the four HR specialists will perform. In addition, the number of staff vary widely, as FTS requires thirteen staff, UIC twenty-three staff, and URS twenty staff. As is the case with the number of toll operations supervisory personnel, the low number of staff compared to the other two proposers requires the evaluation staff to assess the extent to which the positions proposed by FTS are realistic or are too few.

Subcontractors Identified and Appear Qualified and Capable

FTS identifies one subcontractor: HELP Personnel, Inc., a local certified women's business enterprise (WBE) firm that will assist FTS in providing over 125 part-time employees. In addition, FTS states that it is currently working on subcontracts in the areas of (1) uniform services, (2) drug screening, and (3) miscellaneous supplies–materials.

UIC, providing top level management, proposes to work with several subcontractors. MFS Network Technologies provides program management and audit–accounting functions. Wackenhut Services, Inc. would provide the complete toll operations services. Under WSI, a "third tier" of subcontractors are Lyca and Associates, who would provide training and documentation services; PAB Consultants, who would provide temporary, part-time toll collectors; and Ms. Bertica Cabrera, who will help coordinate public relations efforts. These latter three subcontractors all help to achieve goals in the area of minority–women–disadvantaged business participation.

URS proposed to work with three subcontractors. Norrell Services, Inc., which had provided toll collector staffing on the Southern Connector since August 1993, would provide full-time toll collector personnel. U.S. Personnel, Inc., would provide all part-time personnel. Communications, Plus, an Orlando based DBE firm, will provide the lead in developing and delivering training materials.

Analysis

Subcontractors are valuable in that they can provide necessary expertise quickly without the parent firm investing many resources in recruiting, hiring, and training personnel. They can lower costs, since the needed expertise for a given project can be hired only for that project, thus reducing the need to hire full-time in-house staff. Finally, the use of subcontractors can help meet MWD hiring goals. On the other hand, too many subcontractors may cause coordination difficulties and may raise costs if the proposer's management fee or profit is added on top of the subcontractors "profit."

Project Management and Organization Plan: Responsibility and Accountability

This section addresses the soundness and completeness of the proposer's organization and management plan in terms of project responsibility and accountability. The most significant aspect of this section included the organizational charts provided by each bidder. The charts that are provided and the accompanying description of the various planning, operational, and management responsibilities of all management and staff personnel should clearly outline how all are interrelated. In addition, the bidders need to identify the structure and operations of the program office.

Organizational Charts

There are four specific questions that accompany this criteria: (1) Have organizational charts been provided? (2) Do these charts depict the entire organizational structure? (3) Is there an adequate description of the proposers' relationship between it and the corporate organizations? and (4) Has the proposer described the proposed interface relationship with the authority, including subcontractors?

FTS provides two organizational charts, one depicting the staff organization—assuming that it would be awarded the contract—and a smaller one showing the relationship between the parent firms and the management committee. In both, the OOCEA is represented as dealing with both the management committee and the program manager. The one subcontractor identified by the time of the proposal, HELP, Inc., is shown as reporting to the administration manager.

UIC provides three organizational charts, two found in the program organization and management section and the third in the preliminary staffing plan. One shows the relationship among UIC, the corporate backers, and the subcontractors. The second shows the UIC program organization. The third also provides a view of the staff organization and provides a different view of many of the same positions.

In the first chart, OOCEA is shown at the top, with a solid line to the UIC. The owners of UIC, Bechtel and Kiewit, are shown off to one side, with Wackenhut and MFS Network Technologies shown as reporting to UIC. A dotted line runs from Kiewit to MFS Technologies. Finally, the three subcontractors, Lyca, PAB, and Bertica Cabrera, are shown reporting to Wackenhut.

In the program organization chart, a UIC principal-in-charge (PIC) is shown at the top, with the advisory committee and legal counsel also placed there. The program manager is shown as reporting to the UIC PIC, with the toll operations manager and audit–accounting manager reporting to him, along with other staff positions.

The third chart found in the staffing plan also depicts the staff organization, but provides a different view of the organizational relationships. Here the toll operations manager reports to the program manager, with the accounting manager, human resources manager, plaza operations deputy manager, quality–safety, security–investigations, and the public information officer reporting directly to her. A comparison of these latter two charts provides a confusing view of the duties and responsibilities of the program manager and the toll operations manager.

Also, different technical and staff positions are shown on both charts. Auditors–accountants, VES staff, and ETTM system operations are listed under the audit–accounting manager in the former chart, and are not listed at all on the latter chart. Procurement inventory supply and payroll clerks are listed in the latter chart, but not found in the initial chart.

URS provides two organizational charts, one dealing with the mobilization–transition team and the second representing the normal operation organization. All subcontractors are listed on these charts. Both clearly depict all organizational relationships, indicating the two principals-in-charge from URS that represent the link between the program manager and the parent company.

All three provide organizational charts, with URS and FTS providing the clearest picture of which position reports to which other positions. UIC, with contradictory information concerning the staff organization, cannot be rated as highly. FTS provides the most detail concerning how the parent companies–principals-in-charge relate to the OOCEA and the staff organization, and UIC provides more information than does URS.

Preliminary TOC Operations Office SOP

The three respondents each took a different approach to the information provided in the preliminary TOC operations office SOP. FTS indicated that the SOP should outline organization and manning structure, administrative policies, and establish responsibilities and procedures for staff meetings, reports, data automation, and other facets of office activities.

After a quick review of organizational structure, primarily referring to other parts of the proposal where more detail could be found, issues such as a management chain of command, frequency of staff meetings, and security of the office are briefly discussed. Communications, in terms of equipment needed, the FTS newsletter, and communications with patrons are also mentioned.

UIC provides a more extensive operations SOP, outlining policies and procedures for a variety of administrative areas, including those dealing with all aspects of personnel, payroll, equipment, expenses, revenue, contracts, and purchasing. URS took an approach similar to that of UIC, but in only one page provided an extremely brief outline of office policies and procedures. Headings included office operations, audit–accounting, field operations, and accounting for costs.

2-C Project Management and Organization Plan: Work Program

This section requires the evaluators to examine the description of the work program, the reporting requirements, manpower planning, coordination, communication, manpower analysis, and the transition management plan. To a large extent, these criteria ask questions that have been answered elsewhere.[3] How each of the three bidders proposes to integrate manpower planning, coordination, and communication is one part of this section that provides additional information.

Manpower Planning, Coordination, and Communication

Four issues define these criteria:

1. The procedures for supervision and task performance evaluation.
2. Maintenance of financial and time schedule control.
3. The manpower planning and workload projections.
4. Coordination and staff communication.

Task Performance. All three proposers outline procedures for supervision, with FTS including the most amount of detail in its job descriptions. Only a limited amount of information is provided by any of the three concerning performance evaluation, with URS describing a process of comparing employee self-evaluations and supervisor evaluations leading to a discussion of future expectations and performance goals. FTS states that key performance indicators will be developed based on the incorporation of quality performance standards developed for a variety of "operations in the daily work flow processes."

Financial and Document Controls. FTS states that there will be multiple systems of financial controls, to ensure that the correct amount of tolls have been collected. In addition to the ETTM reports, announced and unannounced field visits and direct employee observation, will occur, as fiscal staff will conduct random, in-depth field audits. Also, a document control system will be established. It will include scanning so that any correspondence received or document produced will be available to anyone in the system.

UIC stresses that financial control will first be established because the audit–accounting function will be handled by a subcontractor (MFS Technologies) that will be different from the contractor handling operations (Wackenhut). Plus, the ETTM system will provide additional controls, discussed in detail in the audit–accounting section.

URS will develop a comprehensive document control system. A separate computer system will be installed for office functions that will allow for remote storage of all computer files and documents. Financial controls will be implemented using the ETTM and VES systems.

Manpower Planning and Workload Projections. All three proposers indicated that they had undergone manpower planning by identifying staffing needs at each of the plazas and for the management, technical, and professional staff. FTS and UIC furnished workload projections for each of the plazas, while URS provided an example of one plaza. All three mentioned the capability of using computer-based models for scheduling and workload projections of toll collectors.

Coordination and Staff Communication. FTS links coordination and staff communication to the development of SOPs by seeking input from all plaza personnel. The quality service orientation will also support cooperation, because periodic meetings of all employees will lead to discussions of operations in ways that will improve operational procedures.

In addition, the detailed job descriptions of management personnel and professional and technical personnel outline the ways in which coordination and communication will occur. The audit–accounting manager, for example, will coordinate extensively with the toll operations manager to ensure that ETTM reports of transactions coincide with revenue collected.

UIC approaches coordination and communication in different ways. First, quality work groups will be established as part of the quality control–assurance program. Second, regular weekly staff meetings will address each program area that reports directly to the program manager.

URS also states that regular management meetings will be held to coordinate activities among the management team and the subcontractors. In addition to information furnished in job descriptions, URS also provides examples of how the activity managers will work together. For example, the audit–accounting manager will work with the toll operations manager if there is any unusual report patterns or incidents. The staff development manager will also work with the toll operations manager to coordinate special events.

On the strength of its job descriptions, FTS appears to have better coordination and communication than the other two. It is not clear how UIC intends to communicate among the several contractors and subcontractors that it will employ. The confusing organization charts also detract from a sense of effective coordination.

2-C Project Management and Organization Plan: Quality Control Program

FTS discusses the nature of its quality control program at various places throughout the proposal, calling it a continuous improvement program (CIP). It will be closely linked with training efforts, and will incorporate specific objectives that will also be part of training. Throughout the program, there will be emphasis on monitoring of all operations processes and modification of the system as required.

Both UIC and URS provide a somewhat different approach, emphasizing a quality assurance program that will be integrated into all aspects of operations. Both stress the need for frequent inspections, with results reported to OOCEA.

Of the three bidders, FTS was the only one to link quality assurance to training by combining training and quality control responsibilities in one position. Both UIC and URS linked patron or customer satisfaction to quality assurance by creating procedures that would include close ties to employee performance evaluation.

2-C Project Management and Organization Plan: Financial Control and Security

Evaluators were asked to review the preliminary audit–accounting plan, policies for account verification and the reporting process, and general accounting requirements.

Preliminary Audit–Accounting Plan

For this criteria, the evaluators are asked to rate the preliminary audit–accounting plan according to its policies and procedures concerning how well financial accountability and security is provided, how well "the accumulation, handling, reconciliation, auditing, depositing and reporting of all revenue" (Post et al. 1994, 30) would occur, and how well transaction accountability is addressed.

FTS, in its general policies section, states that strict internal controls and segregation of funds handling, accounting, and auditing will occur. Also, "swift and fair" internal investigations of potential fund mishandling are part of the stated policies. All of the top management team has responsibility in this area, with the toll audit and accounting manager assuming the key management position. This manager constantly monitors the revenue collection process, working with the toll operations manager.

Funds handling procedures are described. The process used by toll service attendants (TSAs) that involves the reconciliation and transfer of tour funds is noted, with the log-in and log-out activities to occur under the surveillance of the toll service supervisor (TSS). The TSS will also have the responsibility of handling funds from the automatic coin machines (ACM), changing the ACM vaults at least once every twenty-four hours. A manual record of revenue in the vaults will be recorded as a back up to the ETTM records. The tasks and duties of the vault couriers and the armored car pickups are also described.

The TSS will perform daily toll audits, with staff auditors responsible for the reconciliation of every lane for every day. Auditors will be periodically rotated among plazas "so that one auditor is not working exclusively on any one plaza location" (United Infrastructure Company 1994, 6-1).

UIC also discusses the audit–accounting procedures in a section separate from the audit–accounting preliminary SOP. Similar to FTS, a "separate and independent sub-contractor not involved in the toll collection process" (United Infrastructure Company 1994, 6-1) will perform the audit–accounting function. Although various specific duties of the supervisors and toll collectors are not presented in this section, some processes, such as that involved with the shift change funds, are described. Each day, the UIC audit staff will account for collector and coin vault deposits. Any discrepancies will be noted.

UIC will also be accountable for 100 percent of all transactions. A sample chart of the various steps in the process for the manual lanes is presented, noting that after the contract award, similar charts will be developed for transactions in all lanes.

In addition, UIC presents an outline of the audit–accounting SOP, with no description of any tasks or duties. Under audit, the outline of the activities dealing with managers and supervisors change funds is described, along with similar activities involving deposits and monthly funds audits. Daily transaction and revenue collections are outlined for manual, ACM, E-PASS, and prepaid lane activities. Tasks concerning deposits and lane fund transfers are outlined under the toll collection SOP.

URS presents a graphic rendition of the revenue collection and reconciliation process. Emphasis is placed on "unusual occurrences" transactions and how these will be reviewed and reconciled. A description of the counting and weighing of coin boxes is also presented. In the audit–accounting preliminary SOP, activities are listed without narrative or description. Under toll auditing, various audit types are listed, along with transaction accountability.

Policies for the Account Verification and Reporting Process

All three provided much the same information, relying heavily on the ETTM reporting process that would be used. All mentioned the need to deal with discrepancies or "unusual occurrences." FTS clearly stated that the operations manager would work with the audit–accounting manager to resolve these difficulties.

Accounting Requirements

All nonrevenue collection accounting requirements are evaluated under this criteria. FTS indicates that the job cost accounting system will be separate from toll revenue accounting, and will be supervised by the administration manager. She will be in charge of developing control and reporting systems that will keep FTS informed of all project expenses. A software program compatible with that used by the OOCEA will be implemented. A job cost accounting report will be submitted each month with the expense invoice to the OOCEA.

Other accounting functions include accounts payable–receivable, payroll inventory, purchasing, utilities, and subcontractor costs and estimates. The senior accountant will direct the overall reporting system, which will also include an inventory control system. Two payroll–human resource management staff will be needed to maintain all aspects of time worked and personnel processes. One staff member will be responsible for purchasing and budgeting functions.

UIC also stresses the need to use a software job cost accounting package that is compatible with that used by the OOCEA. This system will track costs associated with work performance, including accounts payable–receivable, personnel, utilities, subcontractor costs, and inventory. An inventory of all fixed assets will also be conducted and maintained.

URS also reviews the same requirements, mentioning the need for cost accounting that is compatible with the OOCEA's system. The cost information collected will be presented by plaza and TOC operations office as well as by category. A third party invoicing system will be established as well as an inventory of fixed assets.

All three proposers discuss the same information, with FTS providing more detail since it outlined job functions and accounting system characteristics more than the other two. URS provided the least amount of information, not mentioning specific aspects of the cost accounting system.

2-D Affirmative Action Program

This section addresses the proposer's affirmative action program and the minority–women–disadvantaged business enterprise (MBE–WBE–DBE) participation in the proposal.

Proposer Provided Specific Levels of Minorities and
Workmen in the Composition of the
Proposer's Professional–Technical Workforce

The evaluators are asked to assess the proposer's response with regard to the following questions:

1. "Has the Proposer demonstrated an aggressive *Affirmative Action Program* of non-discrimination and equal employment opportunity?"
2. "Has the Proposer adequately described the *promotional history of minorities and women within the proposer's organization*?"
3. "Has the Proposer provided specific levels of minorities and women in the *composition of the Proposer's professional/technical workforce*?" (Post et al. 1994, 32).[4]

Since FTS is an organization created specifically to respond to this proposal, it is at a disadvantage for this criteria in that it cannot describe a history of promotion. It states that if chosen it will create an affirmative action program, complete with identifying the program manager as having final responsibility, as well as maintaining required reports and records.[5] FTS further states that each manager and supervisor is responsible for being sensitive to EEO concerns in the areas of recruitment and placement, promotions and transfers, personnel policies, and in the performance evaluations of all managers and supervisors.

Another approach toward interpreting the "aggressiveness" of an affirmative action program is to examine the results in terms of the numbers of women and minorities in the parent–subcontractor organizations. A categorization by race and sex of professional and technical employees is provided by PB, MK, and Help Personnel, Inc., for those employees of their organizations that are employed in Florida. It reveals, for example, that PB has no females that are officers, management, and supervisors, with two black males and four Asian-American males out of a total of thirty-three in this job category. Of professional employees and technicians, there are eleven women out of 153 total employees listed, with four black males, two Hispanic males, and two black females among this group.

For MK, out of a total of sixty-five officers, management, supervisors, professionals, and technicians, five are female, two of whom are minority, eleven are Hispanic males, and two are black males. For Help Personnel, there are five employees in the same categories, all of whom are women, and none of whom are minority.

UIC is in a position similar to that of FTS, in that it was formed only to respond to this RFP. The parent companies and subcontractors provided the employment data breakdowns. Peter Kiewit shows companywide data. Of 1,480 officers, managers and supervisors, 191 are women (12.9%) with 70 minority males (5%) and 18 minority females (1%). Of the 2,218 professionals and technicians, 313 are women (14%), 216 are minority males (9.7%), and 60 are minority women (2.7%). For Bechtel, of the 217 total employees in the categories discussed, 26 are women (12%), 13 are minority males (6%), and 3 are minority women (2%). MFSN Technologies has only thirteen Florida employees in these categories, none of whom are women and only one is a Hispanic male.

URS, as an already-existing corporation, shows data listing four officers, managers, and supervisors, all of whom are white males, and thirty-five professionals and technicians, five of whom are women, four who are minority males, and one who is a minority woman. U.S. Personnel shows a total of twenty-four officers, managers, supervisors, and professionals (no technicians), twenty-two of whom are women, with one minority female. Norrell Services indicates nineteen officers, managers, and supervisors, eleven of whom are women, with four minority males and two minority females. Of the ninety-seven professionals and technicians, forty-eight are women, twenty-seven are minority males, and eleven are minority women.

It is difficult to agree that an "aggressive" affirmative action program would produce percentages of women and minorities that are below 15 percent in most cases. With PB, for example, showing no women among its officers, and Morrison Knudsen also showing a small percentage of both women and minorities, it is also difficult to support a high score for the second question listed earlier as well.

Participation Goal of 15 Percent

This criteria asks evaluators to note whether the participation of MBE–WBE–DBE meets the 15 percent goal stated in the RFP and if the means by which it is achieved is sound and acceptable.

For FTS, the subcontracting of HELP Personnel, Inc., a WBE firm, to hire the part-time toll service attendants in one sense more than meets the 15 percent goal. Approximately 128 part-time toll service attendants will be hired, out of a total of 402 employees (31.8%). In addition, FTS states that it will make every effort to subcontract with MBE–WBE–DBE businesses, including assisting them "in their pursuit of business opportunities through technical assistance."

UIC proposes to use Lyca Associates, a MWBE firm to provide training, Ms. Bertica Cabrera Agency, a MWBE firm in the public relations area, and PAB Consultants, Inc., a DBE firm to provide part-time toll collectors. As with FTS and URS, 130 part-time collectors out of 437 total personnel equals almost 30 percent participation.

URS will use Norrell Services, a WBE, to hire part-time toll collectors. Since 195 of these will be needed out of 497 employees in the Plaza Staffing system, the percentage is clearly over 15 percent. URS also states that supplies and equipment will be purchased from MBE–WBE–DBE firms.

Table 6.4
Overall Scoring Totals by Evaluator

Evaluator	FTS	UIC	URS
One	242.0	225.0	192.5
Two	260.0	226.0	249.0
Three	258.0	231.0	261.0
Four	178.9	203.0	156.35
Five	261.7	260.4	258.6
Overall Average	240.1	229.1	223.5

Interpreting the 15 percent participation goal by the percentage of employees hired using an MBE–WBE–DBE firms, all three proposers greatly exceed the requirement. FTS and URS also state the intention to contract with other such firms, while URS also has the advantage of an already-in-existence affirmative action plan.

CONCLUSION: THE EVALUATION PROCESS

A comparison of the evaluation team scoring shows the value of creating a thorough and detailed evaluation system. Overall, 280 points were allocated across six major sections, twelve subsections, and fifty-four even more specific sets of criteria. For many of the fifty-four criteria, between three and four questions guided the evaluators' analysis.

The results indicated that there was consistency across all three bidders, even though scores varied across evaluators. See Table 6.4 for evaluators' scoring totals. Two evaluators clearly favored FTS, with FTS and URS in a virtual tie as rated by two other evaluators. The fifth evaluator favored UIC, with FTS a clear second. FTS received two first place votes, tied for two other first places, and received one second place vote; UIC had one first place, tied for another first, one second place votes, and two third place votes; and URS had one first, one tied for first, one second and two third place votes.

Although UIC gave notice that it intended to file a protest, it decided not to follow through. Thus the process was judged to be error free, and the bid was awarded to FTS.

NOTES

1. There was no additional information provided about these "standard measures."

2. There was no requirement in the RFP that the management team personnel identified in the response should be the same people who would manage toll operations, if the bidder won the contract. Presumably, if there were changes in personnel, these would have to be accepted by OOCEA during negotiations that occur after the

awarding of the bid and the signing of the contract. If changes were not acceptable, OOCEA could award the bid to the next highest bidder.

3. The information discussed for manpower planning, for example, is very similar to that found under the section entitled "Staff Loading Capabilities," found earlier in the chapter.

4. The language in the RFP reads as follows:

> Demonstrate that the proposer's Affirmative Action policies and efforts are part of an aggressive program of non-discrimination and equal employment opportunity. Describe the promotional history of minorities and women within the proposer's organization. Give specifics of the level of minorities and women in the composition of the proposer's professional/technical workforce by completing and submitting the "Employment Data Schedule of Minorities and Women with the Technical Proposal." Describe the method, including specific activities, that the proposer intends to use to meet the Authority's MBE/WBE/DBE goal of 15% participation. This 15% goal includes any single category or any combination of the three. (Orlando–Orange County Expressway Authority 1994, 1-27)

5. It could have discussed the parent firms' promotional history, but chose not to do so.

BIDDER RESPONSES
TO THE 266 RFP:
THE PRICING PROPOSALS

7

As indicated in Table 7.1, FTS clearly provided the lowest bid, approximately $6 million less than UIC and more than $7 million less than URS. It did so by significantly bidding the management, professional, and technical labor costs lower than the other two, as well as proposing lower toll operations labor costs. The management fee or profit for FTS, however, was the highest of the three.

Any analysis of pricing proposals from more than one bidder must explain why differences exist for each category of pricing. In general, the proposals of UIC and URS may have been based upon already existing FDOT labor needs. These two bidders may have not sufficiently evaluated appropriate staffing levels. Because they proposed greater numbers of management, staff, and toll operations personnel, their costs were higher.

Second, this analysis must refer to the technical proposal. The pricing proposal should be based upon the labor needs, mobilization activities, and the requirements of the Technical Proposal. To the extent that the pricing proposal does not follow the technical proposal, or to the extent that it does not follow the requirements of the RFP, these items must be identified.

Third, the evaluation of the pricing process must be discussed. Since "lowballing" is a common strategy encountered in contracting, at least two issues are relevant: (1) the extent to which OOCEA examined the FTS bid to determine if the costs identified would be too low, and (2) the extent to which

Table 7.1
Five-Year Summary of Pricing Proposals

		FTS	UIC	URS
I.	Toll Operations Office			
	Labor	4.561	7.965	7.679
	Direct Expense	.887	1.547	1.656
	Mobilization	.795	1.296	1.809
II.	Toll Plazas			
	Toll Operations Labor	34.430	36.948	40.696
	Toll Operations Direct Expense	2.877	1.979	2.769
III.	Management Fee	3.920	3.726	1.117
	TOTALS	**47.470**	**53.461**	**54.609**

Note: All figures are in millions of dollars, rounded to the nearest thousand.

OOCEA analyzed the pricing proposals to ensure that it followed the costs and activities identified in the technical proposal.

TOLL OPERATIONS OFFICE

The costs identified under this section are those related to the management, staff, and costs associated with the toll operations office (TOC). These costs do not include those related to the operations of the toll plazas.

Labor

FTS identified twenty-one personnel that would be part of the TOC. As indicated in Table 7.2, the total of $4.5 million over the five-year period includes assumptions of a 3.5 percent raise per year for all personnel. Fringe benefits average 30.3 percent of total labor costs. Assuming that fringe benefits would not rise quite as much as the 3.5 percent allocated for salaries, the overall increase in labor costs is approximately 3.05 percent per year.

Since not all plazas would be transferred to FTS at the same time during the first year, the budget reflects the need for two toll accountants that would work only a total of 2,000 hours the first year. For years two through four, all twenty-one personnel would be working full-time (2,080 hours per year). The fifth year costs are based upon an assumption of 46.14 weeks.

It is difficult to compare the labor costs provided by UIC and URS since the data is not broken down by individual position (see Tables 7.3 and 7.4). Only by assuming the numbers provided in the technical proposal for the management and support staff are accurately reflected by the pricing proposal are comparisons able to be made.

UIC identified eighteen personnel that comprise this group. There is an apparent assumption that salary raises and fringe benefit costs will rise approximately 4.3 percent per year, as indicated by the amounts in years three, four, and five. Support staff for program management is higher for year one, and then drops significantly in year two. It stabilizes for the remaining three years.

URS identifies twenty-three staff and calculates salary–fringe benefits based upon an assumption of a 4 percent annual increase in salary and fringe benefits. The approximately 25 percent lower first-year costs for full-time personnel assumes that some of these costs are included in the amount listed for mobilization and document preparation.

To compare most accurately UIC and URS with FTS, if labor costs for year three are compared, the underlying assumptions concerning full-time employment of all personnel are most likely to be the same. Comparing UIC with FTS, the labor costs of the program manager, accounting–audit manager, toll operations manager, system administration, and two VES clerks for the first year are almost identical, with FTS costs about 3.5 percent higher ($420,621 versus $406,586). The same six personnel for URS total $501,751, more than 23 percent higher than UIC.

The differences in costs may be due in part to differences in the overhead assumptions. URS may have included overhead charges in the salaries of the management and support staff that were higher than those included by FTS. Conversely, URS bid a lower management fee than FTS.

To some extent, however, the differences in proposed personnel costs are unexplainable. The three bidders must be using significant differences in base salaries in addition to suspected overhead charges. For the clerical–courier category, FTS identified two secretaries and two couriers, paid at an average of $27,548, including fringe benefits. UIC identifies one administrative assistant needed for the program manager, plus one secretary for the toll operations manager and two couriers. Given that both propose to hire staff with similar positions, it is difficult to explain the over $56,000 in difference for this year. URS placed the cost of two assistants in the clerical–courier category, accounting for the $68,319 cost.

Comparing the audit–accounting staff, FTS identified the need for two auditors and two accountants, for a total of $144,640. In the technical proposal, UIC identifies a total of nine personnel: six auditors, two accounting staff, and one ROMW operator. It seems likely that an overhead charge contributes significantly to why these staff would require over $540,000 in labor costs. URS placed eleven staff in this category: one supervisor of toll audit, four auditors, a supervisor of reports and statistics, one computer technician, and the four staff (supervised by the administration manager) in the areas of purchasing and property, human resources, billing and disbursements, and job cost accounting, for a total of $496,823.

Finally, for program management staff, because of the confusing organizational charts mentioned in the discussion analyzing the technical proposal,

Table 7.2
FTS: Five-Year Summary for TOC Operations Office

Item No.	Description	Year 1
		TOC Operations Office
0.0.1	Management Fee	$651,260
0.1.0	**Labor**	
0.1.1	Program Manager	$117,998
0.1.2	Accounting/Audit Manager	$70,462
0.1.3	Toll Operations Manager	$81,272
0.1.5	Support Staff - Program Management	$251,594
0.1.6	Support Staff - Accounting/Audit	$92,430
0.1.7	Support Staff - System Administration & Mgmt.	$70,462
0.1.8	Support Staff - Violation Enforcement	$44,452
0.1.9	Support Staff - Clerical/Courier	$78,626
	Sub-Totals Labor	$807,295
0.2.0	**Direct Expenses**	
0.2.1	Office Building Expenses	$79,050
0.2.2	Telephone	$7,518
0.2.3	Supplies	$15,000
0.2.4	Furnishings and Equipment	$20,404
0.2.5	Vehicles	$22,355
0.2.6	Mileage/Tolls	$9,125
0.2.7	Other Expenses (See Direct Exp List)	$35,000
	Sub-Total Direct Expenses	$188,452
0.3.0	**Mobilization**	
0.3.1	Transition (1st Year Only)	$243,886
0.3.2	Document Development (1st Year Only)	$23,463
0.3.3	Training - Start Up (1st Year Only)	$30,000
0.3.4	Bonds	$42,000
0.3.5	Insurance	$47,798
	Sub-Total Mobilization	$387,147

Table 7.2 (*continued*)

Year 2 TOC Operations Office	Year 3 TOC Operations Office	Year 4 TOC Operations Office	Year 5 TOC Operations Office	Sub Totals
$807,843	$830,308	$851,869	$778,358	$3,919,638
$122,000	$126,129	$130,384	$119,625	$616,138
$72,932	$75,263	$77,611	$70,974	$367,252
$83,809	$86,443	$89,157	$81,628	$422,308
$268,558	$276,535	$284,873	$260,233	$1,342,192
$140,491	$144,620	$148,973	$136,152	$662,686
$72,932	$75,263	$77,611	$70,974	$367,242
$55,909	$57,523	$59,136	$53,985	$271,006
$107,204	$110,192	$113,373	$103,461	$512,856
$923,836	$951,987	$981,121	$897,433	$4,561,671
$79,050	$79,050	$79,050	$70,142	$386,342
$7,725	$7,659	$6,831	$6,268	$36,001
$15,600	$16,224	$16,873	$15,570	$79,267
$20,471	$16,584	$1,884	$1,739	$61,082
$22,789	$23,240	$23,709	$20,405	$112,498
$9,125	$9,125	$9,125	$8,097	$44,597
$31,200	$32,448	$33,746	$35,096	$167,490
$185,960	$184,330	$171,218	$157,317	$887,277
				$243,886
				$23,463
				$30,000
$42,000	$42,000	$42,000	$42,000	$210,000
$52,290	$60,939	$62,522	$57,126	$287,675
$101,290	$102,939	$104,522	$99,126	$795,024

Table 7.3
UIC: Five-Year Summary for TOC Operations Office

Item No.	Description	Year 1
		TOC Operations Office
0.0.1	Management Fee	$644,065
0.1.0	**Labor**	
0.1.1	Program Manager	$115,752
0.1.2	Accounting/Audit Manager	$71,388
0.1.3	Toll Operations Manager	$79,884
1.1.5	Support Staff - Program Management	$473,335
1.1.6	Support Staff - Accounting/Audit	$494,487
1.1.7	Support Staff - System Administration & Mgmt.	$51,114
0.1.8	Support Staff - Violation Enforcement	$54,798
0.1.9	Support Staff - Clerical/Courier	$158,851
	Sub-Totals Labor	$1,499,609
0.2.0	**Direct Expenses**	
0.2.1	Office Building Expenses	$117,277
0.2.2	Telephone	$67,722
0.2.3	Supplies	$11,347
0.2.4	Furnishings and Equipment	$221,507
0.2.5	Vehicles	$16,991
0.2.6	Mileage/Tolls	$7,180
0.2.7	Other Expenses (Please List)	$42,669
	Sub-Total Direct Expenses	$484,693
0.3.0	**Mobilization**	
0.3.1	Transition (1st Year Only)	$81,549
0.3.2	Document Development (1st Year Only)	$65,608
0.3.3	Training - Start Up (1st Year Only)	$15,000
0.3.4	Bonds	$667,530
0.3.5	Insurance	$27,000
	Sub-Total Mobilization	$856,687

Table 7.3 (*continued*)

Year 2	Year 3	Year 4	Year 5	Sub Totals
TOC Operations Office	TOC Operations Office	TOC Operations Office	TOC Operations Office	
$759,032	$761,610	$775,802	$785,339	$3,725,948
$120,984	$126,504	$132,348	$138,444	$634,032
$74,676	$78,156	$81,768	$85,596	$391,584
$82,656	$85,488	$88,524	$91,476	$428,028
$451,070	$467,371	$485,124	$502,469	$2,379,369
$517,243	$541,568	$567,071	$593,582	$2,713,951
$53,488	$56,032	$58,691	$61,469	$280,794
$57,526	$60,406	$63,477	$66,589	$302,796
$159,128	$166,551	$171,064	$178,776	$834,370
$1,516,771	$1,582,076	$1,648,067	$1,718,401	$7,964,924
$118,937	$119,029	$119,029	$119,121	$593,393
$51,005	$52,930	$55,369	$57,449	$284,475
$11,801	$12,310	$12,824	$13,316	$61,598
$10,967	$11,078	$11,192	$11,309	$266,053
$17,557	$18,143	$18,751	$19,383	$90,825
$7,284	$7,391	$7,501	$7,613	$36,969
$42,246	$42,553	$42,866	$43,187	$213,521
$259,797	$263,434	$267,532	$271,378	$1,546,834
				$81,549
				$65,608
				$15,000
$77,875	$77,875	$77,875	$77,875	$979,030
$28,890	$30,912	$88,076	$35,391	$155,269
$106,765	$108,787	$110,951	$113,266	$1,293,456

Table 7.4
URS: Five-Year Summary for TOC Operations Office

Item No.	Description	Year 1
		TOC Operations Office
0.0.1	Management Fee	$206,200
0.1.0	**Labor**	
0.1.1	Program Manager	$124,280
0.1.2	Accounting/Audit Manager	$73,110
0.1.3	Toll Operations Manager	$73,110
1.1.5	Support Staff - Program Management	$396,920
1.1.6	Support Staff - Accounting/Audit	$382,783
1.1.7	Support Staff - System Administration & Mgmt.	$56,145
0.1.8	Support Staff - Violation Enforcement	$59,947
0.1.9	Support Staff - Clerical/Courier	$52,637
	Sub-Totals Labor	$1,218,933
0.2.0	**Direct Expenses**	
0.2.1	Office Building Expenses	$82,292
0.2.2	Telephone	$27,867
0.2.3	Supplies	$56,417
0.2.4	Furnishings and Equipment	$22,958
0.2.5	Vehicles	$36,794
0.2.6	Mileage/Tolls	$12,500
0.2.7	Other Expenses (Please List)	$24,084
	Sub-Total Direct Expenses	$262,912
0.3.0	**Mobilization**	
0.3.1	Transition (1st Year Only)	$524,326
0.3.2	Document Development (1st Year Only)	$225,639
0.3.3	Training - Start Up (1st Year Only)	$66,838
0.3.4	Bonds	$82,240
0.3.5	Insurance	$100,928
	Sub-Total Mobilization	$999,971

Table 7.4 (*continued*)

Year 2	Year 3	Year 4	Year 5	Sub Totals
TOC Operations Office	TOC Operations Office	TOC Operations Office	TOC Operations Office	
$214,448	$223,026	$231,947	$241,225	$1,116,846
$155,100	$161,304	$167,760	$174,468	$782,912
$91,236	$94,884	$98,676	$102,624	$460,530
$91,236	$94,884	$98,676	$102,624	$460,530
$495,356	$515,170	$535,777	$557,208	$2,500,431
$477,714	$496,823	$516,696	$5,537,364	$2,411,380
$70,070	$72,873	$75,788	$78,820	$353,697
$74,813	$77,806	$80,918	$84,155	$377,639
$65,691	$68,319	$71,052	$73,894	$331,593
$1,521,216	$1,582,063	$1,645,343	$1,711,157	$7,678,712
$102,700	$106,808	$111,080	$115,523	$518,403
$34,778	$36,169	$37,616	$39,121	$175,551
$70,408	$73,224	$76,153	$79,199	$355,401
$28,652	$29,798	$30,990	$32,230	$144,628
$45,918	$47,755	$49,665	$51,652	$231,784
$15,600	$16,224	$16,873	$17,548	$78,745
$30,056	$31,258	$32,508	$33,808	$151,714
$328,112	$341,236	$354,885	$369,081	$1,656,226
				$524,326
				$225,639
				$66,838
$85,530	$88,951	$95,509	$96,209	$445,439
$104,965	$109,164	$113,531	$118,072	$546,660
$190,495	$198,115	$206,040	$214,281	$1,808,902

it is difficult to identify accurately how many staff are needed for UIC. Under this category there may be four staff listed under program management support and nine staff listed under toll operations support. These positions are a QA manager, a security manager, document control, customer relations, a human resources manager, two recruitment staff, a training manager, an operations account manager, payroll, procurement, a quality–safety manager, security–investigation, and a public information officer. These thirteen staff members could generate $541,568 in annual labor costs, at an average salary (and fringe benefits) of over $41,000 per year.

In contrast, FTS lists seven program management staff: two secretaries, an administration manager, a project accountant, a payroll clerk, a human resource specialist, and a buyer. The $276,535 cost for these staff members averages $39,505 per staff member in annual salary and benefits.

URS identifies ten program management staff: a security investigator, a QA officer; a customer service–staff development officer who will supervise a public information specialist and a training officer, and an administration manager. Two typists–receptionists will assist in this area as well. In addition, the salaries of the two couriers were placed in this category. The $515,170 averages almost $37,000 per year in salary and benefits.

The explanations for the differences in labor costs clearly are related to the number of management and supporting staff identified by each proposer: for FTS, 21; UIC, 32; and URS, 29. Not only do UIC and URS identifying the need for more staff, these staff are professional positions (e.g., a public information specialist, a security investigator, a computer technician) that are likely to require salaries that are relatively high as well. In addition, salaries for the management staff were much higher for URS than for the other two proposers.

Various conclusions can be drawn from the numbers of staff and the labor costs attached to them. The lower numbers of staff costs for FTS may be ideal, reflecting that FTS has performed a better job of analyzing staffing needs and is willing to propose lower salaries (and a lower raise assumption) because it is more committed to efficiency. On the other hand, FTS may have overlooked the need for additional full-time personnel (e.g., a security investigator). If this is the case, then there is the risk that either FTS would have to hire additional staff after the contract has been issued, thereby lessening their management fee; or management and staff would feel overworked, with resulting possible low morale, high turnover, and resulting lower quality service.

For UIC, it does seem that thirty-two managers and staff may be too high a number, since a number of positions apparently overlap. For example, a QA manager position that may report directly to the program manager seems to overlap with the quality–safety staff member that reports to the toll operations manager. Also, the need for six auditors, when URS needs four and FTS two, may be excessive, especially with the reports generated by the ETTM system.

UIC may have not performed an accurate workload–staffing analysis and thus estimated greater needs than were appropriate. In doing so, it may have overestimated in order to take less of a gamble, with the additional benefit of possibly lowering labor costs after receiving the contract from OOCEA. If this were the case, then UIC risked bidding too high and losing the contract to a competitor that was willing to take more of a risk in accurately estimating workload–staffing needs.

The analysis for URS must be similar to that of UIC, since the number of staff and the labor cost figures were similar. Two of their positions, a report–statistics supervisor and computer technician, were not mentioned by the other two bidders. These positions are listed in addition to four auditor positions.

Direct Expenses

For direct expenses, there is no incentive to estimate low in terms of costs (other than the impact on the overall budget totals), since the cost plus contract means that actual costs will be reimbursed up to the limit provided by the total direct expenses. Since a breakdown of actual items is furnished only by FTS, the analysis will be based on that information. See Table 7.5 for a breakdown of direct expenses.

The office building expense is based upon a need of 5,100 square feet at a rate of $15.50 per square foot. In a recent *Orlando* issue, business lease rates are estimated from $8 to $20 per square foot, with the highest rates in prime locations in downtown Orlando. Given that UIC and URS required additional personnel, it is understandable that their costs would be higher.

For telephones, FTS calculates purchasing three cellular phones at $378 each; three mobile phones at $120 each; and twelve phones at $120 each. Costs of these items are prorated over the phase-in period and the first three

Table 7.5
Direct Expenses—Five-Year Estimated Costs

CATEGORY	FTS	UIC	URS
Office Building Expenses	$386	593	518
Telephone	36	284	176
Supplies	79	61	355
Furnishings and Equipment	61	266	144
Vehicles	112	91	231
Mileage/Tolls	45	37	79
Other Expenses	167	213	152
TOTAL	$887	1,547	1,656

years. No costs are projected for years four and five, assuming apparently that the equipment will not have to be replaced. Toll charges are estimated at $1,000 per year, while line charges for the twelve phones would cost over $5300 per year.

The telephone costs for URS reflect leasing charges, as may the amounts listed for UIC. These must be considerably higher than purchasing telephones. The additional personnel would require more telephones and lines than would FTS. Also, given that the yearly charges for UIC and URS both rise each year from year two through five, perhaps a first-year cost was calculated and the same assumptions used throughout the five-year period.

For supplies, FTS estimated a first-year cost of $15,000, and a 6 percent increase each year. UIC assumes a lower initial cost of $11,347, with increases between 3.8 and 4.3 percent each year. With URS estimating a need of between $56,417 and $79,199 per year, their assumptions must include supplies that are in addition to those needed by the management and support staff. Or, FTS's estimates are unrealistically low.

FTS estimated a need for 71 separate item types, for a total of 349 separate items under the category of furnishings and equipment. The cost of these items was prorated over three years, with only leasing charges for the copy machine appearing in years four and five. Included in these items were desks, chairs, computer equipment, office equipment, software, folding tables, refrigerator, microwave oven, and coffeemaker.

Similar to the analysis provided for the telephone charges, higher costs from UIC and URS would be expected because of more personnel and possibly a different set of replacement (or leasing) assumptions. UIC apparently would charge the entire cost of all items purchased in the first year, with relatively small charges in years two through five. URS may have spread out its charges over all five years, since there is a consistent rise in costs identified. Still, the much higher charges for UIC and URS are difficult to support.

FTS identified the need to purchase one pickup truck, two cargo vans, and two sedans. The $69,800 cost was prorated over five years, after using an 80 percent "salvage balance factor." The other major cost factor was fuel and maintenance, beginning with a $10,842 base in the first year and assuming a consistent 4 percent increase. In comparison, UIC begins with a need for almost $17,000 for vehicles, increasing costs after the second year at a consistent 3.3 percent rate. URS begins with $36,794 first-year cost and uses a 4 percent consistent increase after year two. This amount reflects leasing two sedans and two minivans, plus insurance and potential repair costs.

For mileage and tolls, FTS assumes a consistent $9,125, while UIC reflects a start of $7,180, with a consistent increase of 3.3 percent. URS begins with $15,600 in the first full year of operation (year two). Finally, for other expenses, FTS includes only pension plan start up costs ($5,000) and an annual pension plan administration fee beginning at $30,000 and rising to over $35,000 by year five.

Mobilization

As reflected in Table 7.6, transition costs clearly are related to personnel costs, moving costs, and travel costs, as corporate specialists were to be brought in to help. FTS lists airfare costs for six members of the management team to come to Orlando from Boise, Idaho, and six from McClean, Virginia. Hotel costs are listed at $54 per day for sixty-three days, with an additional $25 per day for per diem. Relocation costs for four management team members is listed at $12,000 each. Initial drug tests and finger printing for sixty people at $388 each cost over $23,000. To assist with document preparation, two technical writers were to be flown into Orlando from Boise, staying forty days at $54 per day, and also receiving $25 per diem.

UIC may have calculated similar transition costs, paying salary and transportation costs for the transition team, plus relocation costs for those management team members who would be both part of the transition and the normal operation functions.

URS took a different approach. Stephen Moon was to head the transition effort, spending thirty weeks preparing each plaza as it transitioned from FDOT. John Ramming would apparently play the dual role of second in command during transition, assuming program manager duties after URS took over the plazas for each phase. In addition, a greater number of the full-time management and support staff would have been hired during the transition period, remaining in their same positions after takeover.

Document preparation costs, for FTS and probably for UIC, were to primarily write the SOPs and documents required by the RFP. For URS, the higher costs reflect the additional cost of a periodic newsletter that would be distributed to all employees.

TOLL OPERATIONS LABOR

Overall toll operations labor costs are presented in Table 7.7. During the first year, since assuming control of plazas would occur in phases, costs are

Table 7.6
Five-Year Summary of Direct Expense Costs

Category	FTS	UIC	URS
Transition (1st year only)	$244	$82	$524
Document Development (1st year only)	23	66	226
Training--Start Up (1st year only)	30	15	67
Bonds	210	979	445
Insurance	288	155	547
TOTALS	$795	$1,296	$1,809

Table 7.7
Toll Operations Labor—Five-Year Summary

Category	FTS	UIC	URS
Plaza Manager	$1311	$1290	$3904
Assistant Manager	NA	2203	NA
Supervisor	6091	6315	9010
Toll Collector (Full-Time)	19866	18254	20505
Toll Collector (Part-Time)	7162	4812	6112
Laborer	NA	NA	1164
PAB Associates	NA	4073	NA
TOTAL	$34430	$36948	$40696

lower compared to those for each year in years two through five. Although these were the transition dates listed in the RFP, the actual dates differed, as discussed in the transition chapter.

Plaza	Transition Date	Toll Collectors Needed
University	1/26/95	39
John Young	1/26/95	36
Boggy Creek	3/01/95	28
Dean Road	3/01/95	22
Holland East	3/01/95	58
Holland West	5/01/95	40
Hiawassee	5/01/95	20
Curry Ford	5/01/95	17
Bee Line	8/01/95	25
Bee Line Airport	9/01/95	37

To obtain a better picture of all labor costs, including percentages of fringe benefits, data are taken from the first full year of operation, year two (see Tables 7.8, 7.9, and 7.10).

Year two FTS base salaries were as follows: plaza manager, $8.96; shift supervisor, $8.18; full-time toll collector, $6.52; and part-time toll collector, $5.17. Fringe benefits included FICA, federal and state unemployment insurance, health benefits, workman's compensation, and bodily injury–property damage. The total fringe benefit costs ranged from 57.6 percent for full-time toll collectors to 34.5 percent for part-time toll collectors. So that comparisons can be made with all three respondents, Table 7.11 shows average hourly rates, including all fringe benefit categories, for all toll operations labor categories.

There are different approaches to determining labor costs, especially the fringe benefit category. FTS calculated one salary and fringe benefit rate for each category, and presented them as a consistent rate for each plaza. UIC presented variable rates, depending in part on the number of hours required for each plaza. It is unclear, however, why plaza managers required different salary rates, since each plaza required one person. URS identified the need for both plaza managers and assistant managers, but chose not to separate these two categories for purposes of pricing. Since there is at least one manager and assistant manager for each plaza, plaza managers will cost more than the averages listed here.

UIC and URS did not furnish information concerning the base salary of each position. In addition, it is impossible to calculate the fringe benefit percentage for each, especially since the health benefit costs are likely to be variable. As was apparent from the technical proposal and the oral presentation, UIC did not provide benefits that were comparable to that of the state of Florida. For URS, the much higher rates could be due to higher salaries as well as health care costs, plus a higher overhead cost added to all salaries.

The identification by UIC of PAB Associates as a line item in the pricing proposal is unique compared to the other two respondents. As UIC was unable to locate a temporary personnel agency willing to furnish toll collectors at the rate bid, PAB Associates agreed to establish an office in the Orlando area to provide these employees. The separate pricing category for them to furnish part-time toll collection personnel, is reflected by the amounts in both Tables 7.7 and 7.11.

As indicated in Table 7.12, the estimates of toll operations expenses vary widely. Again, using the itemized listing provided by FTS, some analysis can be attempted.

Charges for all plazas contained the same items. For telephones, FTS lists each line costing $345. The total amount of $203,000 for five years reflects an average of 11.7 telephone lines per plaza. The lower costs for UIC may have been due to a lower estimate of needed lines, while for URS, the opposite could have been true, plus higher estimated lease charges may have contributed to the $454,000 amount.

The drastically differing amounts for uniforms could have been due to different approaches. FTS indicates that it will lease the uniforms, thus not having to reimburse employees for laundry and cleaning charges. UIC may have made the same assumption. URS perhaps assumed the payment of laundry charges, reflecting a lower figure.

Vehicles are needed to transport toll collectors from the main plazas to ramp locations, among other needs. FTS estimated the purchase of a nine-passenger van for each plaza, at a cost of $15,750, with a 80 percent net salvage factor charged evenly over the five-year period of the contract. Fuel and maintenance charges averaged almost $90,000 for the five-year period for each plaza. The other two bidders either estimated the need for fewer vehicles or underestimated the cost of fuel and maintenance. For mileage and tolls reimbursed to employees, FTS and URS are basing their costs on similar estimates, while UIC estimates are much lower.

Other expenses for FTS include Rifkin bags, coin wrappers, bill straps, safety vests, fingerprinting, and random drug testing. UIC provides a similar

Table 7.8
FTS: Five-Year Summary for All Toll Plazas

Item	Description	Year 1	Year 2
		All Plazas	All Plazas
1.1.1	**Toll Operations Labor**		
1.1.1	Plaza Manager	$201,886	$273,936
1.1.2	Supervisor	$938,508	$1,272,960
1.1.3	Toll Collector (Full-time)	$3,117,114	$4,144,150
1.1.4	Toll Collector (Part-time)	$1,101,997	$1,480,294
	Sub-Totals Toll Operations Labor	$5,359,505	$7,171,341
1.1.10	**Toll Operations Direct Expenses**		
1.1.11	Telephone	$31,636	$41,694
1.1.12	Supplies (inc. Bottled Water)	$23,118	$30,693
1.1.13	Uniforms	$87,984	$91,502
1.1.14	Furnishings and Equipment	$12,694	$17,420
1.1.15	Vehicles	$149,216	$203,540
1.1.16	Mileage/Tolls	$153,835	$193,823
1.1.17	Other Expenses (See Direct Exp List)	$33,914	$12,377
	Sub-Total Toll Operations Direct Expenses	$492,397	$591,049

Total-Toll Operation Cost

Total Contract Amount

Table 7.8 (*continued*)

Year 3	Year 4	Year 5	Totals
All Plazas	All Plazas	All Plazas	
$281,632	$289,536	$264,474	$1,311,454
$1,307,280	$1,344,720	$1,227,324	$6,090,792
$4,257,136	$4,366,086	$3,981,476	$19,865,963
$1,535,672	$1,586,790	$1,457,109	$7,161,863
$7,381,720	$7,587,133	$6,930,383	$34,430,082
$43,361	$45,095	$41,615	$203,401
$31,919	$33,196	$30,632	$149,558
$95,163	$98,970	$91,329	$464,948
$18,120	$18,840	$17,390	$84,464
$210,650	$218,040	$200,370	$981,816
$193,823	$193,823	$171,980	$907,284
$12,720	$13,080	$12,974	$85,065
$605,756	$621,044	$566,290	$2,876,536
			$37,306,618
			$43,550,590

Table 7.9
UIC: Five-Year Summary for All Toll Plazas

Item No.	Description	Year 1
		All Plazas
1.1.1	**Toll Operations Labor**	
1.1.1	Plaza Manager	$163,243
1.1.2	Supervisor	$825,648
1.1.3	Toll Collector (Full-time)	$2,336,812
1.1.4	Toll Collector (Part-time)	$508,386
1.1.5	Assistant Manager	$304,229
1.1.6	PAB Associates	$717,479
	Sub-Totals Toll Operations Labor	$4,885,797
1.1.10	**Toll Operations Direct Expenses**	
1.1.11	Telephone	$16,128
1.1.12	Supplies (inc. Bottled Water)	$10,082
1.1.13	Uniforms	$100,076
1.1.14	Furnishings and Equipment	$0
1.1.15	Vehicles	$52,756
1.1.16	Mileage/Tolls	$225,073
1.1.17	Other Expenses - Locksmith	$6,287
1.1.18	Awards/Savings Bonds	$4,095
1.1.19	Employee Relations/Assistance	$8,608
1.1.20	Background Checks	$7,374
1.1.21	Drug Screening	$6,227
1.1.22	Education Reimbursement	$3,272
1.1.23	Maintenance	$11,587
1.1.24	Propane Gas	$4,580
1.1.25	Recruiting	$3,272
	Sub-Total Toll Operations Direct Expenses	$259,467
	Total Toll Operations Cost	$5,115,264
Total Contract Amount		

Table 7.9 (*continued*)

Year 2 All Plazas	Year 3 All Plazas	Year 4 All Plazas	Year 5 All Plazas	Totals
$274,666	$274,165	$285,332	$292,573	$1,289,979
$1,328,601	$1,337,523	$1,392,894	$1,430,147	$6,314,813
$3,851,806	$3,877,932	$4,038,840	$4,148,893	$18,254,283
$1,027,418	$1,038,480	$1,099,929	$1,138,026	$4,812,239
$459,801	$462,591	$481,851	$494,332	$2,202,804
$838,983	$838,983	$838,983	$838,983	$4,073,411
$7,781,275	$7,829,674	$8,137,829	$8,342,954	$36,947,529
$25,340	$25,970	$26,620	$27,290	$121,348
$15,840	$17,213	$16,650	$17,070	$76,855
$161,390	$151,475	$169,560	$173,800	$756,301
$0	$2,597	$0	$0	$2,597
$85,080	$81,086	$89,390	$91,620	$399,932
$40,440	$39,902	$42,490	$43,550	$191,455
$10,140	$11,948	$10,650	$10,920	$49,945
$6,600	$8,690	$6,940	$7,110	$33,435
$13,880	$15,404	$14,590	$14,950	$67,432
$11,890	$12,190	$12,490	$12,800	$56,744
$10,130	$10,380	$10,640	$10,910	$48,337
$5,280	$5,410	$5,550	$5,690	$25,202
$18,690	$19,160	$19,640	$20,130	$89,207
$7,390	$7,570	$7,760	$7,950	$35,250
$5,280	$5,410	$5,550	$5,690	$25,202
$417,370	$414,405	$438,520	$449,480	$1,979,242
$8,198,645	$8,244,079	$8,576,349	$8,792,434	$38,926,771

Thirty-eight million nine hundred twenty-six thousand seven hundred seventy-one dollars

Table 7.10
URS: Five-Year Summary for All Toll Plazas

Item No.	Description	Year 1
		All Plazas
1.1.1	**Toll Operations Labor**	
1.1.1	Plaza Manager	$490,700
1.1.2	Supervisor	$1,123,779
1.1.3	Toll Collector (Full-time)	$2,553,527
1.1.4	Toll Collector (Part-time)	$761,373
1.1.5	Laborer	$141,929
	Sub-Totals Toll Operations Labor	$5,071,308
1.1.10	**Toll Operations Direct Expenses**	
1.1.11	Telephone	$56,547
1.1.12	Supplies (inc. Bottled Water)	$61,886
1.1.13	Uniforms	$14,451
1.1.14	Furnishings and Equipment	$3,805
1.1.15	Vehicles	$70,984
1.1.16	Mileage/Tolls	$119,377
1.1.17	Other Expenses (Please List)	$17,813
	Sub-Total Toll Operations Direct Expenses	$344,863
Total - Toll Operation Cost		$5,416,171
Total Contract Amount		

Table 7.10 (*continued*)

Year 2 All Plazas	Year 3 All Plazas	Year 4 All Plazas	Year 5 All Plazas	Totals
$803,776	$835,976	$869,397	$904,075	$3,903,924
$1,857,544	$1,931,406	$2,008,574	$208,048	$9,010,351
$4,226,662	$4,397,351	$4,572,307	$4,755,698	$20,505,145
$1,260,352	$1,310,081	$1,362,918	$1,417,312	$6,112,036
$240,860	$250,430	$260,420	$270,820	$1,164,459
$8,388,894	$8,725,144	$9,073,616	$9,436,953	$40,695,915
$93,599	$97,344	$101,238	$105,289	$454,017
$102,440	$106,537	$110,799	$115,231	$496,893
$23,920	$24,876	$25,871	$26,907	$116,025
$6,296	$6,540	$6,811	$7,084	$30,544
$117,498	$122,197	$127,084	$132,166	$529,929
$197,601	$205,504	$213,726	$222,274	$958,482
$29,484	$30,662	$31,888	$33,164	$143,011
$570,838	$593,668	$617,417	$642,115	$2,768,901
$8,959,732	$9,318,812	$9,691,033	$10,079,068	$43,464,816
				$43,464,816

Table 7.11
Average Toll Operations Labor Costs—Year Two

Category	FTS	UIC	URS
Plaza Manager	$13.17	12.42-15.76	17.90-19.48
Assistant Manager		11.04-11.17	
Supervisor	12.24	10.28-10.41	16.85
Toll Collector--FT	10.27	9.46-9.93	10.14
Toll Collector--PT*	6.95	7.96	8.11
Laborer			11.58
PAB Associates		10.50	

*Assumes 1,664 hours per year for FTS and 1,560 per year for UIC.

Table 7.12
Toll Operations Direct Expenses—Five-Year Summary

Category	FTS	UIC	URS
Telephone	$203	$121	$454
Supplies (inc. bottled water)	150	77	497
Uniforms	465	756	116
Furnishings and Equipment	84	3	31
Vehicles	982	400	570
Mileage/Tolls	907	191	958
Other Expenses	85	431	143
TOTAL	$2,877	$1,979	$2,769

Note: Totals are in thousands of dollars, rounded to the nearest one hundred.

list, but adds costs for the cost of awards (savings bonds) for employees, education reimbursement, maintenance, and recruiting efforts. URS probably includes a similar list.

Overall Analysis

Since a varying overhead charge may have been allotted to the labor costs for each of the three bidders, by adding the management fee to the labor cost, a more valid comparison can be made. The $8.481 million for FTS compares favorably with the $8.796 estimated by URS. The considerably higher $11.691 cost bid by UIC for these two categories may indicate a higher total profit–overhead charge was required by the partners for UIC.

Yet this analysis only explains part of the differences, as the variance in the toll operations labor costs, in which presumably overhead charges are also made, is too great a difference to be explained by profit–overhead charges alone. The major cause of the cost difference in the TOC labor category was the smaller number of staff bid by FTS than the other two. More significantly, the lack of assistant plaza managers reduced the labor costs for toll operations for FTS compared to the other two.

The differences here were based on the perception that OOCEA preferred a staff size similar to that provided by FDOT, given that there was a consistent concern with security, accountability for funds, and customer satisfaction levels that would require additional supervisory and management personnel. What was perhaps not realized was that many of the functions performed by assistant plaza managers under FDOT management would be performed by staff in the toll operations office.

With the exception of the mobilization assumptions made by URS, which required more staff during this period of time than did the other two bidders, the direct expense and mobilization totals were not significantly different. Again, FTS bid lower than the other two. But the overwhelming difference in the price bid was the labor assumptions.

CONCLUSION: THE OOCEA ROLE IN PRICING PROPOSAL REVIEW

In preparation for the review of the pricing proposals, PBS&J provided five different estimates of what vendors would bid for the management and toll collection labor costs. Assuming different overhead rates, but consistent wage rates, amounts ranging from $36.88 million to $64.124 million were calculated. Given that the FTS bid of $38.991 million was within this range, OOCEA felt comfortable in accepting the bid.

In the area of direct expenses, OOCEA chose not to provide direct monitoring of actual purchases, but instead requires FTS to bill one-twelfth of the total direct expense amount bid for both the TOC office and the toll collection operations (and for the mobilization costs as well). Bills from FTS do provide itemization by expense category (e.g., office building, telephone, supplies), but there is no backup documentation required. Within each category, there is no explanation of what purchases were made.

This approach limits monitoring costs by OOCEA and lays the groundwork for a trusting partnership. OOCEA assumes that FTS will spend expense dollars in ways that are needed to maintain toll operations effectively. If in doing so, FTS can make additional savings without diminishing quality, then by implication OOCEA approves this practice. The risk of this approach is that the contract manager must be sensitive to signs of cost-cutting practices, and a change in the monitoring practices may be necessary if service quality has decreased below acceptable levels.

THE TRANSITION STAGE: CONTRACT, MOBILIZATION, AND PHASING

8

Once the bid has been awarded and the notice to proceed has been issued, the privatization process enters the stage that transitions the daily operations of the service from the public sector to the vendor. This stage should be guided by the information provided in the RFP and in the winning vendor's response to that RFP. To the extent that this information sets broad guidelines that allow for negotiation between agency and vendor, however, changes are likely to occur during this transition stage.

THE CONTRACT

As discussed in the RFP Section, the 266 contract consisted of a combination of cost plus and fixed price contract types.

The "Toll Facility Operation and Management Agreement" was signed on February 28, 1995, between the OOCEA and Morrison Knudsen Corporation and Parsons Brinckeroff Quade and Douglas, Inc. In many ways, this fifty-two-page contract reflected many of the significant points made in the RFP.

In Article I, the already existing key documents are brought into the contract:

All terms and provisions of the RFP, the SOP manual and the Contractor's Proposal are incorporated by reference in this Agreement as though fully set forth herein.

Whenever possible, the provisions specifically set forth in this Agreement and those set forth in the RFP and SOP manual shall be construed to supplement each other, so as to give effect and meaning to all terms and provisions. (1.1 (b), p. 2)

In the subsequent sections of Article I, it is made clear that the SOP manual will provide more detailed information concerning the "Contractor's obligations and standards." This manual may be amended "to take into account changing circumstances and new information." Likewise, the Contractor's Proposal "shall be the determinative document with respect to consideration to be paid by the Authority."

The contract thus identifies two key documents that act as the basis of determining the partnership between the OOCEA and FTS. The SOP manual, later described as those documents described in the RFP that establish all policies and procedures relevant to FTS toll operations, is the "living document" which can be altered as deemed necessary. Using this document allows for the maximum degree of flexibility concerning the daily relationship between OOCEA and FTS.

Employee Transition

On February 17, 1995, Christine Speer, director of the Office of Toll Operations, FDOT, sent a memorandum to all toll collection employees in the Orlando Barrier and Orlando Turnpike regions. In this memo she outlined the personnel selection process that was to occur during the transition to FTS operations.

Of the 470 total full-time, career service positions in the toll collector series available in the OOCEA toll plazas and in the Orlando Turnpike plazas, a total of 288 were to be reduced, leaving 182 positions remaining with FDOT in the turnpike plazas. In order of seniority, all 448 full-time employees, as of February 17, 1995, were given the option of choosing employment with the turnpike or employment with FTS. If there were no FDOT position available for an employee, he or she would be considered laid off, whether he or she chose to work for FTS.

According to the rules of the Department of Management Services, state of Florida, Chapter 60K-17, *Work Force Reduction*, seniority was measured by assigning each employee a number of retention points. One point was assigned for each month of continuous service in a full-time career service position.

Four other rules affected the number of retention points held by these employees. First, if an employee resigns from one career service position to take another career service position within thirty-one days, there is no break in service. Second, if an employee who is laid off from a career service position is recalled within one year, there is no break in service. Third, within the last five years, five points were deducted for each month an employee spent in an performance improvement plan or for each month spent in a below performance standards status. Finally, veterans received an additional 5 or 10 percent added to their retention point total.

Once this retention list was created, ranked from the employee with the highest number of points to the employee with the lowest number of points, "bumping rights" were used to determine which positions would be filled in what order. Given that all employees held one of five classes in the toll collector series: Toll Facility Supervisor II, Toll Facility Supervisor I, Toll Collector Supervisor, Toll Collector, and Toll Collection Courier—the employee at the top of the list has the option of selecting any position in their current class or a lower class not already selected by an employee with more retention points. Employees were provided a listing of all turnpike positions, with shift times, locations, and a map of the locations.

An employee who was required to demote to retain a position with FDOT would retain his or her salary, provided it was within the salary range of the new position. If an employee voluntarily chose a position that was a demotion, he or she would receive a 5 percent reduction in pay for each level demoted or the maximum of the new class, whichever was lower, as long as the amount was above the minimum of the class.

Using a question and answer format, FDOT provided other relevant information to help the employee make a choice. If the employee chose a position with FTS, he or she would be placed on a callback list for a period of one year.

If the employee was vested with the state of Florida (i.e., had ten years experience), early retirement was possible. Also, if the employee left the employ of FDOT, he or she would be paid for (1) up to 240 hours of unused annual leave, if employed at least twelve months; (2) special compensatory leave; and (3) accumulated sick leave, if the employee had at least ten years experience, with one-quarter of sick leave hours reimbursed (a maximum of 480 hours) for time accrued after October 1, 1973.

FTS

To help the FDOT employee choose, FTS also provided information prior to the job fair. In a letter from "The Director's Desk," part of an employee-generated newsletter, employee questions and concerns were anticipated. First, FTS provided a positive message: its goals were to focus on "reducing costs to the Expressway Authority and improving the quality of services to the users. To meet these goals requires operational and organizational changes, clear lines of communication, and most importantly, cooperation."

The underlying message was that FTS is committed to creating a positive work environment, but that changes from the FDOT organizational procedures will occur.

Next, job security is addressed. Even though FTS has a contract for up to five years, FTS stated that it is committed to a long-term partnership with the OOCEA. The issue of pay is neatly connected to job security, by suggesting that "if FTS followed the procedures used by government, with annual increases, we would price ourselves out of the market when the next contract competition is issued."

In place of annual increases, FTS offers performance bonuses for top performers. Even though the average pay for TSAs would be $6.30, employee health costs would be less than what most toll collectors would be paying under FDOT: $10 per month for each employee; $20 per month for an employee and one dependent; and $30 per month for family coverage with an employee and two or more dependents.

FTS would furnish a retirement plan that is portable. FTS will match any funds contributed to the retirement plan up to 5 percent. All employee contributions are taken from pretaxed income. FTS's share is vested at 20 percent per year, with 100 percent vesting after five years.

Other benefits are identified. Clean uniforms would be furnished to each employee. Employees would be reimbursed for tolls going to and from work. Most TSAs would have the same shift but different days off, rotating lane assignments once an assignment is made to a plaza. Eight hours of leave per pay period covers eighty hours of vacation, eight paid holidays, six sick days, and two days of administrative leave. Vacation days must be taken during the year, but unused sick leave could be cashed out at one-half hourly paid rate.

The final statements are significant, providing a strong commitment to a promotion from within policy and a statement that attempts to reassure the potential employee: "We have designed a program to reduce overall operating costs compared to FDOT. Therefore, we have no bottom line reason to cut employees and replace them with lower wage workers."

The final statement is perhaps the most significant. It is correct because all toll operations labor costs are fully reimbursed. Although the reason for its accuracy is not fully explained in this letter, it may be considered important by the potential employee seeking long-term employment with the chance for promotion.

Beginning on February 27, 1995, for each hour between 8:00 AM and 5:00 PM, five to seven employees were brought into Job Fair headquarters. Nine of the next ten days (excluding Sunday, March 5, 1995) were devoted to the Job Fair, with employees transported to the fair in order of their retention points. Sixty percent of the employees had fewer than sixty points, indicating less than five years experience.

RESULTS

By the conclusion of the Job Fair, as indicated in Table 8.1, FTS had hired 159 TSAs, 40 supervisors, and 9 plaza managers from the 450 eligible FDOT employees. Almost all of the TSAs had less than five years experience (90%). Of the 40 supervisors, 18 (45%) were given promotions upon joining FTS. Similarly, of the 9 plaza managers hired, 7 (78%) were promoted into those positions.

Table 8.1
Job Fair Results

YRS EXP	FTS: TSA'S	FTS: TSS'S	FTS: MGRS	FDOT LD/OFF	TOTAL
OVER 5	16	5 (0)	3 (1)	155	179
UNDER 5	143	35 (18)	6 (6)	87	271
	----	----------	-----	----	----
TOTAL	159	40 (18)	9 (7)	242	450

Note: Numbers in parentheses are those promoted by FTS.

Assuming that 182 of the remaining 242 positions remained with FDOT, there were 59 employees who refused employment with FTS and were laid off (one was hired by OOCEA and one by FTS in an audit capacity). Clearly the most experienced employees remained with FDOT. FTS hired as many as were willing to work for it, promoting twenty-five into supervisory and management positions. Many of the FTS hires were employees without much experience who, when given the choice of unemployment or working with FTS, chose the latter option.

TRANSITIONAL LOGISTICS

The transitional issues facing the OOCEA staff were more challenging than may be the case in other privatization efforts. The role of OOCEA was changing, from one of having little influence over FDOT operational policies and procedures to one of being in a great deal of control as the contractor. Yet since the RFP had allowed FTS to create its own SOPs for much of the operations, at the beginning of the transitional period much of this information was still incomplete.

Since the ETTM systems were also being implemented at the same time as the change in operations, OOCEA staff had to deal with SAIC/Syntonic as well. TELOS Corporation was the consulting firm that had been hired to oversee the implementation of the ETTM system. OOCEA had to coordinate among TELOS and SAIC/Syntonic, as well as to ensure the creation of a working relationship between FTS and SAIC/Syntonic.

Even though the contract with FTS was not signed until February 28, 1995, toll operations coordination meetings began on February 3, 1995. Representatives from OOCEA, FTS, FDOT, SAIC/Syntonic, and PBS&J participated. The major subject of the first meeting was a review of the eighty-three transition tasks as identified by FTS. A chart was provided identifying the person who held the key responsibility for each task; the person or persons (if any) that held additional responsibility; the percentage complete; whether a draft would be provided; and the days due after the contract was completed. The items identified included the SOPs due as required by the RFP, as well as other smaller transitional items, including, for example, procurement procedures, personnel files, cash inventory, daily time sheets, and a police courtesy meeting.

The group began to meet every week, with the next meeting held on February 10, 1995. Of immediate importance was getting the TSAs, TSSs, and plaza managers ready for phase one, the takeover of University, Boggy Creek, John Young, and Dean Road plazas on April 1. The Holland East plaza was scheduled for takeover on April 23.

Several topics were of high priority. The TSAs needed to be trained to use the ETTM system. At the February 10 meeting, a main topic of discussion was the location of an FTS facility and the set up of appropriate training facilities. Syntonic needed to work with FTS to ensure that all equipment and telephone lines were in place by no later than March 15.

OOCEA was also concerned that uniforms would be available when plazas were under FTS operation, as no FDOT uniforms would be permitted. Employee policies, especially those impacting recruitment, needed to be finalized. These included finger printing, drug testing, sick leave, and hiring dates. If the drug testing was to be subcontracted, drafts of the subcontracts needed to be given to OOCEA.

There were logistical issues concerning the transfer of employees from FDOT to FTS. With the Job Fair scheduled to begin on February 27, FTS needed to know how many employees would be eligible to transfer; and OOCEA requested that FDOT send another newsletter to the employees answering questions and concerns.

One week later on February 24, there were still last minute Job Fair issues. On the first day, FTS would take applications, but not hire. Norrell employees needed applications and consideration for full-time employment, while OPS (and Norrell) needed Help applications for part-time employment. Schedule rotation was important for some FDOT employees. Their preferences needed to be surveyed at the Job Fair. FTS needed a list of existing FDOT personnel who were transferring. It wanted to meet with supervisors and managers one week before changeover, providing drug testing information and uniform fitting on that day.

The weekly transition task list was updated, plus a finalized transition day checklist, complete with names of those responsible for which tasks. FTS also needed a specific schedule when FDOT would remove the cash vaults. Additional meetings were needed with PBS&J and FDOT regarding the construction of uniform lockers.

At the March 10 meeting, a final timeline was agreed to by all parties. Arrangements with the First Union Bank and armored car services were to be completed by March 14, followed by a tour of the Bank Cash Management facility. Plaza inventories for University, Dean, John Young Parkway, and Boggy Creek plazas were to be completed by March 24. Training for toll collection personnel was to occur from March 13 through 31, with training schedules due from FTS by March 15. Employee orientations from FTS were scheduled for March 15 to 18, and for Help Temporary Services from March 21 to 23. By March 27, all personnel relocations were to be complete, with all personnel entered into the ETTM system personnel list. At 6:00 AM on April 1, plaza keys were to be turned over from FDOT to FTS.

Other last minute transition items still remained. Neither FTS plaza supervisors nor vault couriers had yet been hired. The Cardkey security system was still not active for University and Dean. There was a need to rekey all four plazas during the first week of FTS operations. PBS&J was to meet with FTS to discuss monitoring the construction work for OOCEA areas.

By the March 17 meeting, much of the transition work had occurred. FTS reported that staff had been hired the previous week, and that four of the five orientation meetings had occurred. The employees seemed to be handling the change well, and orientations had been effective, especially in explaining the benefit package. Five training classes had occurred. Meetings with First Union regarding banking and armored car services had occurred without problems. All new FTS employees were working at their assigned plazas.

One potential problem still remained. Norrell temporary employees were quitting before the transition period. Help Services were trying to keep them at their current plazas, but with mixed success.

The next week, FTS reported that all staff would be in place by March 27. All but one employee had been trained. The final SOP, audit procedures, had been distributed. FTS was moving that day into its permanent headquarters.

FDOT had several transition items. A schedule of the tour funds transfer for all four plazas was identified, also indicating that keys and combinations would be handed over to FTS plaza managers after a check for the tour funds had been received. FDOT also requested a list of FTS employees by plazas, as it needed to send out lay off letters by March 27 for the May 7 phase two plaza transfers. FDOT money would be taken from vending machines; locker keys of employees leaving need to be retrieved; and Rifkin bags need to be transferred to FTS or replaced.

The following week's meeting, one day before the phase one plaza takeovers, had a much more limited agenda, as many of the items previously mentioned had been accomplished. All FTS staff were in place; one audit employee needed to be trained; FTS was in the new office; and all SOPs had been submitted. New lockers were to be installed at two of the plazas. The "3-C" (comment, complaint, and contact) cards had been ordered, although OOCEA staff needed to review these.

On Friday, April 7, six days after the phase one four-plaza takeover, FTS reported few glitches. Cash deposits by collectors were at 97 percent accuracy. OOCEA responded that this was acceptable for the first week, but that the accuracy level needed to improve. Most employees had uniforms, but some had sizes that were incorrect.

FTS reported that the next hiring routine for phase two, Holland East–West, was to begin on April 19. One innovation suggested by FTS, the use of disposable, plastic cash bags, instead of the Rifkin cloth bags, apparently was well received by the bank.

On the important issue of quality control: FTS reported that the audit process was still being fine tuned. The quality review committee, consisting of representatives from OOCEA, FTS, Syntonic, and ZHA, would begin to meet every two weeks. Training for Holland East staff would begin April 17, in time for the May 1 takeover. Since this was a high volume plaza, it was stressed by OOCEA that it would be extremely important to have well-trained employees at Holland East.

OOCEA gave a status report at the next meeting, held on April 14. There was concern expressed that staffing levels for various lanes were less than what was indicated in the RFP. It was stressed that Holland East must be fully manned during rush hours. FTS was to correct this situation as soon as possible. At this time, there were still issues to be resolved concerning the audits and audit procedures. The need for a "customer service" attitude among toll collectors was stressed again.

On a more positive note, OOCEA felt that customer service was good, in that collectors appeared friendly, happy, and helpful. Uniforms looked good so far. Collector fund shortages were less as well.

A similar status report was provided by OOCEA at the meeting one week later. Staffing levels had improved. Gates were being left open too frequently. New lockers needed to be installed.

Auditing remained an issue of importance. OOCEA announced that FTS had to keep records for a three-year period, requiring investment in storage facilities. Audits had been received for the University plaza, but not for the other three that were part of the phase one takeover. FTS is working on apparent discrepancies and improving procedures.

FTS announced that John Simonese, operations manager, would be leaving at the end of April. Four training–orientation sessions had been completed, with Holland East–West orientation the following week. VES processing should be operational this week. Most uniform problems had been resolved, with HTS temporary employees having uniforms in the near future. VES and ACM vault turnover procedures needed to be discussed and agreement reached in the near future.

CONCLUSION

The transition meetings were discontinued in April 1995. The same group has continued to meet, however, discussing quality review issues. The coordination and cooperation begun at this time has also carried over and provided the foundation for the public–private partnership that characterizes the current contract management stage.

The relatively quick acceptance of the SOPs created by FTS, with the exception of the auditing SOP, indicated that the approach of letting FTS have discretion concerning how to accomplish a particular function or activity was successful. That there were no major problems found with the human resource management system or the quality management–assurance system, for example, helped both FTS and OOCEA weather the initial transition period.

The major success of this stage was the results of the Job Fair. It would seem likely that there were few FDOT employees who were unhappy with the result. All the supervisory and management personnel that wanted to remain with FDOT were able to do so. All long-term FDOT employees, those for whom a transfer to FTS would very likely meant a salary reduction, were also allowed to remain with FDOT. Many of the FDOT employees with less experience were given promotions by FTS, while others found more money in their paycheck because of lower medical premiums. FTS had to offer positions to former part-time employees to fill all their full-time TSA positions.

CONTRACT MANAGEMENT AND RENEWAL   9

The essence of most public–private partnerships lies in the management of the privatization contract by the government agency or organization. On a smaller, more focused level, contract management is concerned with monitoring. Reports are collected and reviewed for accuracy, and performance is measured and compared to agreed-upon standards that are spelled out in the RFP and the contract.

On a larger level contract management deals with providing incentives to the vendor to increase and maintain a high level of performance. In other words, the vendor must focus on achieving the goals set forth by the RFP and contract. Incentives must not only be present to reward performance in ways already agreed to, but ideally they must also induce the vendor to suggest new and better ways of achieving the goals. These activities and suggestions may mean contract adjustments.

Both creating incentives and monitoring efforts must be directed toward goal achievement. The contract manager has discretion concerning which more specific activities are chosen. When a government service is contracted out or privatized, it is useful to consider two sets of incentives that must be provided by the government: those to the owners or management team that administers the service; and the nonmanagement personnel or employees that work for the vendor. Monitoring efforts can include different sets of activities or types, different ways to collect performance data, and different approaches.

In addition, principal-agent theory, found in the study of organizations from an economics viewpoint, offers insights into the parameters that limit the ability of the government to manage contracts in an ideal fashion.

This chapter begins with a discussion of the major aspects of the principal–agent theory, moving to a consideration of monitoring. A more detailed discussion of contract management follows, identifying the ways in which it differs from more specific monitoring efforts. The OOCEA experience is then analyzed, focusing on monitoring issues and concerns within the three major goals of the privatization effort. Contract renewal or termination considerations, which provide an overall standard by which to judge the performance of the vendor, are also discussed.

Principal–Agent Theory

The basic goal of any contractual relationship is "to structure an agreement that will induce agents to serve the principal's interests even though their actions and information are not observed by the principal" (Pratt and Zeckhauser 1991, 2). In the case where the principal is the government that privatizes or contracts out a service to an agent or private vendor, the contract–RFP must identify the service delivery goals that the government wishes the vendor to achieve. Beyond simply stating the goals, though, there must be incentives for the vendor to achieve these goals, especially during those times when the government cannot closely watch or monitor his or her behavior.

Even though the vendor has signed a contract in which he or she agrees to achieve the specified service delivery goals, there is a natural tendency for other self-interests to have high priority. This nongoal achievement behavior is termed shirking (Kettl 1993). Shirking has two primary types: leisure activity or self-regarding behavior (Perrow 1986). The latter term refers to behavior that benefits only the vendor (or its management team) and not the government; or benefits an individual employee of the vendor and does not benefit other employees.[1]

Shirking is also inevitable because of information asymmetries. At any given point in time, the vendor will know more about the tasks needed to deliver the service than will the government (Pratt and Zeckhauser 1991, 3). Also, the vendor and its employees will have more opportunities to shirk than the government will be able to control (Kettl 1993, 24).

The government attempts to reduce shirking in two ways: by providing incentives and by monitoring behavior. Incentives can, first, reward goal-directed, nonleisure activity, and second, limit self-regarding behavior. These two categories of incentives are not necessarily mutually exclusive.

The first category of incentives includes (1) monetary rewards for high quality performance, (2) nonmonetary rewards such as recognition within the organization by awards, and (3) reputational rewards within the service delivery industry for high quality performance. If there are cost savings due to greater efficiency, for example, these savings can be shared by both the management team and by the employees.

Within the boundaries created by the contract, the government can also limit self-regarding behavior. According to Perrow (1986), self-regarding behavior is supported by the following conditions:

1. Continuing interactions are minimized.
2. Storage of rewards and surpluses by individuals is encouraged.
3. The measurement of individual effort or contribution is encouraged.
4. Interdependent effort through design of work flow and equipment is minimized.
5. A preference for leadership stability and generalized authority dominates.
6. Tall hierarchies are favored (1986, 232).

Assuming that Perrow's analysis is correct, a government agency can limit self-regarding behavior by helping as much as possible to create conditions that are the *opposite* of these. The government can require frequent interactions between itself and the vendor management team. It can also require employees to interact with each other through stating in the RFP the need for training, and the creation of quality assurance teams and other organizational structures that support employee interaction.

To the extent that rewards can be shared through the use of team recognition or effort, self-regarding behavior will be limited. To the extent that employees can be empowered, supervisors rotated, and strict lines of authority not clearly defined, employees will be less likely to act in their own self-interest in a way that does not coincide with the service delivery goals.

In order to be the most effective, the principal (government agency) needs to provide incentives that reward high levels of performance and to encourage the agent to limit or lessen the conditions that favor self-regarding behavior among its employees. Depending upon factors such as the nature of the work performed, the efforts by the principal to lessen these conditions will have limits as well. The quality of the performance of a parking lot attendant, cashier, or lawn service person depends primarily on individual effort. To the extent that the work performed is routine, and thus performance is largely judged by an "error rate" or the number and frequency of mistakes, it may be difficult to encourage behavior that is directed toward lessening the errors. Even if valid measures of performance can be identified and agreed upon, it is often difficult to establish standards of performance, especially if the service is customer based, resulting in a workload that may vary greatly.

Under these conditions, a principal can encourage the agent to create an organizational culture committed to high quality performance. To the extent that a subjective commitment to the agent or to a suborganizational unit can be created, the limits imposed by the nature of the job can be overcome.

MONITORING

The second approach to inducing goal-achieving behavior on the part of the agent is monitoring. There are several ways to interpret or classify monitoring. These include (1) different sets of activities or types of monitoring, (2) the different ways in which data regarding agent performance can be collected, and (3) principal approaches to monitoring.

Monitoring Types

As reviewed by Rehfuss (1989, 91) types of monitoring include

1. Reports
2. Periodic inspections
3. Citizen complaints
4. Level of citizen satisfaction
5. Performance standards

Reports can be checked for accuracy and reviewed for timeliness. More important, the degree to which the reports' content responds to the requirements of the RFP or contract must be assessed. Reports can also be analyzed for the purpose of identifying trends regarding service, workload, or expenses. Periodic inspections can be scheduled or unscheduled. Physical surroundings and conditions can be inspected, and work performance can be observed. Citizen complaints are counted, compared to service delivery units, and addressed. A complaint resolution process must be established, and monitoring includes reviewing the responsiveness of this process. Citizen satisfaction levels act as an overall reflection of how well the agent is performing. Usually determined by surveys, satisfaction with more specific aspects of the service can be tapped as well. Performance standards reflect data collected by identified performance measures. These standards can reflect negotiated thresholds between the principal and the agent, they can reflect service industry standards, they can be represented in terms of an acceptable range of behavior, and they can be established by analyzing trends of behavior over longer periods of time.

Data Collection

The way data are collected can be grouped into direct, follow up, and monitoring by exception (Harney 1992). Direct monitoring occurs by observing or inspecting the service delivery as it is happening. Follow-up monitoring occurs after the service has been delivered, often in terms of reports, survey results, and comparing performance levels to predetermined standards. Monitoring by exception occurs only when problems are sufficiently severe as to warrant immediate response. The more the five previously mentioned monitoring types are employed, the less likelihood monitoring by exception will be used.

Monitoring Approaches

Harney (1992) identifies two monitoring approaches: output and outcome. Although these two approaches are interrelated, it is important to note their differences. Output monitoring involves measuring, reviewing, and inspecting. Output monitoring measures the number of people served or units of service delivered. In a "check off" fashion, it notes whether reports have been delivered on time. It compares the information found in SOPs with actual policies and activities. It measures the time needed to perform activities that are specified in the RFP–contract.

In terms of the employing the five monitoring types, the first three—reports, inspections, and citizen complaints—are the most likely to be found. All three of the data collection methods are used.

Outcome monitoring, in contrast, focuses much more on analyzing the extent to which the goals specified in the RFP–contract have been achieved. In doing so, it relies in part on the information gathered by output monitoring. Although it employs all five monitoring types, it much more emphasizes the latter two—levels of citizen satisfaction and performance standards—as these two types are typically more closely related to goal achievement.[2] Data are collected primarily by follow-up efforts, as performance is reviewed after it has occurred.

The two monitoring approaches have aspects that overlap, especially since the monitoring types interrelate, often in a causal fashion. An increasing number of citizen complaints or a complaint resolution process that is not sufficiently responsive, measured by the number of days between receiving a written complaint and the resolution of that complaint, for example, is probably an indicator that the level of citizen satisfaction is low. If reports contain inaccuracies or are not submitted in a timely fashion, it is probable that performance standards are not being met.

Principal–Agent Theory: Additional Insights

Principal–agent theory does not provide the level of detail concerning the types and approaches of monitoring discussed above. It does not specify how incentives are to be provided, or what type of monitoring is preferable. Most important, it does not address how the principal is to solve problems that arise, institute changes that are needed, or ultimately, decide to seek another agent. Contract management encompasses these activities.

Ultimately, the theory does not support the existence of a true partnership between public and private organizations. By implication, principals must always assume there will be shirking, as information flow will not be sufficiently timely to ever allow the principal to become fully aware of the activities and behaviors of the agent.

With the advances in information and communication technology, it is now possible to significantly reduce delays in the principal receiving information concerning key aspects of the agent activities that are crucial to goal achievement. Although shirking cannot be totally eliminated, technology can help to establish a more positive relationship than is implied by the principal–agent theory.

CONTRACT MANAGEMENT

The management of a contract can include all types and approaches to monitoring. The contract manager goes beyond collecting and analyzing data by implementing changes that lead to the resolution of performance problems. Contract amendments may have to be proposed, revised, and accepted. The agent may have to perform additional duties that will help to achieve stated service delivery goals. Additional compensation may be due to the agent. If there are subcontractors whose performance influences goal achievement, the contract manager may have to intervene between the agent and the subcontractor, establishing a relationship that had not previously existed.

More important, the contract manager must be sensitive to the evolving nature of the service delivery goals as stated in the RFP–contract. These goals must be prioritized, as there may be insufficient resources or will to give them all equal weight. If an efficiency goal, a customer satisfaction goal, and a responsiveness goal all exist, conditions such as the demand for service and the nature of the local economy may influence the prioritization of these three goals.

The Contract Management Experience of the OOCEA

The toll operations privatization contract between OOCEA and FTS was signed on February 24, 1995. The transition period overlapped with contract management, since the takeover of all ten plazas was phased in over time, with FTS operating the first four as of April 1, 1995. The operations of the final plaza was handed over to FTS by FDOT on October 1, 1995.

Given the multifaceted nature of the contract management team, the dynamic nature of the public–private partnership can be viewed from a variety of perspectives. The issues that are discussed below have evolved through a variety of discussions at all levels of the contract management team and their counterparts at FTS. These relationships have been built upon the foundation established by the contract and the RFP.

There is a common thread throughout all of these issues and the likelihood that they will represent successful partnership efforts. If an issue will add to management profit of FTS because it requires the hiring of additional full-time personnel, for example, it is more likely to be suggested by FTS. Issues of service quality and safety are secondary to issues of efficiency for FTS, especially if additional profit will result.

Those issues suggested by OOCEA that do not lessen FTS management profit, requiring fewer manned toll lanes, for example, are not opposed by FTS. Furthermore, OOCEA is more likely to give higher priority to issues of service quality and safety than to efficiency.

Contract Management:
Goal Achievement Efforts and Issues

Any assessment of contract management efforts must include analysis of how well the goals stated in the RFP–contract have been met. As stated, in terms of the principal–agent theory, the more the principal is successful in limiting shirking by providing incentives and limiting self-regarding behavior, the greater the likelihood that goals will be achieved. Incentives must be divided into those provided by the RFP–contract and those that occur after the contract has been implemented.

For any contract, the degree of goal achievement can be attributed to several sources. These include the following: (1) the extent to which the RFP–contract clearly identifies the goals and provides measures to adequately assess goal achievement; (2) the extent to which performance standards are identified and agreed upon during the transition period; (3) the clarity and extent of incentives which influence the performance of the agent–vendor; (4) the physical limits of the technology and machinery needed to deliver the service; (5) the contract management efforts; and (6) conditions or events outside the control of either principal or agent.

It is extremely difficult to distinguish between the degree to which ongoing contract management efforts by OOCEA have contributed to goal achievement, compared to the contributions made by FTS in response to the terms set forth in the RFP–contract. Any assessment of goal achievement must represent a review of efforts made at one point of time, understanding that contract management is an ongoing process. The following evaluation of goal achievement must include reference to all the factors that have contributed to it.

The four primary goals of the toll operations privatization contract are stated in the RFP:

1. Efficient toll collection operation including a reduction in current operating costs.

2. Sound financial accounting of revenues and assets.

3. Responsive, courteous customer service.

4. Serves the best interest of the people of Central Florida and the OOCEA.

The efforts and activities needed to achieve all of the first three goals are not mutually exclusive. In many respects, the degree of goal achievement for one goal positively influences achievement of another goal.

The first goal clearly wishes to achieve lower operating costs, one that primarily involves both fewer toll collector hours and lower expense dollars. Efficiency also refers to the ratio of revenue to expense. Efforts that increase use of the toll roadways will increase revenue. With the use of E-PASS, plus increased friendly, courteous service from toll collectors, revenue is likely to rise.[3]

A comprehensive, consistent auditing–accounting system will also help both efficiency and quality of service. With the introduction of the ETTM system, the collection of data that records traffic, revenue, and collector performance is greatly facilitated. Also, with the use of the vehicle enforcement system, more violators will be caught, thereby increasing revenue. Similarly, with the reports generated by the ETTM system, collector errors can be identified easier, thereby leading to improved collector performance and improved service quality.

The goal of customer satisfaction and improved service quality is the most complex and multifaceted, as it encompasses policies and activities that refer to security, customer satisfaction, training, performance evaluation, safety, maintenance, and turnover. In many cases, efforts to improve this goal require additional expense dollars, thereby reducing efficiency. Since toll collection generates a revenue stream, however, in a greater sense this goal positively affects efforts to achieve greater efficiency, as better service quality will lead to greater usage and more revenue. Likewise, the incentive performance program that is part of the efforts to achieve efficiency provides incentives to toll collectors to provide better service.

Efficiency and Lower Operating Costs

Compared to the cost of operations under the agreement with FDOT, costs under FTS have lessened considerably. Savings are approximately $1 million per year. Much of this savings is due to (1) the lower overhead and profit costs charged by FTS compared to the FDOT overhead costs, (2) the leaner management and support staff proposed by FTS, and (3) the lower toll operations costs bid by FTS.

In addition, greater efficiencies have been achieved because the number of toll customers continues to rise. Even though OOCEA operating costs have risen as a result of privatization, greater efficiencies are occurring because of increased revenue.

Without the specific guidance of contract language, a financial incentive system has been negotiated and agreed to by both OOCEA and FTS. Entitled the "incentive performance program," it has led to a decrease in operating costs without full-time employee layoffs and without decreasing customer satisfaction. It represents a classic incentive system that significantly contributes to the greater achievement of all three goals. It also represents a prime example of the increased management flexibility that OOCEA has gained from the privatization efforts.

Incentive Performance Program

Savings from reductions in toll operations costs are placed in a dollar pool that is distributed to toll operations employees in the form of bonuses. These dollars are distributed according to ratings achieved as the result of a performance evaluation system created and implemented by FTS.

These savings can come from a number of sources. There is an employee suggestion program through which suggestions to save operating expenses can be made. The quality review program, required by the RFP–contract, can also produce suggestions to save operating costs.

All of the presently identified savings, though, have come from reduced toll operations labor costs. As the use of E-PASS has increased, the number of manned lanes needed has decreased. Similarly, the use of the VES system at ramp locations has eliminated the need for toll service attendants at these ramps, especially during low traffic times. For 1995, a total of $213,000 was saved. In order to ensure that an incentive was available for TSAs over a longer period of time, 50 percent of this savings was distributed in December 1995, 25 percent in 1996 (12.5% in July 1996 and 12.5 in December 1996), with 15 percent to be distributed in 1997 and 10 percent in 1998.

Beginning in December 1995 and for every six months after that time, the performance of all TSAs, toll service supervisors, and plaza managers is reviewed and ranked according to nine factors, using a ten-point scale. As indicated in Table 9.1, two of the factors are weighed more than 1—money handling and job knowledge—while appearance is given a weight of .5.

Bonuses are distributed according to an agreed-upon formula, with higher ranked employees receiving a higher percentage bonus. To be eligible for the bonus, a collector must have worked at least ninety-one days of the base or six-month period and not have been formally reprimanded during that period.

Table 9.1
Performance Evaluation–Appraisal System: FTS–TSAs

Factors	Weight	Total Poss. Points
1. Money Handling	2	20
2. Vehicle Classification	1	10
3. Productivity	1	10
4. Customer Relations	1	10
5. Appearance/Attire	0.5	5
6. Job Knowledge	1.5	15
7. Cooperation/Attitude	1	10
8. Attendance	1	10
9. Attention to Safety	1	10
TOTAL		100

As part of the agreement establishing the IPP, FTS does not lose any of its management fee even though toll collector labor dollars are reduced. Plus, since it is a bonus system, the base pay of collectors does not rise. This has two advantages. If the dollars were added to the base pay, raising salaries, fewer numbers of collectors would be eligible for pay increases in subsequent base periods. Also, when contract renegotiation occurs at the end of the five-year period, FTS would be able to rebid the contract using the same lower base salaries. Otherwise, if the IPP dollars were added to the base, and FTS did not wish to lower any collector salaries if it won the contract, it would face a serious challenge from competitors who would bid the contract using lower base salaries.

As with any monetarily based incentive system, however, there is the risk that the employee will come to expect the bonus dollars in his or her paycheck. If at a future time there are no savings to distribute, then morale may fall if paychecks are significantly smaller.[4]

Achieving Greater Efficiency: Ongoing Issues

The primary causes of increased revenue may be outside the control of contract management efforts. To the extent that toll roadway usage is increasing in Central Florida because the population continues to increase while the unemployment rate remains low, there is little that can be done by the OOCEA beyond efforts to increase customer satisfaction and increase E-PASS usage. One issue that may have bearing on the revenue production is the increased sensitivity paid to the VES. Recent changes in enforcement policies may lead to fewer violators and/or increased revenue.

The major efforts that could lead to increase efficiency focus on reducing operating costs. There are several potential areas for reduction. These include closing additional manned lanes as E-PASS usage increases; reducing manned lane coverage during time when traffic volume is low; reducing the number of plaza managers; allowing toll collection couriers to deposit collected funds at the most convenient plaza instead of the "home" plaza; allowing FTS to be responsible for counting collected funds; and reducing the amount of paper needed throughout the toll collection system.

All these issues have service quality concerns. All are in various stages of discussion and consideration by both OOCEA and FTS.

Reduction of Manned Lanes as E-PASS Usage Increases

Current E-PASS users total over 100,000, with a total average of 30,000 E-PASS transactions each day. Since E-PASS users can use any lane when passing through the toll plaza, the replacement of a manned lane with an E-PASS lane should occur only when the number of transactions handled by a given manned lane lessens. Both traffic counts for manned lanes and E-PASS usage must be monitored. If both are increasing, however, then the manned lanes for a given plaza should not be closed. If the closing would increase the waiting time for traffic progressing through the manned lanes beyond an acceptable limit, then the quality of service would lessen.

Ideally, a traffic rate for a given period of time should be identified that would constitute a standard below which the manned lane should be closed and replaced with a E-PASS lane. At present, no such standard exists. Both OOCEA and FTS should work together to identify and agree upon such a standard.

Reducing the Number of Hours Needed for Manned Lanes

A similar consideration is to compare the amount of revenue collected during a given number of hours during a twenty-four-hour time period for a manned lane or ramp. If the amount collected is relatively small, especially when compared to the amount of salary and benefits paid to the collector, then it may be cost effective to close the lane for that period of time.

Other conditions must be considered before the decision would be made. At least one manned lane must be open in each direction twenty-four hours per day. Second, scheduling logistics must be taken into account. Reduced lane hours may mean fewer part-time or full-time toll collector hours would be required. Reducing full-time hours would save more toll labor dollars than reducing part-time hours, but it may mean that service quality would be reduced.

Reducing the Number of Plaza Managers

FTS responded to the RFP by indicating that there would be a need for one plaza manager for each of the ten plazas, with no assistant plaza managers needed. This organization structure, different from the one used by FDOT to operate the plazas, was strongly supported by the RFP selection committee as reflected by its high ratings for this item. Also, FTS indicated its desire to review this structure:

Initially, a Plaza Service Manager will be assigned to each of the ten toll plazas. During the transition and the first year of contract operation, an ongoing review by FTS management in conjunction with the Authority will determine if the Plaza Service Managers duties can be realigned to improve consistency and service quality. (Florida Toll Services 1994, 31)

FTS has proposed reducing the number of plaza managers to eight, assigning two plazas to one manager. One manager would become assistant to the director of operations, working a Wednesday through Sunday shift, as well as manage the Curry Ford plaza. Two managers, one assigned to the Northern Area plazas and one to the Southern Area plazas, would have four-day work weeks, working twelve hours on every weekend and eight hours for each of two days either just before or after the weekend. According to the redistricting proposal, the benefits include that the five plaza assigned managers would have every weekend off; higher level of managerial decision-making capability would be available on the weekends without calling out the director of operations; and salary savings would be available to raise the salaries of the plaza managers.

In assessing this request, several factors must be considered. First, under the present structure, the ability of the managers to complete their assigned duties at a high level must be assessed. As stated in the RFP response, these duties include to

Assist with the employee selection process, providing support to Toll Service Supervisors, directing emergency responses, performing field inspections, training and re-training supervisors and attendants, and assisting with patron disputes and other complaints. Prepare performance evaluations for supervisors, review performance evaluations of Toll Service Attendants, assist supervisors with the disciplinary and grievance process, ensure the dissemination and understanding of information (Florida Toll Services 1994, 31)

If FTS and OOCEA agree that these are the appropriate duties, then there must be an assessment of how well managers are performing them. There must be confidence that the managerial process already established with ten managers is running well before an organizational structural change could occur.

More important is the related issue of appropriate workload. If the above duties are performed well in less than forty hours per week, then a redistribution of workload could be considered. Most important, though, is the availability of managers to provide timely response to emergencies, customer complaints, and other urgent communication. Perhaps what needs to be avoided is the public perception that a given plaza is not important enough to warrant a full-time manager.[5] On this issue, achieving greater efficiencies through lessening the number of managers may lessen both the appearance and reality of a lowering of service quality.

Security versus Efficiency

The final two issues also have quality of service and efficiency aspects. If policies and procedures are changed so that there is a reduction in operating costs, there may be increased security concerns. First, allowing FTS to have more responsibility and control over the funds collected before they are transported to the bank could allow for more flexibility in fund pick up than under current policy. Couriers could deposit collected funds at the nearest main plaza rather than at the "home" plaza. Also, FTS could be responsible for counting the funds collected from the vaults prior to bank transport and deposit. Second, the number of required hard copy forms could be reduced, thus lessening the amount of paper needed.

Policies Regarding FTS Control over Funds Collected

With the ETTM system, there is now an accurate count of the number of vehicles who travel through the toll plazas and the amount of tolls that should be collected. This increased accuracy, currently operating at an average of 99.86 percent, is much greater than the accuracy achieved under a manual treadle system. This accuracy also opens the potential for changes in policy regarding fund handling. It is now more conceivable that more control over the funds could be given to FTS, with the ETTM system ensuring accountability. Although more research and analysis is needed than will be provided here, two areas of policy that could be changed will be discussed.

First, the routes taken by couriers who travel to pick up funds from ramp locations could be more efficiently specified. Current policy requires couriers to pick up coin vaults from ramp locations and return them to the main or "home" plaza. If instead they could return them to the nearest main plaza, it would decrease travel time and expense.

Second, counting of the coins collected in vaults could be performed less expensively by allowing FTS to count them rather than requiring the banks to count these funds. Couriers could pick up funds at all ramps and plazas, and transport them to a central location at the FTS operations center for counting. At present, armored cars pick up the funds from each plaza and transport them to the bank where they are counted and deposited.

If the counting of the funds were removed from the "Armored Car and Depository Banking Services" contract, and FTS were allowed to count these funds, operating costs could be lessened. Travel costs allocated for the armored cars would be greatly diminished, as they would travel to one location instead of ten plazas to pick up the collected funds.

Alternatively, couriers could return the vaults to each plaza for counting. Savings would still result if the costs associated with additional personnel required to count these coins would be less than presently charged by the bank. In addition, the damage to vaults would be less, as the vaults would not have to be transported by armored car to the banks and returned to the plazas. Replacement costs for vaults would be lowered.

In theory, to maximize fund collection security, armored car pick ups could be made at each ramp location as well as at each plaza, and couriers would not be needed. Minimal fund collection security would occur if nonarmored personnel and vehicles (e.g., couriers traveling in cars or vans), were used to pick up and deliver funds directly to the bank, bypassing plazas or the toll operations center. In reality, the policies and procedures that maximize security with reasonable efficiency identify routes and responsibilities for couriers and armored cars that fall between these two extremes.

Common practice for toll operations without ETTM systems is to use couriers to transport funds from ramp locations to main plazas. If more discretion were to be given to FTS to choose their own courier routes, as well as to count the funds prior to deposit, the ETTM system could provide sufficient accountability. Further analysis would be needed to identify the amount of savings more precisely and to clarify the responsibility of FTS if there were a shortfall of funds. In addition, the potential need for greater monitoring efforts by OOCEA would have to be explored.

Reducing the Need for Hard Copy Forms and Paper

Although additional study is needed, there may be additional operating cost savings by lowering paper needs. The ETTM system could be used more efficiently. Duplicate copies of system reports that are printed at each plaza could be eliminated with software and hardware adjustments. Reports generated by the ETTM system could be reduced or consolidated, especially in the area of accounting and fund handling. Requirements that TSAs must "sign in and sign out" could be replaced with other data generated by the ETTM system.

The issues discussed earlier remain the same, as greater security risks and increased opportunities for TSA shortages may be the result of lessening the number of hard copy forms. Although, as the FTS audit staff achieves greater capabilities, high quality TSA performance could be ensured even with fewer hard copy forms.

The brief review of these issues indicates that there are many possibilities for lowering operating costs. In most cases, the issues are multifaceted, involving concerns that greater efficiency may be gained at the risk of lowering service quality. Since revenue from toll collections is increasing, the need to lower operating costs is less urgent. As is discussed in the next section, ensuring that service quality remains high has become a more important goal than efficiency.

Maintaining and Achieving High Service Quality

Three of the monitoring types focus more on assessing quality than on efficiency. These are (1) reviewing citizen complaints and the process established to respond to them, (2) evaluating overall levels of citizen satisfaction, and (3) establishing and interpreting performance standards. These types also impact the achievement of efficiency and sound auditing goals, especially since the key measure of toll collector performance is the "shortage" or error rate in terms of funds collected.

FTS has established a responsive citizen complaint system. Monitoring efforts require a consistent review of the number of complaints and compliments, as well as the ratio of complaints to the number of vehicles that have traveled through the toll lanes. In addition, there needs to be follow up concerning the actions taken to correct the problems noted in the complaints.

Evaluating overall levels of citizen satisfaction is a monitoring type that has not been used by OOCEA or FTS since the privatization effort was implemented. Although a recent survey of E-PASS and non-E-PASS users was completed, the results focused on the reasons why (or why not) citizens obtained an E-PASS account, with limited reference to overall levels of satisfaction. A consistent, periodic written survey is needed to more fully assess the degree of citizen or customer satisfaction.

Performance standards can be interpreted in a variety of ways. Individual levels of toll collector performance, discussed above as part of the IPP, need to be reviewed by OOCEA. Other performance issues are discussed in the next section, reviewing the efforts to achieve a sound financial system.

In addition, there are three current, ongoing issues that require additional discussion. These are the impact of collector turnover on service quality and efficiency; the ideal full-time to part-time collector ratio; and the evolving nature of the quality management plan.

Citizen Complaints

Customers who wish to complain, compliment, or comment can do so on a "3-C" card that can be obtained at each toll booth. There is a sign on each booth encouraging a response: "How's my service? Ask for a comment card." In addition, a toll-free telephone number is provided for those who wish to respond vocally. The FTS Director of Training and Quality Management, responds to each card or call. For those who have complained, he offers to make them "Mystery Drivers" (explained in the following paragraphs).

Each month, a report is given to OOCEA. Several measures are used. For example, during November 1996, there were 13 complaints, 27 compliments, and 44 "general concern" comments, for an overall total of 84 comments. Since a total of 5.052 million manual lane transactions occurred during that month, there was one comment for every 60,147 vehicles, and one complaint for every 388,644 vehicles.

Customers are generally increasingly happy with the service they are receiving. Interestingly, the number of compliments is increasing, as is the ratio of compliments to vehicles. In 1995, for example, there was one compliment for every 444,148 vehicles, while for 1996 (through November) the ratio is one compliment for every 204,852 vehicles, an improvement of almost 54 percent. Also, the ratio of compliments to complaints has been increasing. From July 1996 through November 1996, the ratio has been more than 2.5 to 1 (145 to 55). In comparison, for all of 1995, there were 103 complaints and 88 compliments.

Likewise, the number of complaints is decreasing and the complaint to vehicle ratio is improving. The six-month period from June to November 1996 has seen fewer average monthly complaints compared to the average for the first five months of the year (11.7 versus 20.2). Similarly, the average monthly ratio of complaints to vehicles is one for 281,493 for the first five months of 1996, compared to an average monthly ratio of one for every 477,636 vehicles for June to November, a 70 percent improvement! Most of the complaints and comments refer to attitude and treatment from the TSAs. Increasingly, they are friendly, provide customers with a smile, and say "thank you."

The focus of contract management must be on ensuring that these trends continue. There must also be an assessment of why complaints are decreasing and compliments increasing so that the efforts that are causing these positive results can continue and improve. There are several possible causes. First, the IPP may be providing enough of an incentive to encourage TSAs to provide high quality customer service. Second, the increased ratio of full-time TSAs compared to the part-time temporary employees may have helped. Third, the FTS policy of hiring part-time TSAs to fill full-time position vacancies may also be providing incentives. Finally, the quality management process created by FTS and reinforced by the quality review committee meetings, may be a contributing factor.

Quality Management–Assurance Program

In response to the RFP, FTS has created a quality management–assurance program (QMP) that has many components.

Suggestion Program

The goal of the suggestion program is to encourage plaza managers, supervisors, and TSAs to come up with improvements in a variety of areas. These include practices and procedures that will lower operating costs, change configuration of lanes, improve the location of signs, increase safety, and provide more equitable employment practices. All suggestions are reviewed by an FTS suggestion committee. The quality control–training manager responds to each suggestion with a letter. The letter explains the procedures that have been changed as a result of the suggestion or explain why the suggestion cannot be followed.

From April 1995 through November 1996, fifty-nine suggestions were made. None of those that have been adopted have led to lower operating costs. For example, there was a suggestion that wearing a safety vest with the OOCEA logo over clothes of the TSAs choice would be preferable to wearing uniforms. The cost of leasing uniforms would be saved, although offset by the cost of purchasing safety vests. It was determined that this suggestion would not lower costs, plus dress code standards would be lowered. The use of scrap paper in the printers at the plazas was not feasible either, as this paper would jam the printers and not produce clear results.

Other suggestions, such as the need for window tinting in the lane booths because the glare of the sun makes the screen difficult to read, have been brought to the Quality Review meetings and action has resulted. Even though savings have not been realized, improved working conditions and other positive changes have resulted.

Employee Incentive Programs

In addition to the IPP, FTS has established several smaller incentive programs.

Employee of the Quarter

One full-time TSA per plaza is eligible for this award. TSAs are nominated by plaza managers, supervisors, or by other TSAs. A favorable comment card (compliment) will also enter a TSA for consideration. All audit reports and performance reviews are examined. Some TSAs who have faced disciplinary action are eliminated from contention. The winners receive a certificate, recognition through the FTS employee newsletter, and a reserved parking space for the succeeding quarter.

Employee of the Year

All winners of the Employee of the Quarter award are eligible for the Employee of the Year award. With additional supporting comments from supervisors and managers, one TSA is chosen in January for the preceding year.

Florida Toll Services Excellence Award

This award is designed to honor the TSA for his or her contributions outside the workplace. Exceptionally outstanding performance to charitable causes or community projects may win this award for an employee. It may be given anytime, upon recommendation from a supervisor, manager, or fellow employee. As of November 1996, no one had been given this award.

Mystery Driver Awards

Those customers who complain are offered the chance to become "mystery drivers." Each customer who agrees is given five postpaid cards. If a TSA greets the mystery driver with a smile and says "thank you," the mystery driver has the discretion to mail in the card to FTS. The award is one day of vacation with pay. Approximately fifty mystery drivers have issued 240 cards since the program began.

Outstanding Plaza Performance

This annual award is given to the plaza that has demonstrated the best overall performance for the year, according to performance standards developed for each plaza. No group awards have been given, as performance standards are still being developed.

Quality Review Meetings

As part of the evolving nature of the quality management program, monthly quality review meetings are held. Initially, from April through October 1995, meetings were held every two weeks, with monthly meetings beginning in November 1995. Participants in these meeting include representatives from OOCEA and FTS, but also from Syntonic, the ETTM systems contractor, and ZHA, the general maintenance contractor. The purpose of these meetings is to convey problems and other issues that can be discussed by more than one of the participants. Solutions can be identified and implemented in a more timely fashion. Topics range from those dealing with operations, auditing, maintenance, and equipment.

Initially, the meetings were a continuation of transitional issues. There was a concern with TSA shortages and overages that were unacceptably high, as well as sufficient staffing for lane coverage. OOCEA also expressed concern with the training that occurred, urging that logistical concerns be eliminated and that TSAs that needed refresher training on the ETTM system did receive it.

ZHA was introduced as the maintenance contractor, and it apparently took a few months to establish procedures and policies regarding janitorial and pressure cleaning services. In July 1995, ZHA reviewed the services that it performed for the plazas. The relationship between plaza managers and ZHA contracted staff was clarified. If there were concerns about the quality of janitorial–maintenance services, ZHA was to be contacted directly, with ongoing concerns raised at these quality management meetings. As of January 1996, some janitorial services were still receiving complaints. In June, there were several concerns about appearance and condition of the plazas, with agreement by all participants that better effort could be made.

The ETTM system has continued to require updating and refinement since April 1995. Both software and hardware issues have been raised. In May 1995, OOCEA noted that there were continuous gate problems at University, Holland East, and Holland West, requesting that gates remain in a locked up position during peak traffic hours. As of the June 1995 meeting, Syntonic needed to provide instructions regarding how to clean the "touch screen" on the TSA computers. An additional technician was hired to handle service calls. Problems were noted with the VES computers back up process taking excessive time to complete its function. At the meeting held on July 7, 1995, Syntonic was directed to complete the wiring hook ups for the MLT terminals in the FTS training room. Three weeks later, at the meeting on August 4, 1995, it was announced that a Syntonic technician would be present to adjust the exposed wiring in the training room.

In October 1995, the first mention of the need for new receipt printers was made. TSAs were to contact Syntonic directly for resolution, not just discuss the problem with a technician. Lane computers were reprogrammed to allow a single touch "Two Axle Paid" function for TSAs. The OOCEA directed plaza managers to refer problems with VES cameras to Syntonic. Problems with individual treadle counts or vault counts were noted and referred to Syntonic.

The issues and problems raised during 1995 were related more to start up problems that were identified and solved as new procedures were established, personnel from different organizations began to work together more closely, and equipment was installed and "fine tuned." Throughout much of 1996, the issues discussed were not as crucial to service delivery, but nonetheless had a bearing on quality service and efficiency. The OOCEA identified dress code violations among toll employees, and FTS enforced the existing policy. There is an ongoing issue of damaged coin vaults and whether repair or replacement is needed. It is also recognized that the ACM coin baskets need to be repaired, modified, or replaced. Window tinting and shade hoods for the TSA booths was mentioned as a need to enable TSAs to view the computer screen more closely. Some refurbishing of plazas is occurring, while general painting has also begun.

There is a greater value to the interaction among all the participants at these meetings. It creates a forum for all voices to be heard, resulting in specific actions. A stronger commitment to achieving the goals of higher quality service has resulted. At various times, participants have thanked others for their assistance and complimented them on improved performance. Since communication lines have been opened, plaza managers, for example, are now more willing to contact ZHA directly if maintenance work is not performed adequately, thereby helping OOCEA with contract management issues. All participants are more willing to work together to solve problems and resolve issues.

Achieving Service Quality: Current Issues

There are two issues that impact both service quality and efficiency goals. In both cases, higher levels of service quality may be achieved, but higher operating costs are the likely result. Both issues are related to the issue of what causes TSAs to provide a high level of customer satisfaction.

The Ratio of Full-Time TSAs to Part-Time TSAs

The RFP identified a ratio of full-time TSAs to part-time TSAs to be no more than 40 percent part-time, temporary (without full benefits) and no less than 60 percent, full-time, permanent (with full benefits). This ratio has been a "rule of thumb," originally used by FDOT operations. If part-time employees are more than 40 percent, then customer satisfaction levels were felt to be less than acceptable, personnel issues and disciplinary problems would be higher, occupying an inordinate amount of supervisory time and effort, and turnover would be too high, costing too much in terms of training, payroll, and other personnel costs.

Furthermore, the assumption has been that full-time TSAs will perform at a higher level than their part-time counterparts. Their base wage is higher, and the benefits are substantially greater. The IPP is available only to full-time employees. There is a greater identification with working for FTS, and therefore adopting a stronger commitment to customer service is much more likely.

Of greatest importance is that full-time TSAs are much more likely to have fewer dollar amounts of negative discrepancies or shortages than their part-time counterparts. With greater experience, the full-time TSA is better able to classify the vehicle correctly, make correct change, and greet the customer courteously. Because most part-time TSAs have less experience, they are concentrating more on avoiding shortages, and are less likely to be comfortable with the customer.

Because of logistical and scheduling issues, employing some part-time TSAs will always be preferable. Since they can be assigned less than an eight-hour shift, they provide more flexibility for FTS. If ramp or manned lane closings are implemented, full-time TSAs do not have to be laid off. If there are unexpected reasons for requiring additional TSAs, there is less need for overtime.

Additional study will be needed to more accurately identify the optimal ratio of full-time to part-time TSAs. The relationship between performance and hours of experience needs more investigation. Unacceptable levels of service quality as well as total labor costs that are considered less than efficient could both be related to this ratio. Both OOCEA and FTS favor additional analysis, as a higher percentage of full-time TSAs would improve service quality as well as increase the management profit of FTS.

The Relationship of TSA Turnover to Performance

For many of the same reasons as identified above, the issue of acceptable levels of employee turnover should be addressed. With less turnover among TSAs, performance levels among the entire workforce should improve or be maintained at a high level. With greater turnover, more training is required, and there are more TSAs with less experience.

Using a basic measure of turnover, the full-time TSAs and TSSs who were employed by FTS in October 1995, after all plazas had been transitioned to FTS management, were compared to those still employed by FTS in December 1996. The turnover rate for TSAs was 25.7 percent, as 35 of the 136 full-time TSAs on the payroll in October 1995 were not employed by FTS fourteen months later. For TSSs, 10 of the 45 had left FTS employment, for a turnover rate of 22.2 percent.

For similar time periods for the part-time TSAs, only 2 of 106 that were employed in May 1995 were still with FTS by December 1996, and only 6 of the 141 employed in October 1995 were TSAs in December 1996. Since many employees likely became employees and left between the beginning and ending of these two time periods, the turnover rate in both cases is probably much higher than 100 percent.

It is difficult to assess whether any of these turnover rates is "too high." When performance decreases significantly as the turnover rate rises, then the reasons for the turnover need to be more fully investigated. To the extent that employees have been terminated for theft, for example, the ETTM and auditing systems could be improved to prevent future such occurrences.

Lowering the turnover rate for part-time employees is a much more challenging task. Raising the wage rate may help, as the alternative of a higher paying position is less likely or feasible. Ensuring that part-time TSAs have more hours may also assist those who prefer full-time employment and who wish to make as much money as possible. If performance measures, including the number of complaints and compliments, are at acceptable levels, however, then a higher turnover rate may be tolerated without raising wages or hours.

Achieving a Sound Financial Auditing and Accounting System

Before privatization of toll operations could occur, it was deemed necessary that the ETTM system be implemented to provide maximum possible accountability for revenue collected from the private sector vendor. There would also be the additional benefit of much greater system accuracy in terms of counting the actual number of vehicles that traveled through plazas and ramps. Greater efficiencies could be achieved because the ETTM system would produce reports that would much more greatly facilitate the auditing of revenue collected compared with the same activities under the manual system. Fewer auditors–auditor hours would be spent on auditing collector accounts to achieve a much greater accurate collection of revenue.

Given these positive expected changes, the goal of the RFP was to create a system of reports and data collection procedures that would maximize the capabilities of the ETTM system. In terms of reviewing TSA performance, the daily exception report (DER) is the key document. Provided for each TSA at each plaza on a daily basis, it furnishes information from which the monthly exception report is created. In response to the data provided on the DER, FTS auditors must investigate all shortages or overages that are $3 or over and provide adjustments on the transaction accountability exception report (TAER). To provide examples of the reports generated by the ETTM, a brief description of these two reports is provided, with an assessment of their implications for contract management.

Daily Exception Report

With the identification and name removed of actual TSAs, Table 9.2 provides an actual example of a daily exception report. The information found in the middle columns provides an indication of the accuracy of the system: Axles indicated are the number recorded by the TSA, while the actual axles are the number that actually went through the lanes. The differences range from .0 percent to 1.6 percent, for an overall error rate of .32 percent (both overages and shortages are added together). In other words, the system was 99.68 percent accurate.

The latter nine columns deal with the nature of vehicle classification and how each vehicle was classified as it traveled through the lanes. Next to the column listing the total vehicles traveling through the lane and responded to by each TSA are five classifications of vehicles: (1) MLT, or manned lane transaction, in which the patron stopped, paid a toll, and received change and/or a receipt; (2) NR, or nonrevenue, in which the patron, usually law enforcement personnel, is exempt from paying a toll; (3) AVI, or automatic vehicle identification, which has counted an E-PASS customer that had traveled through the manned lane; (4) VIOS, or violations, that count those travelers who did not pay a toll, and (5) UOS, or unexplained observations.

The latter category is a miscellaneous classification, which includes the following vehicles: (1) police, fire and ambulances, and emergency vehicles (that do not have a nonrevenue card); (2) an E-PASS customer that pays cash; (3) if the E-PASS system is malfunctioning, the result will be a UO or a violation on the collectors screen; and (4) a vehicle pulling a trailer.

For the purposes of auditing revenue collection, the key data are found in the first four columns. Revenue expected is the amount identified by subtracting the amount based upon the number of axles indicated as traveling through the lanes from the vehicles listed under the MLT column. Many of the collectors have overages. This may be due to a TSA shortchanging the customer, or it could be due to the ETTM system, such as pushing the wrong button on the touch screen, thereby creating a false violation (e.g., the four-axle vehicle button is pushed when the vehicle only had two axles).

FTS auditors focus on all variances over $3, and all over 1 percent. Full explanations are sought for these errors, including wrong change, false violations, and unexplained shortages or overages.

The Transaction Accountability Exception Report

On this form, explanations for the revenue discrepancies are provided (see Table 9.3). The comment form indicates the number of false violations, amount of insufficient funds, and any bank adjustments. The dollar amounts reflecting these reasons is found in Column B, in which all adjustments except those due to bank adjustments are made; and in Column E, in which bank adjustments are made. Unexplained variance is listed in Columns F and C.

Contract management of the audit function could vary over time. If there are a lot of shortages or overages, then OOCEA auditors closely check the work of the FTS auditors, acting as a double check to ensure that all errors are noted and explained. As the performance of the TSAs improves, and as the FTS auditors also improve their capability to accurately discover and explain all discrepancies, then the OOCEA auditors only have to "spot check" the data on these forms. In the future, when there is more confidence in the ETTM system as well as with all auditing functions, fewer forms will be needed.

Current Issues: Violation Enforcement System

An ideally working VES should identify all vehicles that travel through toll lanes without paying. A camera, part of the ETTM system, photographs the license plate of all vehicles. From these files, violators are identified. According to the present policy, once a vehicle has violated the lanes three times, a warning letter is sent urging payment of due tolls. If the warning letter is ignored, and an additional violation occurs, a uniform traffic citation (UTC) is issued.[6] Part of the charge for the UTC is returned to the OOCEA to help pay administrative costs.

The challenge for OOCEA, FTS, and Syntonic is to create a system that more closely resembles this ideal. The problems faced are multifaceted. Although violations total only 2.8 percent of all vehicles (as of November 1996), in some locations the rate approaches 7 percent. Given the volume of traffic experienced by the total OOCEA system, the number of violations for November 1996 was over 300,000. Due to factors such as glare, speed of the vehicles traveling through the E-PASS lanes, and other lighting problems, only about 50 percent of the images captured by the present ETTM equipment are readable. Furthermore, only about 30 percent of the images captured are usable, as a vehicle may have no license plate or have placed it in an unusual location, plus towing balls, other obstructions, fog, smoke, and dust prevent the license plate number from being read accurately.

All participants have responded to these problems. OOCEA has committed additional resources to hire staff, as FTS now manages a staff of fourteen who are processing images, issuing warning letters, and handling administrative functions. Syntonic has hired an additional technician, will monitor equipment and improve maintenance, and will support an automated image processing system being developed by Telos that will lead to greater processing efficiency. OOCEA has also given this a high priority for quality management discussions.

The VES affects revenue collection, service quality, and efficiency goals. Less revenue is collected in the lanes. Service quality is a potential issue, as a

Table 9.2
Orlando–Orange County Expressway Authority Daily Exception Report

Rev. Expt	Rev. Dep + CPU	Rev. Var.	% Var	Axle Ind.	Axle Act.	Axle Diff	% Diff
624.00	435.26	188.74	30.2	1686	1680	6	.4
1,234.50	1,249.40	14.90	1.2	3342	3341	1	.0
165.50	167.00	1.50	.9	813	318	0	.0
127.50	128.50	1.00	.8	613	607	6	1.0
1,016.00	1,008.35	7.65	.8	2739	2736	3	.1
309.00	311.00	2.00	.6	1338	1337	1	.1
1,243.75	1,236.06	7.69	.6	3349	3349	0	.0
1,052.50	1,056.75	4.25	.4	2830	2832	2-	.1
973.25	976.43	3.18	.3	2643	2633	10	.4
158.00	158.50	.50	.3	689	689	0	.0
372.50	371.39	-1.11	.3	1670	1670	0	.0
320.75	319.80	-.95	.3	1054	1051	3	.3
837.25	839.49	2.24	.3	2248	2240	8	.4
1,309.00	1,312.43	3.43	.3	3535	3538	3-	.1
433.75	434.74	.99	.2	1410	1414	4-	.3
925.50	927.50	2.00	.2	2504	2501	3	.1
382.00	382.75	.75	.2	1653	1655	2-	.1
955.75	957.49	1.74	.2	2573	2581	8-	.3
796.25	797.50	1.25	.2	3124	2133	1	.0
1,013.25	1,012.35	-.90	.1	2740	2745	5-	.2
674.50	675.01	.51	.1	1814	1805	9	.5
433.50	433.30	-.20	.0	1160	1161	1-	.1
1,174.25	1,173.85	-.40	.0	3148	3148	0	.0
741.25	741.50	.25	.0	1988	1984	4	.2
853.50	853.50	.00	.0	2292	2296	4-	.2
18,127.00	17,959.85	-167.15		51965	51939	26	

Source: Florida Toll Services.

Table 9.2 (*continued*)

Tot. Vehs	MLT	NR	AVI	VIOS	% VIO	UOS	% UOS	DEP CT
842	818	2	4	7	.8	13	1.6	1
1652	1624	1	5	22	1.3	31	1.9	1
405	331	2	66	6	1.5	7	1.7	1
304	255	3	40	6	2.0	6	2.0	1
1334	1315	6	8	5	.4	26	1.9	1
664	618	1	38	7	1.1	10	1.5	1
1651	1632	7	6	6	.4	40	2.4	1
1400	1386	0	7	7	.5	20	1.4	1
1314	1289	4	12	9	.7	41	3.1	1
341	316	1	24	0	.0	5	1.5	1
831	745	2	76	1	.1	12	1.4	1
523	506	0	17	0	.0	6	1.1	1
1116	1107	0	1	8	.7	25	2.2	1
1740	1715	8	6	11	.6	31	1.8	1
696	672	5	17	2	.3	12	1.7	1
1239	1219	6	12	2	.2	32	2.6	1
821	764	2	44	11	1.3	6	.7	1
1268	1253	4	8	3	.2	25	2.0	1
1048	1039	1	4	4	.4	22	2.1	1
1333	1312	1	18	2	.2	19	1.4	1
902	893	1	1	7	.8	27	3.0	1
575	572	1	1	1	.2	9	1.6	1
1555	1545	0	10	0	.0	23	1.5	1
958	948	2	5	3	.3	19	2.0	1
1129	1118	3	7	1	.1	20	1.8	2
25630	24992	70	437	131		487		26

Table 9.3
Florida Toll Services Transaction Accountability
Exception Report

Rev. Exp	Adj. Amt.	Adj. RevExp	Rev Dep + CPU	Adj. Amt.	Adj. Rev. Dep + CPU	$ Var	% Var
1, 635.75	26.25	1,662.00	1,662.00	(0.07)	1,662.43	0.43	0.0%
422.00	7.50	429.50	427.48	(0.06)	427.42	(2.08)	-0.5%
704.25	5.50	709.75	711.00		711.00	1.25	0.2%
717.25	4.25	721.50	722.27		722.27	0.77	0.1%
213.00		213.00	211.59		211.59	(1.41)	-0.7%
1757.50	5.50	1763.00	1766.23	0.09	1766.32	3.32	0.2%
538.75	0.25	539.00	536.10		536.10	(2.90)	-0.5%
267.00		267.00	268.25		268.25	1.25	0.5%
813.00	(3.00)	810.00	809.33		809.33	(0.67)	-0.1%
1,654.50	6.35	1,660.85	1,661.82		1,661.62	0.97	0.1%
723.00	2.00	725.00	720.00	0.01	720.01	(4.99)	-0.7%
262.50		262.50	263.55		263.55	1.05	0.4%
130.50		130.50	131.01	(0.30)	130.71	0.21	0.2%
1,615.00	(0.50)	1,614.50	1,608.70		1,608.70	(5.80)	-0.4%
915.50	(0.50)	915.00	912.45		912.45	(2.55)	-0.3%
1,000.25	1.50	1,001.75	1,003.45		1003.45	1.70	0.2%
1,626.25	3.75	1,630.00	1630.12		1,630.12	0.12	0.0%
1,652.50	0.75	1,653.25	1,656.08		1,656.08	2.83	0.2%
1,778.00	2.00	1,780.00	1,781.83		1,781.83	1.83	0.1%
246.50		246.50	247.00		247.00	0.50	0.2%
1,648.25	3.00	1,651.25	1,651.45		1,651.45	0.20	0.0%
1,394.25		1,394.25	1,396.75	0.02	1,396.77	2.52	0.2%
300.00		300.00	299.50	0.01	299.51	(0.49)	-0.2%
564.00		564.00	564.72		564.72	0.72	0.1%
1,412.25		1,412.25	1,413.95	0.01	1,413.96	1.71	0.1%
330.50		330.50	330.64		330.64	0.34	0.1%
832.25		832.25	831.52	0.25	831.77	(0.48)	-0.1%
1,582.75		1,582.75	1583.85		1,583.85	1.10	0.1%
679.50		679.50	679.86		679.86	0.36	0.1%
1,318.75	16.50	1,335.25	1,319.26	0.01	1,319.27	(15.98)	-1.2%
637.25		637.25	637.45		637.45	0.20	0.0%
214.00		214.00	214.00		214.00	0.00	0.0%
599.00		599.00	599.00		599.00	0.00	0.0%

Table 9.3 (*continued*)

Comments	Attend Deposit	Bank Deposit	Var. Bk Dep - At Dep
36 False Viol. @ .75, -.75 Insuf. Funds, -.07 Bank Adj.	662.50	662.43	(0.07)
15 False Viol.@ .50, -.06 Bank Adj.	427.48	427.42	(0.06)
6 False Viol. @ .75, -.75 Insuf. Funds, 1.75 Under Class.	86.00	86.00	0.00
6 False Viol. @ .75, -.25 By Cust.	172.27	172.27	0.00
	211.59	211.59	0.00
See Below, #1	366.23	366.32	0.09
10 False Viol @ .75, -.75 Insuf. Funds, -6.50 Over Class	286.10	286.10	0.00
	268.25	268.25	0.00
2 False Viol. @ .75, -1.50 Insuf. Funds, -3.00 Over Class	359.33	359.33	0.00
See Below, #2	511.82	511.82	0.00
See Below, #3	720.00	720.01	0.01
	263.55	263.55	0.00
-.30 Bank Adjustment	131.01	130.71	(0.30)
2 False Viol. @ .75, -2.75 Insuf. Funds, .75 Under Class.	358.70	358.70	0.00
False Viol. @ .75, -1.25 Insuf. Funds.	182.45	182.45	0.00
2 False Viol. @ .75	163.45	163.45	0.00
6 False Viol. @ .75, -.75 Insuf. Funds	460.12	460.12	0.00
2 False Viol. @ .75, -.75 Insuf. Funds	376.08	376.08	0.00
False Viol. @ .75, -2.25 Insuf. Funds, 3.50 Under Class	451.83	451.83	0.00
	247.00	247.00	0.00
5 False Viol. @ .75, -.75 Insuf. Funds	701.45	701.45	0.00
02 Bank Adjustment	576.75	576.77	0.02
01 Bank Adjustment	299.50	299.51	0.01
	564.72	564.72	0.00
01 Bank Adjustment	703.95	703.96	0.01
	330.84	330.84	0.00
.25 Bank Adjustment	381.52	381.77	0.25
	983.85	983.85	0.00
	679.86	679.86	0.00
19 False Viol. @ .75, 2.25 Under Class, .01 Bank Adj.	279.26	279.27	0.01
	187.45	187.45	0.00
	214.00	214.00	0.00
	599.00	599.00	0.00

potentially growing perception that enforcement is "lax" may lead to increasing violations. Depending upon the amount of revenue collected as a result of warning letters and UTC citations, compared to the increased administrative costs, lower efficiency may be the result. The OOCEA has identified the present number of violations as unacceptably high, with the goal of decreasing the number and stabilizing the violation rate. Further analysis of the costs and benefits associated with VES could help to identify an acceptable level of violations.

CONTRACT TERMINATION OR RENEWAL

The nature of contract management can be very positive, as both the public agency and the private vendor work together harmoniously to achieve their common goals. When contract renewal is needed, this positive relationship manifests itself in the private vendor rebidding, being awarded the contract, and renewing the partnership.

At the other extreme, the performance of the vendor deteriorates to the point that contract termination occurs. This negative relationship may be due to low levels of performance among those providing the service, or due to repeated violations of the contract agreement, or to overall shirking, as goal achievement is low.

Part of the responsibility of the contract manager is to identify criteria under which either renewal or termination would occur. For renewal purposes, assuming that a second RFP is let, the contract manager can contribute to the creation of this process, identifying conditions, standards, and criteria necessary for a continued positive relationship with the original vendor (or with a new vendor).

Identifying criteria under which termination would occur is more challenging. In one sense, a "disciplinary" process should be established, in which if performance deteriorates, the vendor is given the opportunity to correct mistakes and solve problems. As much as possible, a sense of what is the lowest acceptable standard should be agreed upon by the government agency during the contract management period. As conditions and service requirements change, this standard needs to be revisited and redefined.

Contract renewal or termination is often an unspoken threat for the vendor. Assuming that there is sufficient competition among potential service providers and that the government agency has devised a contingency plan to quickly replace the vendor in the event of termination, the vendor must be ever aware of the possibility of termination and of the evaluation opportunity that the contract rebidding offers the government agency. If the vendor performance is acceptable but not outstanding, there is the risk that when the contract renewal RFP is let, the vendor's responses will be rated lower than a potential competitor.

CONCLUSION

To evaluate fully the effectiveness of contract management, several issues must be clarified and decisions made concerning appropriate action. Many of these center around the actions needed to prevent or alleviate apparent shirking behavior. In the spirit of providing a true public–private partnership, the appropriateness of actions may also change over time as the nature of the partnership evolves.

First, after appropriate reports and performance standards, for example, have been identified and agreed upon, the contract manager must decide which data to scrutinize in greater detail. If there are obvious problems or clearly identifiable high priority issues, then data that measures the success of efforts to solve the problem must be analyzed more closely.

Second, the monitoring and management activities relevant to a startup period are different from those of a later period. As the contract manager becomes more confident in the vendor's capability to perform an audit function, for example, there is less need to analyze the reasons for negative discrepancies. Also, the operations activities that involve new contracting relationships with other contractors (e.g., FTS with Syntonic and ZHA), will have to be monitored more closely during start up periods. Once there is assurance that all parties are working together to achieve the goal of keeping the plazas clean, for example, then OOCEA contract management does not have to spend as much time on this issue.

Third, the choice of monitoring by exception may be made as part of the public–private partnership arrangement. In line with the thinking that bidders responding to the RFP should be allowed discretion to create SOPs and choose how to implement a human resource management plan, for example, once the original SOP is approved, monitoring does not occur unless there is a problem. If there were activities listed in the SOP that are not presently implemented, unless this is brought to the attention of the contract manager, no monitoring is deemed necessary.

NOTES

1. Shirking encompasses a wide range of behavior. For the individual employee, it can range from sleeping on the job, taking breaks that are too long, or using the company telephone for personal calls. For the vendor, it could include behavior that saves money or lessens inconvenience. A policy may not be updated because it may require overtime on the part of managers. Lower than satisfactory performance may be tolerated because it may be perceived as too costly to fire and replace the employee.

2. With these two types of monitoring, performance is measured by comparing changes in performance that occur after an initial collection of data are used to establish a baseline. For example, overall citizen satisfaction with a service after the first year of the contract may be rated a 3.2 (on a scale where 5 equals excellent, and 1

equals unsatisfactory). A year later another citizen satisfaction survey indicates that satisfaction levels have risen to 3.8, an increase of 19 percent.

3. E-PASS is the name given to an automatic vehicle identification system established by the OOCEA in May 1994. A customer establishes an E-PASS account with a $50.00 deposit. A transponder is permanently fixed to the vehicle. Each toll plaza has dedicated E-PASS lanes, which allow vehicles to travel through the plaza without having to stop, often at speeds of forty miles per hour. The E-PASS has become increasingly popular, with an average of over 500 customers per week obtaining an account. Present vehicles using E-PASS number over 100,000. There are a number of potential impacts on revenue collection. Economic growth for the greater Orlando area would have an impact on revenue, as positive growth would result in greater usage of the tollways. The accompanying increase in population would also have a positive impact on revenue, because the more crowded alternative roadways become, the more use of tollways will occur. Factoring out impacts such as these, the attraction of E-PASS, with its marked decrease in waiting time as vehicles travel through toll plazas, would lead to increased tollway usage and revenue.

4. Bonus checks have typically ranged from 2 to 9 percent of base salary, distributed every six months. A TSA whose performance is consistently rated among the top 10 percent could receive a bonus of almost 20 percent annually.

5. It is true that the percentage of travelers that would have occasion to speak with a manager would be very small. Only those who have a serious complaint may ask to speak with the plaza manager. The risk that one such incident may result in adverse publicity, however, is one reason to retain full-time managers for each plaza.

6. The VES policy represents a more cautious approach. OOCEA is interested in making sure that when warning letters and UTCs are sent to violators, no errors have been made in identifying those who habitually violate.

ASSESSMENT AND CONCLUSION

10

The last six years have been a period of tremendous growth and change for the OOCEA. The introduction of AVI and ETTM technology, along with privatizing operations, created a highly challenging and complex situation for OOCEA staff. The decision to privatize was innovative for the transportation industry from 1992 to 1994. In retrospect, the effort has been successful, as the goals of the OOCEA set out in the RFP have largely been achieved.

Overall, the assessment of any privatization transfer process must be judged by the degree to which the goals identified by the public agency have been achieved by the existing private–public partnership. Each stage or step can be judged by using this criteria as well, although it is most appropriate in evaluating the first stage, the decision to privatize.

There are more specific assessment criteria, however, that can be used to judge each stage. The following assessment reviews each stage in the chronological order presented.

THE DECISION TO PRIVATIZE

As reflected in the RFP and discussed in Chapter 4, the decision to privatize toll operations was based on expectations that: (1) greater efficiency and lower operating costs would be less; (2) customer service would be improved; (3)

sound financial accounting procedures would be provided; and (4) increased managerial flexibility for OOCEA would be achieved. It is difficult to determine the extent to which FTS has performed better than FDOT would have if it had remained in control of operations. One major factor that influences any assessment must be the implementation of the ETTM and AVI equipment. Since the introduction of both has had a positive impact on operations, it is impossible to totally separate out their impact from that of the change in control of operations from FDOT to FTS. Yet the flexibility of the public–private partnership has clearly lead to benefits that would not have existed with the OOCEA–FDOT lease arrangement.

Another confounding factor in the analysis is that efforts to achieve the four goals mentioned above were not mutually exclusive. Increased managerial flexibility facilitated efforts that have and will lead to greater customer satisfaction. Also, policies that have increased costs (e.g., hiring a higher percentage of full-time TSAs), have hopefully led to increased customer satisfaction.

The following does focus on the major achievements for each of the four goals mentioned above. Overall, the decision to privatize, and the privatization transfer process initiated by that decision, have had successful results.

Greater Efficiency–Lower Operating Costs

The total number of transactions and toll revenue has continued to grow, exceeding projections. Since the Southern Connector main toll plazas became fully operational in FY 1994, FY 1995 was the first full fiscal year that all ten main toll plazas were operational for the entire twelve months. Toll revenues for FY 1996 are over $82 million, an increase of 12.2 percent over the more than $73 million for FY 1995. Similarly, ridership is over 119 million transactions for FY 1996, an increase of 12.3 percent over FY 1995.

Several factors could explain this growth. The general population of Central Florida grew approximately 8 percent. Unemployment remains at record low levels, at 4.1 percent to 4.3 percent, indicating that more discretionary income may be available to spend on a toll road rather than to travel alternative nontoll routes.

The technological changes and the privatization effort have contributed to increased ridership as well, as the tollways have become the preferred choice of travel for many Central Florida commuters. The introduction of the E-PASS has been extremely successful, with almost 70,000 transponders in use by June 30, 1996, a number that has grown to over 85,000 by December 1996. Travel time for many businesses have been significantly reduced. Efforts to improve customer service have been effective, as comment card compliments outnumbered complaints by a two to one ratio for June to November 1996. A systemwide maintenance program, started by OOCEA in FY 1994, has increased safety and improved the beauty of the landscaping, further making the toll ways a more pleasant ride.

To support the assessment that privatization has led to lower operating costs, a comparison must be made of operating and administrative costs that are in similar categories. First, the choice of which two fiscal years to compare is made difficult by the transition timetable. Since the first plazas were transitioned near the end of FY 1995 (April 1995), FY 1994 is the last full year of FDOT operations. Even though the two plazas from the Southern Connector, Boggy Creek, and John Young, began operation in July 1993, since this occurred at the beginning of the fiscal year, FY 1994 will be used for comparative purposes.

Likewise, in FY 1996, OOCEA paid operating expenses to both FDOT and FTS, since the final plaza was handed over to FTS in October 1995. FY 1997 was the first full year that all ten plazas are under FTS operating control. Assuming that the operations costs for the Southern Connector plazas represent all of FY 1994, then a rough comparison can be made with similar costs for FY 1997, even though these latter cost figures are estimated.

Some costs that appear in the OOCEA budget must be excluded from the comparison. Since OOCEA took over maintenance for all plazas in FY 1994, expanding the maintenance program considerably ($.78 million in FY 1993 compared to $ 4.2 million in FY 1994), maintenance costs are not comparable. Likewise, since the ETTM system was not implemented before FY 1995, all equipment and maintenance costs for this system must be excluded, as does equipment and maintenance costs concerning the equipment in place under FDOT operations.

It is also difficult to compare administrative office expenses and toll collection expenses. They are higher in 1997 than they were in 1994, but many of the expenses are those associated with the ETTM system. In addition, it seems as though some expenses charged by FTS are in the same category as those included in the overhead charge made by FDOT.

Operating costs were reimbursed by OOCEA for seven of the ten toll plazas that were managed by FDOT. What is easiest to compare are those operating costs under FDOT management with similar categories of costs under FTS management.

See Table 10.1 for a comparison of operating costs between FY 1994 and FY 1997. The amounts listed under ADM include management salaries for both FDOT and FTS, and management fees (profit) and mobilization costs for FTS. The FDOT overhead charge is included in the ADM amount for FY 1994. Included in the TCS amounts are all salaries of toll collectors, supervisors, and plaza managers. The amount of ADM for FY 1997 is proportionally divided among all plazas.

Using this rough comparison, the results indicate a savings of over $1 million annually for the OOCEA. In addition, it is assumed that FDOT would have comparable lower operating costs for the three plazas that they have been paying for throughout this time period.

Table 10.1
A Comparison of Operating Costs for Seven Plazas: FY 1994 to FY 1997

PLAZA		FY94	FY97	DIFFERENCE
Hiawassee	ADM	$178.8	133.4	- 45.4
	TCS	1078.0	503.5	-574.5
University	ADM	$146.6	212.6	+ 66.0
	TCS	978.2	831.0	-147.2
Dean	ADM	$144.7	133.8	- 9.9
	TCS	710.8	546.3	-164.5
Curry Ford	ADM	$108.6	111.8	+ 3.2
	TCS	523.4	449.3	- 74.1
Bee Line	ADM	$142.3	122.8	- 13.5
	TCS	743.1	590.8	-152.3
Boggy Creek	ADM	$108.2	201.6	+ 93.4
	TCS	842.3	645.0	-197.3
John Young	ADM	$74.7	223.6	+148.9
	TCS	779.2	786.6	+7.4
TOTAL OPERATING COST DIFFERENCE				-1059.8

Some costs are higher, including expense items as mentioned. OOCEA administrative costs are higher as well. Total administrative costs in FY 1994 were $1.308 million, compared with $1.790 million for FY 1996. Of these costs, twenty-two staff incurred salary and fringe benefit costs of $887,545 in FY 1994. Comparably, although not all were hired for a full twelve-month period, thirty-six staff cost $1.025 million in FY 1996, an increase of $137,455. Not all these additional staff have been hired to assist with the privatization of toll operations, though, as the ETTM system and other OCCEA efforts have required more staff.

Overall, there have been substantial increases in efficiency and lower operating costs because of privatizing toll operations. Lower administrative and toll collection labor costs have contributed the most to these savings.

Improved Customer Service

It is difficult to "parcel out" the degree to which customer service has improved because of privatization. Customer satisfaction is high today because of the technological improvements such as E-PASS and the ETTM system. The maintenance program referred to earlier has also made the drive on OOCEA tollways safer and more aesthetically pleasing.

To some extent, though, the increase in compliments and the decrease in complaints must be attributed to the incentive performance program, the mystery driver program, and the other incentive programs sponsored by FTS. The emphasis on interacting with the customer in a friendly, courteous manner is communicated to TSAs in training sessions by both FTS and OOCEA. The organizational culture of FTS, with its emphasis on quality service, also contributes to the service provided by the TSAs.

Sound Financial Accounting and Auditing System

Using the ETTM system, many reports have been created that allow auditors to much more easily identify problem areas such as TSA shortages (negative discrepancies) or overages. The ETTM system, 99.86 percent accurate, now provides a much more accurate identification of the amount of revenue that should be collected as vehicles travel through the toll lanes. These features make it much more difficult (or impossible) for TSAs who wish to consistently steal funds from the revenue collected. Coupled with termination policies that make it more easy to fire nonperformers, shortages are kept lower because the ETTM system acts as a deterrent.

TSAs, as they have become more familiar with the ETTM system and have been retrained as necessary, have greatly improved their performance. One measure that reflects the effectiveness of the accounting–auditing system as well as of overall operations is the amount paid to the OOCEA by FTS as a result of all TSA shortages over $10 on any given day. For January to November 1996, the total returned was $19,679.83. Although this amount is only a little more than .01 percent of the total revenue collected, it does reflect a number of separate incidents of shortages that over time could be lessened.

Increased Managerial Flexibility

There are a number of ways in which the managerial flexibility of the OOCEA has been increased. Most significantly, a consistent factor in all of the OOCEA–FTS partnership induced changes is the speed and ease at which these changes have been implemented. Although it is impossible to fully assess the nature of a continued OOCEA–FDOT partnership, the personnel, budgetary, and political constraints faced by FDOT would have made it very difficult—if not impossible—for it to have responded as quickly.

The incentive performance program is an example of this increased flexibility. Both OOCEA and FTS agreed to a formula by which the savings from reduced staffing would be distributed. FTS devised a performance evaluation system which was then used to distribute the additional funds. The IPP was outlined in an addendum to the original contract (signed in February 1995), that was approved by the OOCEA board in July 1995. The first bonuses were distributed in January–February 1996.

FDOT would have potentially faced legislative, union, and personnel regulative hurdles in implementing such a plan. It may have been difficult to provide incentive dollars to only some of its employees (i.e., those working on the OOCEA), and not to those working on the Florida Turnpike or in other parts of the state. The Florida Legislature may have had to approve such an incentive plan. If so, it may have been difficult to get its approval by the end of the 1995 legislative session, thereby delaying implementation of the IPP.

More significantly, OOCEA has been able to easily add full-time personnel to the FTS toll collector staff as changing operations needs and policies have required. As reflected in the change orders to the original contract in October 1995, additional staffing was approved for the Bee Line Main plaza and for the ramp locations at the Hiawassee plaza. In October 1996, the higher priority given to dealing with the VES issue has resulted in the hiring of additional full-time and part-time VES processing personnel.

If approved positions and accompanying approved salary rate were not already in FDOT's budget, it would find it difficult to quickly add full-time positions in response to a request from OOCEA. Given that the state political climate favors reducing the number of state employees, it may also have been difficult for FDOT to add significant numbers of employees for this reason as well.

RFP Creation and the Responses to the RFP

The creation of the RFP and the consideration of responses to it are two stages that are closely intertwined. If the RFP is written clearly, and its goals are communicated well to potential bidders, then the responses are likely to be better written, and rated higher, and the public agency will feel much more confident about transferring the service to the private vendor.

The OOCEA achieved its goal of greater operating efficiencies with the staffing and pricing plan proposed by FTS. With fewer management and support staff than bid by the other two bidders, plus significantly lower toll collection labor costs because no assistant plaza manager positions appeared in the bid, FTS was able to bid the lowest cost. FTS received the highest score on the technical portion of the evaluation as well, primarily because it presented a better organizational and staffing plan, with greater amounts of toll operations experience among its proposed management personnel.

The evaluation of the technical proposals, however, indicated that all three bidders were more than qualified to provide effective toll operations. Knowing that there are qualified competitors for FTS both provides an incentive for FTS to maintain a high level of service and a degree of confidence for OOCEA to know that if FTS does not perform acceptably, alternative vendors could bid on a new RFP.

TRANSITION

To assess this stage, the fate of the public employees must first be considered. The RFP gave all FDOT toll collection employees the "right of first refusal." All parties were fortunate that FDOT was able to broaden the field of options for all OCCEA system toll employees by including positions at nearby non-OOCEA plaza and turnpike locations as part of their choices. The long-term FDOT employees could remain in state employ by exercising their "bumping rights" and switching to non-OOCEA system plazas. The vast majority of those with over five years experience chose to make that change.

As a result, plaza manager and supervisory positions were available as promotional opportunities for toll collectors. Many of them accepted the promotion, and all FTS supervisory–managerial personnel were filled by former FDOT employees. Toll collectors who retained the same position, in many cases at the same plaza, may have received a lower starting wage, as all TSAs began at $6.30 per hour, but lower medical insurance costs meant an increase in the take-home pay for these employees.

Furthermore, since the turnover rate among TSAs has remained steady at less than 2 percent per month, there has been no exodus among FTS personnel indicating low morale or general unhappiness with either wages or working conditions. There are many indications that the opposite condition exists, as there are signs of a developing FTS organizational culture that realistically reflects a commitment to quality service.

CONTRACT MANAGEMENT

Both OOCEA and FTS have grown together in this public–private partnership, experiencing growing pains in the process, as both learned what needed to be done. The responsiveness of FTS has been commendable, as transitional issues of too high TSA shortages and inadequate lane staffing have been corrected. Customer satisfaction has probably never been higher, thanks in large part to the everyday management skills and commitment of FTS.

The contract management issues faced by both OOCEA and FTS have been made easier by the introduction of the ETTM and AVI technology. The auditing function is greatly facilitated by the ETTM system, easing efforts in this area. On the other hand, additional challenges have been faced, as violations in the E-PASS lanes have grown, and the ETTM system still needs adjustment.

The technological advances have thus caused new management and operations problems that had to be solved. Many of these are still creating ongoing issues, as the needed software and hardware changes are not forthcoming as quickly as many would prefer. It is not that there is deliberate resistance to solving these problems. It is that time and resources must often be spent solving higher priority problems, leaving others to wait for a technological fix. In the meantime, contract management must try to resolve issues through training, communication among affected parties, and exchanges at the quality review meetings that often must seem like patches on problems that really require longer term, more technologically based solutions.

For its part, OOCEA has exercised excellent leadership in coordinating and implementing the technological advances simultaneously with the privatization efforts, continuing to do so throughout the transition period and into contract management. It has been innovative, as shown by the incentive performance program. Now that privatization has given it the managerial flexibility to quickly meet a problem, such as that faced by increasing violations, OOCEA has shown resolve in changing priorities and applying resources to solve problems.

If the contract management stage and the future of the private–public partnership is to continue its success, both OOCEA and FTS must continue to be willing to exchange new ideas, consider the other's viewpoint, and resolve any differences, keeping the goals of the toll operations in mind. This effort will require continued trust and mutual respect by both parties. Without it, the partnership risks becoming stagnant, making contract management much more difficult, as coming change and innovation will face more difficult implementation issues.

FUTURE DIRECTIONS: IMPROVING TOLL OPERATIONS AND THE OOCEA–FTS PARTNERSHIP

By all measures, the privatization of toll operations has been a success. Revenue continues to be collected at an increasing amount, E-PASS continues to grow, and customer service is never better. Given this evidence of an effective and growing public–private partnership, the following are ideas that reflect both current issues and future efforts that could "fine tune" toll operations.

Customer Satisfaction Surveys

Additional data concerning customer satisfaction could be collected using mail and/or telephone surveys of both toll road users and nonusers. Collected on a consistent basis, perhaps every six months, this data could add greatly to contract management efforts by identifying areas of dissatisfaction. More important, it could provide additional evidence of high quality performance that could be shared with the Central Florida public and FTS employees and could strengthen the OOCEA–FTS partnership.

Additional Measures of Performance and Accompanying Performance Standards

The ETTM system provides a wealth of easily obtainable data that could be used in a variety of ways to more objectively track performance. In the process of doing so, performance standards could be set that could aid in contract management efforts and could help to set nationwide industry standards.

For example, although all agree that the performance of TSAs has greatly improved since the first plazas were transitioned in April 1995, additional measures could more validly document this conclusion. The percentage of TSAs who are more than $3 (or $5 or $10) short on a daily basis could be identified and monitored over time. This information could be collected monthly and/or by plaza. Once collected, a reasonable standard could be established, both for full-time and part-time TSAs. Similarly, the ratio of negative discrepancies to revenue collected could add additional relevant information.

Cost–Benefit Analyses

There are a number of policy–operational issues that could benefit from efficiency or cost–benefit analyses. Adding more VES staff to process warning letters and UTCs will lower the violation rate. An optimal violation rate to cost ratio could be identified. Similarly, the issue of identifying the optimal full-time–part-time TSA ratio deserves additional study, such as what turnover rate for both full-time and part-time TSAs is acceptable, given the measures of performance used as part of the IPP as well as those generated by the ETTM. A similar study could be made of the auditing function, both for FTS and OOCEA. For all of these issues, the size and cost (salaries and benefits) of the staff plus expenses needs to be compared to the benefits accrued.

There are many instances in which efforts to improve customer service cost more or efforts to improve efficiency may negatively impact customer service. For example, in the area of staffing, more analysis could be made of the impact of closing manned lanes more frequently during different times within a twenty-four-hour period.

Increased–Improved Incentives

The incentive performance program has contributed significantly to improved TSA performance. It needs to be monitored over a long-term basis to ensure that the incentives provided continue to improve or maintain high-quality performance. Reduced staffing will continue to be the major contributor of funds to the program unless suggestions to increase the efficiency of other aspects of operations are forthcoming.

Nonfinancial (or low cost) incentive programs need to be developed or expanded. Group incentives, such as those that are plaza based, should be implemented. Overall, efforts to maintain TSA motivation toward high performance need to be continuous, with different approaches taken over time. Incentives that may be effective at one time may not work as well at a later period.

CONCLUSION: FUTURE CONSIDERATIONS

The healthy public–private partnership that currently exists between OOCEA and FTS must be maintained. As long as there is a willingness to engage in a dialogue to solve problems, resolve issues, and make improvements, then the partnership will continue to be successful.

As additional technological improvements change the nature of toll operations, along with the expansion of the OOCEA system to include the Western Beltway, and potential greater consideration of traffic management issues, the partnership will face additional challenges. This study is only an initial look at a continuing, evolving partnership, whose nature can grow and mature in order to keep pace with the continuing change that faces the OOCEA.

GLOSSARY

Automated Vehicle Identification System (AVI)

This system allows vehicles to travel through toll plazas without stopping to pay tolls. It identifies the vehicle through the use of a radio transponder that sends a signal from the vehicle to a central receiver that automatically deducts the cost of the toll from a predetermined account. The OOCEA has named its system E-PASS.

Joseph Berenis

Deputy Executive Director of the OOCEA. He was Acting Executive Director from August 1991 to May 1992.

Thomas Boyd

Comptroller of the Florida Department of Transportation.

Milissa Burger

Regional Toll Operations Manager, Florida Department of Transportation.

Philip Burkhard

A consultant who helped write both toll operations privatization RFPs.

Greg Dailer

Chief Finance Officer of the OOCEA.

Electronic Toll Collection and Traffic Management System (ETTM)

This system is fully computerized. It was built for the OOCEA by SAIC/Syntonic. It was installed prior to the privatization of toll operations.

Donald Erwin

General Engineering Consultant Contract Administrator. He is employed by PBS&J.

Jorge Figueredo

Director of Operations of the OOCEA since August 1996.

Florida Toll Services

A Morrison Knudsen/Parsons Brinckerhoff joint venture. This company was awarded the OOCEA toll operations privatization contract.

Charles Gilliard

Operations Manager for OOCEA from August 1992 to January 1993. Prior to this position, he was Regional Toll Operations Manager for the Florida Department of Transportation.

D. W. "Bill" Gwynn

OOCEA Executive Director until August 1991.

Robert Harrell

Chairman of the OOCEA Board of Directors from October 1990 until January 1992.

Robert Hawkins

President of RCH and Associates, the consulting company that assisted the OOCEA in writing the first toll operations privatization RFP.

Robert Mandell

Chairman of the OOCEA Board of Directors from January through December 1992.

William McKelvey

Director of Construction for OOCEA.

Norrell Temporary Services

The firm that provided temporary toll collectors on the Southern Connector toll plazas.

Orlando–Orange County Expressway Authority (OOCEA)

Founded in 1963, it is an agency of the state of Florida governed by a five-member board. Three members are appointed by the governor. The other two members are the Chairman of the Orange County Commission and the District Five Secretary of the Florida Department of Transportation.

David Pope

Operations Manager of the OOCEA from October 1993 to May 1996.

Post, Buckley, Schuh and Jernigan

An engineering consulting firm that provides services to the OOCEA.

Project 256

The number assigned to the ETTM–AVI project, awarded to SAIC/Syntonic.

Project 266

The number assigned to the toll operations privatization contract, awarded to Florida Toll Services.

RCH and Associates

A consulting company that assisted the OOCEA in authoring the first toll operations privatization RFP.

A. Wayne Rich

Chairman (1999) of the OOCEA Board. His term began in December 1992.

Science Applications International Corporation (SAIC)

In conjunction with Syntonic, SAIC was awarded the contract to devise the software and hardware that comprise the ETTM and AVI systems for the OOCEA.

The Southern Connector

Name for the newest toll plazas that are part of the OOCEA system. These were completed by July 1993.

Christine Speer

Director of the Office of Toll Operations, Florida Department of Transportation.

Ben Watts

Secretary of the Florida Department of Transportation.

Dr. Harold Worrall

Executive Director of the OOCEA since May 1992. Prior to accepting this position, he was an Assistant Secretary in the Florida Department of Transportation.

BIBLIOGRAPHY

BOOKS, MONOGRAPHS, AND GOVERNMENT PUBLICATIONS

Allen, Joan W., Keon S. Chi, Kevin M. Devlin, Mark Fall, Harry P. Hatry, and Wayne Masterman. 1989. *The Private Sector in State Service Delivery: Examples of Innovative Practices*. Washington, DC: Council of State Governments, Urban Institute Press.

Ammons, David N. 1991. *Administrative Analysis for Local Government: Practical Application of Selected Techniques*. Athens, GA: Carl Vinson Institute of Government, University of Georgia.

Bowman, Gary, Simon Hakim, and Paul Seidenstat, editors. 1992. *Privatizing the United States Justice System*. Jefferson, NC: MacFarland.

————. 1994. *Privatizing Correctional Institutions*. New Brunswick, NJ: Transactional Publishers.

Brooks, Harvey, Lance Liebman, and Corinne S. Schelling, editors. 1984. *Public–Private Partnership: New Opportunities for Meeting Social Needs*. Cambridge, MA: Ballinger.

Butler, Stuart M. 1985. *Privatizing Federal Spending*. New York: Universe Books.

Carroll, Barry J., Ralph W. Conant, and Thomas A. Easton. 1987. *Private Means Public Ends: Private Business in Social Service Delivery*. Westport, CT: Praeger.

Chandler, Timothy David. 1991. *Public Sector Unions and the Privatization of Municipal Services*. Champaign: University of Illinois at Urbana–Champaign Press.

Cibinic, John, Jr., and Ralph C. Nash, Jr. 1986. *Formation of Government Contracts.* Washington, DC: George Washington University.

Cohen, Steven, and William Eimicke. 1998. *Tools for Innovators: Creative Strategies for Managing Public Sector Organizations.* San Francisco: Jossey-Bass.

Colman, William G. 1989. *State and Local Government and Public–Private Partnerships.* Westport, CT: Greenwood Press.

Davis, Perry, editor. 1986. *Public–Private Partnerships: Improving Urban Life.* New York: Academy of Political Science.

Donahue, John D. 1989. *The Privatization Decision.* New York: Basic Books.

Downs, Anthony. 1967. *Inside Bureaucracy.* Boston: Little, Brown.

Farr, Cheryl A. 1989. *Service Delivery in the 90's: Alternative Approaches for Local Governments.* Washington, DC: International City Management Association.

Florida Toll Services. 1994. *Proposal to Orlando–Orange County Expressway Authority for Toll Facility Operations and Management Services, Part I Technical Proposal, Contract 266.* Orlando, FL: Author.

Fosler, R. Scott, and Renee A. Berger, editors. 1982. *Public–Private Partnership in American Cities: Seven Case Studies.* Lexington, MA: D. C. Heath.

Garvey, Gerald. 1992. *Facing the Bureaucracy.* Boston: Houghton Mifflin.

Gomez-Ibanez, Jose A., and John R. Meyer. 1993. *Going Private: The International Experience with Transportation Privatization.* Washington, DC: The Brookings Institution.

Hakim, Simon, Paul Seidenstat, and Gary W. Bowman, editors. 1994. *Privatizing Education and Educational Choice: Concepts, Plans, and Experiences.* Westport, CT: Praeger.

———. 1996. *Privatizing Transportation Systems.* Westport, CT: Praeger.

Hanrahan, John D. 1983. *Government by Contract.* New York: W. W. Norton.

Harney, Donald F. 1992. *Service Contracting: A Local Government Guide.* Washington, DC: International City Management Association.

Heilman, John G., and Gerald W. Johnson. 1992. *The Politics and Economics of Privatization: The Case of Wastewater Treatment.* Tuscaloosa: University of Alabama Press.

Hilke, John C. 1992. *Competition in Government-Financed Services.* Westport, CT: Quorum Books.

Hirschman, Albert O. 1982. *Shifting Involvements: Private Interest and Public Action.* Princeton, NJ: Princeton University Press.

Horn, Murray J. 1995. *The Political Economy of Public Administration: Institutional Choice in the Public Sector.* New York: Cambridge University Press.

Hula, Richard C., editor. 1988. *Market Based Public Policy.* New York: St. Martin's Press.

Kamerman, Sheila B., and Alfred J. Kahn. 1989. *Privatization and the Welfare State.* Princeton, NJ: Princeton University Press.

Kelley, Joseph T. 1984. *Costing Government Services: A Guide for Decision Making.* Chicago: Government Finance Officers Association of the United States and Canada.

Kelman, Steven. 1990. *Procurement and Public Management: The Fear of Discretion and the Quality of Government Performance.* Washington, DC: American Enterprise Institute.

Kemp, Roger L., editor. 1991. *Privatization: The Provision of Public Services by the Public Sector.* Jefferson, NC: McFarland.

Kent, Calvin A. 1987. *Entrepreneurship and the Privatizing of Government.* Westport, CT: Greenwood Press.

Kettl, Donald F. 1988. *Government by Proxy: (Mis?) Managing Federal Programs.* Washington, DC: Congressional Quarterly.

———. 1993. *Sharing Power: Public Governance and Private Markets.* Washington, DC: The Brookings Institution.

Kettner, Peter M., and Lawrence L. Martin. 1987. *Purchase of Service Contracting.* Beverly Hills, CA: Sage.

Knowlton, Winthrop, and Richard Zeckhauser, editors. 1986. *American Society: Public and Private Responsibilities.* Cambridge, MA: Ballinger.

Lavery, Kevin. 1999. *Smart Contracting for Local Government Services: Processes and Experiences.* Westport, CT: Praeger.

Lawther, Wendell, Kathryn Denhardt, Andrew Judd, Jay Jurie, and Ellen Rosell. 1993. *Privatization of Toll Collections: Feasibility Study.* Orlando: University of Central Florida.

Linden, Russell M. 1994. *Seamless Government: A Practical Guide to Re-Engineering in the Public Sector.* San Francisco: Jossey-Bass.

Linowes, David F. 1988. *Privatization: Toward More Effective Government.* Urbana: University of Illinois Press.

MacManus, Susan A. 1992. *Doing Business with Government.* New York: Paragon House.

Marlin, John Tepper, editor. 1984. *Contracting Municipal Services: A Guide for Purchase from the Private Sector.* New York: John Wiley and Sons.

Moore, Mark H. 1995. *Creating Public Value: Strategic Management in Government.* Cambridge: Harvard University Press.

National Commission for Employment Policy. 1988. *Privatization and Public Employees: The Impact of City and County Contracting out on Government Workers.* Washington DC: U.S. Government Printing Office.

National Institute of Governmental Purchasing. 1986. *General Public Purchasing.* Falls Church, VA: The Institute.

O'Leary, J., and W. D. Eggers. 1993. *Privatization and Public Employees: Guidelines for Fair Treatment.* Los Angeles: Reason Foundation.

O'Looney, John A. 1998. *Outsourcing State and Local Government Services: Decision-Making Strategies and Management Methods.* Westport, CT: Quorum Books.

Orlando–Orange County Expressway Authority. 1994. *Request for Proposal—Toll Operation, Management and Maintenance Services for Holland East–West Expressway, Central Florida Greeneway, and Bee Line Expressway Mainline Toll Plazas and All Associated Ramp Toll Plazas—Project 266.* Orlando, FL: Author.

Osborne, David, and Peter Plastrik. 1997. *Banishing Bureaucracy: The Five Strategies for Reinventing Government.* Reading, MA: Addison-Wesley.

Perrow, Charles. 1986. *Complex Organizations: A Critical Essay.* New York: Random House.

Post, Buckley, Schuh & Jernigan, Inc., in association with Telos Consulting Services, Inc. 1994. *Evaluation Guidelines and Scoring Forms for Qualification Statements and Technical Proposals, Orlando–Orange County Expressway*

Authority, Project 266, Toll Facility Operations and Management Services. Orlando, FL: Author.

President's Commission on Privatization. 1988. *Privatization: Toward More Effective Government.* Washington, DC: U.S. Government Printing Office.

Pratt, John W., and Richard J. Zeckhauser, editors. 1991. *Principals and Agents: The Structure of Business.* Boston: Harvard Business School Press.

Reason Foundation. 1992. *Privatization* Los Angeles: Reason Foundation.

Rehfuss, John A. 1989. *Contracting Out in Government: A Guide to Working with Outside Contractors to Supply Public Services.* San Francisco: Jossey-Bass.

Ross, Randy L. 1988. *Government and the Private Sector: Who Should Do What?* New York: Crane Russak.

Salamon, Lester M., editor. 1989. *Beyond Privatization: The Tools of Government Action.* Washington, DC: Urban Institute Press.

Savas, E. S. 1987. *Privatization: The Key to Better Government.* Chatham, NJ: Chatham House.

Seidenstat, Paul, editor. 1999. *Contracting Out Government Services.* Westport, CT: Praeger.

Short, John. 1987. *The Contract Cookbook for Purchase of Services.* Lexington, KY: Council of State Governments.

Smith, Steven Rathgeb, and Michael Lipsky. 1993. *NonProfits for Hire: The Welfare State in the Age of Contracting.* Cambridge: Harvard University Press.

Stein, Robert. 1990. *Urban Alternatives: Public and Private Markets in the Provision of Local Services.* Pittsburgh: University of Pittsburgh Press.

Tompkins, Jonathan. 1995. *Human Resource Management in Government.* New York: HarperCollins.

United Infrastructure Company. 1994. *Part I Technical Proposal RFP-266 Orlando–Orange County Expressway Authority.* Chicago: Author.

U.S. General Accounting Office. 1985. *Comparisons of Federal and Private Sector Pay and Benefits* (September). Washington, DC: U.S. General Accounting Office.

URS Consultants, Inc. 1994. *Contract 266, Toll Facility Operations and Management Services for the Orlando–Orange County Expressway Authority, September 23, 1994.* Tallahassee, FL: Author.

Weicher, John C. 1988. *Private Innovations in Public Transit.* Washington, DC: American Enterprise Institute for Public Policy Research.

DISSERTATIONS

Aronson, David L. 1992. *Examining Contracting Processes: Implications for Municipal Government.* Wayne State University, Detroit.

Carver, Robert Howard. 1988. *Privatization and Organizational Choice: Chaos and Calculation.* University of Michigan, Ann Arbor.

Donahue, John David. 1987. *Private Agents, Public Acts: The Architecture of Accountability.* Harvard University, Cambridge, Massachusetts.

Jackson, Cynthia Yvonne. 1994. *Production and Financing Choices for Municipal Services: Contracting and Franchising.* University of Southern California, Los Angeles.

Korosec, Ronnie Patricia La Course. 1994. *Privatization of Local Governments: Contracting Out as a Service Delivery Option.* State University of New York at Binghamton.

Marrow, Donald B., Jr. 1994. *Three Essays on Environmental Policy and Institutions.* Massachusetts Institute of Technology, Cambridge, Massachusetts.

Shiang, Jing. 1995. *Successful Privatization: Contractual Policies and Performance of Public Service Contractors.* Ohio State University, Columbus.

Walker, John Spencer. 1994. *A Financial Agency Analysis of Privatization: Managerial Incentives and Financial Contracting.* Lehigh University, Bethlehem, Pennsylvania.

JOURNAL ARTICLES AND BOOK CHAPTERS

Ammons, David N., and Debra J. Hill. 1995. "The Viability of Public–Private Competition as a Long-Term Service Delivery Strategy." *Public Productivity and Management Review* 19, no. 1 (September): 12–24.

Avio, Kenneth L. 1993. "Remuneration Regimes for Private Prisons." *International Review of Law and Economics* 13: 35–45.

Baden, John, and Laura Rosen. 1983. "The Environmental Justification." *Environment* 25, no. 8 (October): 7, 38–43.

Ban, Carolyn. 1998. "The Changing Role of the Personnel Office." In *Handbook of Human Resource Management in Government,* ed. Stephen E. Condrey. San Francisco: Jossey-Bass.

Barnekov, Timothy K., and Jeffrey A. Raffel. 1990. "Public Management of Privatization." *Public Productivity and Management Review* 14 (Winter): 135–152.

Barnes, John A. 1986. "The Failure Of Privatization." *National Review* 38 (July 18): 38–40, 61.

Bean, Richard C. 1988. "Practical Considerations In ADP Acquisition." *The Air Force Law Review* 29 (Fall): 265–276.

Becker, Fred W., Gail Silverstein, and Lee Chayin. 1995. "Public Employee Job Security and Benefits: A Barrier to Mental Health Services." *Public Productivity and Management Review* 19 (September): 25–33.

Behn, Robert D. 1995. "The Benefits of the Private Sector." *Governing* 8 (June): 103.

Bellush, Sandra Mokuvos. 1985. "Private Choices." *American City and County* 100, no. 10 (October): 62–65.

Bennett, James T., and Thomas J. DiLorenzo. 1983. "Public Employee Unions and the Privatization of 'Public' Services." *Journal of Labor Research* 4, no. 1 (Winter): 33–45.

Bennett, James T., and Manuel H. Johnson. 1980. "Tax Reduction without Sacrifice: Private-Sector Production of Public Services." *Public Finance Quarterly* 8 (October): 363–396.

Bennett, Julie. 1992. "Private Prison Industry Booms in the South." *City and State* 9 (September 7): GM-4, GM-8.

Benson, Robert. 1985. "Privatizing Public Services." *Congressional Quarterly, Editorial Research Reports* 2, no. 4 (July 26): 559–576.

Berenyi, Eileen Brettler, and Barbara J. Stevens. 1988. "Does Privatization Work? A Study of the Delivery of Eight Local Services." *State and Local Government Review* 20 (Winter): 11–20.

Bernard, Paul. 1989. "Managing Vendor Performance." *Production and Inventory Management Journal* 30, no. 1 (First Quarter): 1–7.

Birnbaum, Owen. 1956. "Government Contracts: The Role of the Comptroller General." *American Bar Association Journal* 42 (May): 433–436.

Bovbjerg, Randell R., Philip J. Held, and Mark V. Pauly. 1987. "Privatization and Bidding in the Health-Care Sector." *Journal of Policy Analysis and Management* 6, no. 4: 648–666.

Brotman, Andrew. 1992. "Privatization of Mental Health Services: The Massachusetts Experiment." *Journal of Health, Politics, Policy, and Law* 17 (Fall): 540–551.

Brudney, Jeffrey L. 1986. "Coproduction and Local Governments: Exploring Other Options for Privatization." *Public Management* 68, no. 12 (December): 11–13.

Bruggink, Thomas H. 1982. "Public versus Regulated Private Enterprise in the Municipal Water Industry: A Comparison of Operating Costs." *Quarterly Review of Economics and Business* 22, no. 1 (Spring): 111–125.

Callison, Charles H. 1983. "The Fallacies of Privatization." *Environment* 25, no. 8 (October): 7, 17–20, 37.

Campbell, A. K. 1986. "Private Delivery of Public Services: Sorting Out the Policy and Management Issues." *Public Management* 68, no. 12 (December): 3–5.

Capell, Kerry. 1995. "Paying for Public Works." *Governing* 8 (August): 63–64.

Carver, Robert H. 1989. "Examining the Premises of Contracting Out." *Public Productivity and Management Review* 13 (Fall): 27–40.

Chandler, Ralph Clark. 1986. "The Myth of Private Sector Superiority in Personnel Administration." *Policy Studies Review* 5, no. 3 (February): 643–653.

Chandler, Timothy, and Peter Feuille. 1991. "Municipal Unions and Privatization." *Public Administration Review* 51, no. 1 (January–February): 15–22.

Chang, Cyril F., and Howard P. Tuckman. 1996. "The Goods Produced by Nonprofit Organizations." *Public Finance Quarterly* 24, no. 1 (January): 25–43.

Chang, Stanley Y., and Roberta Ann Jones. 1992. "Approaches to Privatization: Established Models and a U.S. Innovation." *Government Finance Review* 8 (August): 17–21.

Chi, Keon S. 1993. "Privatization." *State Trends and Forecasts* 2, no. 2 (November): 1–39.

———. 1998. "State Civil Service Systems." In *Handbook of Human Resource Management in Government*, ed. Stephen Condrey. San Francisco: Jossey-Bass.

Coe, Charles K., and Elizabeth O'Sullivan. 1993. "Accounting for the Hidden Costs: A National Study of Internal Service Funds and Other Indirect Costing Methods in Municipal Governments." *Public Administration Review* 53 (January–February): 59–64.

Cole, Ed. 1993. "Partnering: A Quality Model for Contract Relations." *The Public Manager/The New Bureaucrat* 22 (Summer): 39–42.

Corbin, Lisa. 1995. "Culture of Fear." *Government Executive* 27 (September): 40–45.

Daniels, Alex. 1995. "Making a Connection Between Day Care and Commuting." *Governing* 8 (August): 60.

David, Irwin T. 1988. "Privatization in America." In *The Municipal Year Book*. Washington, DC: International City Management Association, 43–55.

DeHoog, Ruth Hoodland. 1985. "Human Service Contracting: Environmental Behavioral, and Organizational Conditions." *Administration and Society* 16 (February): 427–454.

———. 1990. "Competition, Negotiation, or Cooperation: Three Models for Service Contracting." *Administration and Society* 22, no. 3 (November): 317–340.

Denhardt, Kathryn, J. Raffel, E. Jacobson, M. Manlove, D. Auger, and J. Lewis. 1995. "Employee Issues in Privatization." *MIS Report* 27, no. 10 (October).

Dilger, Robert Jay, Randolph R. Moffett, and Linda Struyk. 1997. "Privatization of Municipal Services in America's Largest Population Cities." *Public Administration Review* 57, no. 1 (January–February): 21–26.

Dixon, Richard B. 1992. "Reducing Service Delivery Costs through Public/Private Partnerships." *Government Finance Review* 8, no. 3 (June): 31–33.

Ferris, James M. 1986. "The Decision to Contract Out: An Empirical Analysis." *Urban Affairs Quarterly* 22 (December): 289–311.

Ferris, James M., and Elizabeth Graddy. 1991. "Production Costs, Transaction Costs, and Local Government Contractor Choice." *Economic Inquiry* 29, no. 3 (July): 541–554.

Ferris, James M., and E. Graddy. 1986. "Contracting Out: For What? With Whom?" *Public Administration Review* 46 (July–August): 332–344.

Fitch, Lyle C. 1988. "The Rocky Road to Privatization." *The American Journal of Economics and Sociology* 47 (January): 1–14.

Fitzgerald, M. R. 1986. "The Promise and Performance of Privatization: The Knoxville Experience." *Policy Studies Review* 5, no. 3: 606–613.

Flanagan, Jim, and Susan Perking. 1995. "Public Private Competition in the City of Phoenix, Arizona." *Government Finance Review* 11, no. 3 (June): 7–12.

Gaebler, Ted. 1992. "Reinventing Government Offers Officials Hope." *City and State* 5 (July): 27.

Globerman, Steven, and Adrian R. Vining. 1996. "A Framework for Evaluating the Government Contracting Out Decision with an Application to Information Technology." *Public Administration Review* 56, no. 6 (November–December): 577–586.

Goodman, John B., and Gary W. Loverman. 1991. "Does Privatization Serve the Public Interest?" *Harvard Business Review* 69 (November–December): 26–38.

Gormley, William T., Jr. 1994. "Privatization Revisited." *Policy Studies Review* 13, no. 3–4 (Autumn–Winter): 215–234.

Greene, Jeffrey D. 1996. "How Much Privatization? A Research Note Examining the Use of Privatization by Cities in 1982 and 1992." *Policy Studies Journal* 24, no. 4: 632–639.

Gurwitt, Rob. 1994. "Entrepreneurial Government: The Morning After." *Governing* 7, no. 8 (May): 34–40.

Guzek, Robert S. 1992. "Privatization Ahead." *City and State* 9 (September 7): 7.

Hames, Peter. 1984. "When Public Services Go Private: There's More Than One Option." *National Civic Review* 73 (June): 278–282.

Harney, Donald F. 1986. "A Purchasing Agent's View of Privatization." *Public Management* 68, no. 12 (December): 16–18.

Hass, Nancy. 1993. "Philadelphia Freedom: How Privatization Has Worked Wonders in the City of Brotherly Love and Beyond." *Financial World* 162, no. 16 (August 3): 36–37.

Hebdon, R. 1995. "Contracting Out in New York State: The Story the Lauder Report Chose Not to Tell." *Labor Studies Journal* 20, no. 1 (Spring): 3–29.

Henderson, André. 1994. "Blotting Out the Red Ink: For Most States, the Fiscal Picture Is Suddenly Looking Brighter. But How Long Will It Last?" *Governing* 7 (August): 37–44.

Hiller, John R., and Robert D. Tollison. 1978. "Incentive Versus Cost-Plus Contracts in Defense Procurement." *The Journal of Industrial Economics* 26 (March): 239–248.

Hirsch, Werner Z. 1989. "The Economics of Contracting Out: The Labor Cost Fallacy." *Labor Law Journal* 40 (August): 536–542.

———. 1995. "Factors Important in Local Governments' Privatization Decisions." *Urban Affairs Review* 31, no. 2 (November): 226–243.

Hoffman, Donald B. 1995. "Privatization: Signing Away the Whole Public Works Department." *Financing Local Government* 7, no. 14 (January 15): 3.

Honig, Bill. 1990–1991. "Why Privatizing Public Education Is a Bad Idea." *The Brookings Review* 9, no. 1 (Winter): 15–16.

Howlett, Michael, and M. Ramesh. 1993. "Patterns of Policy Instrument Choice: Policy Styles, Policy Learning and the Privatization Experience." *Policy Studies Review* 12, no. 1–2 (Spring–Summer): 3–24.

Hula, Richard C. 1993. "The State Reassessed: The Privatization of Local Politics." In *The New Localism: Comparative Urban Politics in a Global Era*, ed. Edward G. Goetz and Susan E. Clarke. Newbury Park, CA: Sage.

Jensen, Michael. 1989. "Eclipse of the Public Corporation." *Harvard Business Review* 67, no. 5 (September–October): 61–74.

Jensen, Ronald W. 1989. "New Wave Privatization." *Privatization Review* 4 (Spring): 24–39.

Kellam, Susan. 1995. "Reinventing Government." *CQ Researcher* 5, no. 7 (February 17): 145–168.

King, Ralph. 1990. "We Have to Keep this Growth Machine Going." *Forbes Magazine* 145, no. 7 (April 2): 46–48.

Kostro, Charles. 1994. "The Road to Cheaper Services." *American City and County* 109, no. 9 (August): 16.

Lavery, Kevin. 1995. "The English Contracting Revolution." *Public Management* 77 (August): 20–24.

Lemov, Penelope. 1995. "The Tax Revolt That Wasn't." *Governing* 8 (January): 22–23.

Linsley, Clyde. 1995. "Government Inc." *Government Executive* 27, no. 2 (February): 38–44.

Liwer, Robert. 1993. "Privatization Not Always Solution." *City and State* 10 (September 13): 8.

Lyons, William, and Michael R. Fitzgerald. 1986. "The City as a Purchasing Agent: Privatization and the Urban Polity in America." In *Research in Urban Policy*, ed. Terry N. Clark. Greenwich, CT: JAI Press.

Mahtesian, Charles. 1994a. "The Precarious Politics of Privatizing Schools." *Governing* 7 (June): 46–51.

———. 1994b. "Taking Chicago Private." *Governing* 7 (April): 26–31.

Makar, Scott D. 1994. "Local Government, Privatization and Antitrust Immunity." *The Florida Bar Journal* 68, no. 4 (April): 38–46.

Manchester, Lydia D. 1986. "Delivering Services with Vouchers: An Option Worth Considering." *Public Management* 68, no. 12: 23–24.

Mardikes, George M., Pamela Cone, and Julie Van Horn. 1986. "Governmental Leasing: A Fifty State Survey of Legislation and Case Law." *The Urban Lawyer* 18, no. 1: 1–187.

Martin, Lawrence L. 1993a. "Evaluating Service Contracting." *MIS Report* 25, no. 3 (March): 1–14.

———. 1993b. "Bidding on Service Delivery: Public–Private Competition," *MIS Report* 25, no. 11 (November): 1–12.

McGroarty, Daniel. 1994. "School Choice Slandered." *The Public Interest* 117 (Fall): 94–111.

McTague, Jim. 1995. "So Long, Projects?" *Barron's* 75 (February 6): 17–18.

Miranda, Rowan, and Karlyn Andersen. 1994. "Alternative Service Delivery in Local Government, 1982–1992." In *Municipal Yearbook*. Washington, DC: International City Management Association, 26–35.

Moe, Ronald C. 1987. "Exploring the Limits of Privatization." *Public Administration Review* 47, no. 6 (November–December): 457–465.

Morgan, David R., and Robert E. England. 1988. "The Two Faces of Privatization." *Public Administration Review* 48, no. 6 (November–December): 979–987.

Murin, William J. 1985. "Contracting as a Method of Enhancing Equity in the Delivery of Local Government Services." *Journal of Urban Affairs* 7 (Spring): 1–10.

Perlman, Ellen. 1992. "Public–Private Competition Win–Win for Governments." *City and State* 9 (June 1): GM5.

Perry, James L., and T. T. Babitsky. 1986. "Comparative Performance in Urban Bus Transit: Assessing Privatization Strategies." *Public Administration Review* 46, no. 1 (January–February): 57–66.

Poole, Robert W., Jr., and Philip E. Fixler, Jr. 1987. "Privatization of Public-Sector Services in Practice: Experience and Potential." *Journal of Policy Analysis and Management* 6, no. 4: 612–625.

Posner, Bruce G., and Lawrence R. Rothstein. 1994. "Reinventing the Business of Government: An Interview with Change Catalyst David Osborne." *Harvard Business Review* 72 (May–June): 133–143.

Rangazas, Peter. 1995. "Vouchers in a Community Choice Model with Zoning." *The Quarterly Review of Economics and Finance* 35, no. 1 (Spring): 15–39.

Rehfuss, John. 1983. "Contract Management Keeps Vehicles Moving for Less." *American City and County* 98, no. 7 (July): 35–36.

———. 1990. "Contracting Out and Accountability in State and Local Governments: The Importance of Contract Monitoring." *State and Local Government Review* 22 (Winter): 44–48.

Sappington, David E. M., and Joseph E. Stiglitz. 1987. "Privatization, Information, and Incentives." *Journal of Policy Analysis and Management* 6, no. 4 (Summer): 567–585.

Savas, E. S. 1989–1990. "A Taxonomy of Privatization Strategies." *Policy Studies Journal* 18, no. 2 (Winter): 343–355.

———. 1990. "Privatization: A Strategy for Structural Reform." *National Forum* 70, no. 2 (Spring): 9–13.

Schneider, Mark. 1989. "Intermunicipal Competition, Budget-Maximizing Bureaucrats, and the Level of Suburban Competition." *American Journal of Political Science* 33, no. 3 (August): 612–628.

Seader, David. 1986. "Privatization and America's Cities." *Public Management* 52 (December): 6–9.

Seglem, Lee. 1992. "Turning State Street Upside Down." *State Legislatures* 18, no. 6 (July): 21–25.

Semmens, John. 1993. "From Highways to Buy-Ways." *Spectrum* 66 (Fall): 20–27.

Setzer, Steven W. 1991. "Contracting Out Effort Catches Fire." *ENR* 227, no. 23 (December 9): 11–13.

Sharkansky, Ira. 1980. "Policy Making and Service Delivery on the Margins of Government: The Case of Contractors." *Public Administration Review* 40 (March–April): 116–123.

Shoop, Tom. 1994. "From Citizen to Customers." *Government Executive* 26, no. 5 (May): 27–30.

———. 1995. "Going, Going, Gone." *Government Executive* 27, no. 6 (June): 16–20.

Shubart, Ellen. 1993. "Privatization Is Coming Slowly; Services Still the Main Area, but Infrastructure Seems Next." *City and State* 10 (October 25): 14.

Sloane, Todd. 1992. "All Eyes on Michigan's Privatization Plan." *City and State* 9 (September 7): 2, 21.

Stevens, Barbara J. 1984. "Comparing Public and Private Sector Productive Efficiency: Analysis of Eight Activities." *National Productivity Review* 3 (Autumn): 395–406.

Stein, Lana. 1994. "Privatization, Work-Force Cutbacks, and African-American Municipal Employment." *American Review of Public Administration* 24, no. 2 (June): 181–191.

Sullivan, Harold J. 1987. "Privatization of Public Services: A Growing Threat to Constitutional Rights." *Public Administration Review* 47, no. 6 (November–December): 466–473.

Vickers, John, and George Yarrow. 1991. "Economic Perspectives on Privatization." *Journal of Economic Perspectives* 5, no. 2 (Spring): 111–132.

Wade, Beth. 1995. "The Business of Educating." *American City and County* 110, no. 1 (January): 24–31.

White, Wendell. 1994. "Competition: A Privatization Strategy." *American City and County* 109, no. 2 (February): 16.

Wisniewski, Stanley. 1992. "A Framework for Considering the Contracting Out of Government Services." *Public Personnel Management* 21, no. 1: 101–117.

Worsnop, Richard L. 1992. "Privatization: Should the Private Sector Provide Public Services?" *CQ Researcher* 2, no. 42 (November 13): 978–999.

Yager, Edward M. 1994. "An Organizational Perspective on Municipal Contracting Decisions." *National Civic Review* 83 (Winter–Spring): 73–76.

Zolkos, Rodd. 1992. "Arizona Toll Road Could Cost Less; But Project May Not Be Politically Feasible." *City and State* 9 (October 5): 24.

NEWSPAPER ARTICLES

Albright, Mark. 1995 "Chiles Turns Up Heat on Agency." *St. Petersburg Times* (April 7), 1-E.

Arenson, Karen W. 1995. "Large Charities Pay Well, Survey Finds." *The New York Times* (September 5), A-12.

Aucoin, Don. 1993. "Weld's Privatization Plans Dealt a Double Blow." *Boston Globe* (June 17), 42.

Barlow, Jim. 1994. "Why Privatizing Is Tough, Alluring." *Houston Chronicle* (August 2), C-1.

Barro, Robert. 1995. "The Imperative to Privatize." *The Wall Street Journal* (June 29), A-16.

Bryant, Web. 1995. "Banks Cash In, Taxpayers Lose on Loan Program." *USA Today* (September 18), 14-A.

Butterfield, Fox. 1995. "For Privately Run Prisons, New Evidence of Success." *The New York Times* (August 19), A-7.

"Catholic Schools." 1995. *The Wall Street Journal* (August 28), A-12.

"Chile's Trap." 1991. *St Petersburg Times* (October 4), 14-A.

Debenport, Ellen. 1995. "A Test for School Vouchers." *St. Petersburg Times* (October 13), 1-A.

Emshwiller, John R. 1995. "More Small Firms Complain about Tax-Exempt Rivals." *The Wall Street Journal* (August 8), B1, B2.

Finder, Alan, and Richard Perez-Pena. 1995. "For the M.T.A., Critics Abound, but So Do Fiscal Successes." *The New York Times* (August 13), 31, 34.

Finn, Chester, E. 1995. "Charter Schools—Beware Imitators." *The Wall Street Journal* (September 7), 14.

Firestone, David. 1995a. "Giuliani Says City May Elect to Keep Hospital or Three." *The New York Times* (August 19), B-22.

———. 1995b. "Giuliani Sees Catholic Schools as Model for City." *The New York Times* (August 15), A-1, B-2.

Glass, Stephen. 1995. "Job Training of the Future." *USA Today* (July 10), 11-A.

Goldberg, David. 1995. "Privately Owned Toll Roads May Make a Return." *The Atlanta Constitution* (July 23), G1.

Henry, Tamara. 1995. "Good Grade So Far from Pupils and Teachers." *USA Today* (September 13), 1-D, 2-D.

Hershey, Robert D., Jr. 1995. "G.O.P. Wants I.R.S. to Use Bill Collectors." *The New York Times* (September 26), A-1, C-7.

Janofsky, Michael. 1995. "New Toll Road Offers Glimpse at Future." *The New York Times* (September 29), A-16.

Johnson, Dirk. 1995. "In Privatizing City Services, It's Now Indy-A-First-Place." *The New York Times* (March 2), A-14.

Keefe, Robert. 1993. "Tampa, Orlando Vie for New State Agency." *St. Petersburg Times* (May 26), 1-E.

Kettl, Donald F., and Louis Winnick. 1995. "Privatize City Jails? Here's the Hitch." *The New York Times* (August 22), A-15.

Kotkin, Joel. 1995. "Privatizing Health Care for the Poor." *The Wall Street Journal* (August 23), A-12.

Krawzak, Paul. 1995. "A Business Touch on Government Difficult Analysts Claim the Two Can't Be Managed the Same." *The State Journal–Register* (May 26), 3.

Kreuzer, Terese Loeb, Francis Petit, Hector Lindo-Fuentes, Deborah Meier, and Timothy P. Mulhearn. 1995. "Can Parochial Schools Teach Public Schools?" *The New York Times* (August 22), A-14.

Larrabee, John. 1995. "Charter Schools Follow a Mandate for Change." *USA Today* (September 13), 7-D.

"Leasing the City Hospitals." 1995. *The New York Times* (September 16), L-18.

Lueck, Thomas J. 1995. "Giuliani Is Gauging Companies' Interest in Operating Jails." *The New York Times* (August 12), A-1, A-24.

Mazzarella, David. 1995. "Vouchers Use Tax Money to Benefit Church Schools." *USA Today* (August 23), 10-A.

McGrath, Dennis J. 1993. "Study Sweeps Out Privatization Idea for State Janitors." *Minnesota Star Tribune* (March 20), 5-B.

McKeon, Buck. 1995. "Bank Program Is Better." *USA Today* (September 18), 14-A.

McKinnon, John D. 1991a. "Governor to Propose Reforms in Civil Service." *St. Petersburg Times* (October 9), 4-B.

———. 1991b. "Group Says 'Right-Sizing' Should Grow." *St. Petersburg Times* (August 21), 4-B.

———. 1992. "Government Reorganization Moves along No Straight Lines." *St. Petersburg Times* (March 3), 4-B.

Miller, Sabrina. 1995. "Private Prison Goes Public." *St. Petersburg Times* (March 18), 1-A.

Morgan, Lucy. 1992. "Deja Vu in State Government." *St. Petersburg Times* (May 3), 3-D.

Morgan, Lucy, and Charlotte Sutton. 1991. "Legislature Blamed for Added Jobs." *St. Petersburg Times* (October 1), 1-A.

Morgan, Lucy, Charlotte Sutton, and Bob Port. 1991. "Right-Sized, State Has Growing Staff." *St. Petersburg Times* (September 28), 1-A.

Moss, Bill. 1993a. "Chiles Record on State Reform Is a Mixed Bag." *St. Petersburg Times* (August 29), 8-A.

———. 1993b. "Governor Considers Merging More Agencies." *St. Petersburg Times* (December 11), 7-B.

Myers, William G. 1995. "Let Ranchers Keep Working." *USA Today* (July 26), 8-A.

Myerson, Allen R. 1995. "The Garbage Wars: Cracking the Cartel." *The New York Times* (July 30), F-1, F-11.

Ochs, Adolph. 1995. "Glib Advice on Selling Hospitals." *The New York Times* (August 19), A-18.

Peirce, Neal R. 1991. "Florida Seeks to Redesign the Way It Runs Itself." *St. Petersburg Times* (June 24), 8-A.

Petzinger, Thomas, Jr. 1995. "He Ran Up against Latest Business Foe: Private Regulators." *The Wall Street Journal* (September 22), B-1.

Poole, Robert W., Jr., and David Yardas. 1995. "A Shocking Approach to Privatization." *The Wall Street Journal* (September 26).

Prince, Pat. 1993. "Ramsey County; Board Renews Private Firms Contract." *Minnesota Star Tribune* (March 18), 7-B.

———. 1993. "Business Regulatory Agencies Merge Today." *St. Petersburg Times* (July 1), 4-B.

Rado, Diane. 1992. "State Agencies Told to Trim Staffs Again." *St. Petersburg Times* (November 5), 4-B.

"Reducing the City's Monopoly." 1993. *The Washington Post* 116 (January 8), A-18.

Rodgers, Will. 1991. "Chiles Looks Again for the 'Right-Size.'" *St. Petersburg Times* (September 29), 1-B.

Rosenthal, Elizabeth. 1995. "Ailing Poor Will Get Care, Panel Asserts: Hospital Plan Hinges on Private Cooperation." *The New York Times* (August 17), B1, B2.

Sack, Kevin. 1995. "Public Hospitals around Country Cut Basic Service." *The New York Times* (August 20), A-1, A-24.

"Schools on Contract." 1992. *The Wall Street Journal* (July 24), 10.

Shanker, Albert. 1995. "Where We Stand." *The New York Times* (August 27), E-7.

"Showdown in Wilkinsburgh." 1995. *The Wall Street Journal* (August 29), A-14.

Steinberg, Jacques. 1995. "3,100 New York Teachers Planning to Retire Early: Despite Wide Acceptance of Offer, Layoffs Still Appear Possible." *The New York Times* (August 15), B-2.

Sulllivan, John, and Matthew Purdy. 1995. "In Corrections Business, Shrewdness Pays." *The New York Times* (July 23), 1.

Sutton, Charlotte. 1991. "Firings Called Wrong Way to 'Right-Size.'" *St. Petersburg Times* (December 13), 1-B.

———. 1992. "Reorganization Bill Jumps Hurdle." *St. Petersburg Times* (February 27), 4-B.

"Taxpayers Taken for Ride by Western Ranchers." 1995. *USA Today* (July 26), 8-A.

Thompson, Tommy G. 1995. "Vouchers Help All Students." *USA Today* (August 23), 10-A.

Tobar, Hector. 1992. "County's Use of Private Firms May Be Revised." *Los Angeles Times* 111 (April 10), B-1.

"Two Towns Torn Asunder as Private Bridge Is Closed." 1995. *The New York Times* (August 27), L-24.

Van Natta, Don Jr. 1995. "Despite Setbacks, a Boom in Private Prison Business." *The New York Times* (August 12), A-24.

Wilke, John R. 1995. "Gtech Loses a Bid to Dispense Welfare, Food-Stamp Benefits." *The Wall Street Journal* (September 8), 6, 14.

Winslow, Ron. 1995. "New York Is Urged to Privatize System of Public Hospitals." *The Wall Street Journal* (August 16), B-5.

INDEX

ABOUT THE AUTHOR

Wendell C. Lawther is Associate Professor of Public Administration at the University of Central Florida. His areas of research include privatization, human resource management, and transportation policy. He has published eighteen articles in these fields.

ISBN 0-275-96900-2

90000>

EAN

9 780275 969004

HARDCOVER BAR CODE